The Grabbing Hand

The Grabbing Hand

Government Pathologies and Their Cures

Andrei Shleifer

Robert W. Vishny

HARVARD UNIVERSITY PRESS

Cambridge, Massachusetts
London, England

Library of Congress Cataloging-in-Publication Data
Shleifer, Andrei.
    The grabbing hand : government pathologies and their cures /
Andrei Shleifer, Robert W. Vishny.
        p.   cm.
    Includes bibliographical references (p.   ) and index.
    ISBN 0-674-01014-0 (alk. paper)
    1. Government ownership.   2. Government business enterprises.
3. Privatization.   4. Trade regulation—Political aspects.
5. Political corruption.   I. Vishny, Robert W. (Robert Ward)
II. Title.
HD3850.S5   1998
338.9—dc21   98-7440

Second printing, 1999

To Emma and Mark Shleifer
and to Betty-Ann Vishny
and in memory of
Seymour Vishny

Contents

Acknowledgments

We would first like to thank our collaborators on some of the chapters in this book, Maxim Boycko, Brad DeLong, Florencio Lopez-de-Silanes, and Kevin Murphy, for both working with us and allowing us to include joint work in this volume. We would also like to thank James Hines for suggesting (the first part of) the title.

Over the last decade, many colleagues have offered us valuable comments on the various chapters of this book. We would particularly like to thank Philippe Aghion, Alberto Alesina, Joshua Angrist, Abhijit Banerjee, Robert Barro, Robert Bates, William Baumol, Marco Becht, Roland Benabou, Abram Bergson, Tim Besley, Olivier Blanchard, Maxim Boycko, Suzanne Cooper, Avinash Dixit, Mark Duggan, Steven Friedman, Timothy Frye, Edward Glaeser, Claudia Goldin, Oliver Hart, Jonathan Hay, Carol Heim, Igal Hendel, James Hines, Bengt Holmstrom, Caroline Hoxby, Guido Imbens, Steve Kaplan, Lawrence Katz, Daniel Kaufmann, Janos Kornai, Michael Kremer, Alan Krueger, Anne Krueger, Paul Krugman, Rafael La Porta, David Laibson, Florencio Lopez-de-Silanes, Eric Maskin, Sam Peltzman, Anne Piehl, James Poterba, Robert Putnam, Paul Romer, Ilya Segal, Carl Shapiro, Lawrence Summers, Timothy Taylor, Daniel Treisman, Robert Waldmann, and Michael Whinston.

The research described in this book was financed by a number of organizations: the Bradley Foundation, the Harvard Institute for International Development, the Institute for Policy Reform of the United States Agency for International Development, the National Bureau of

Economic Research, the National Science Foundation, the Sage Foundation, and the Sloan Foundation. We thank them all for their generous support.

Finally, we would like to thank our editors at Harvard University Press, Michael Aronson and Elizabeth Gretz, for improving the manuscript, and Clare MacLean for making sure that the many steps involved in putting this book together were actually taken.

1.1 Three Models of Government

In the center of a nation's sprawling capital, the imposing tower of the country's largest commercial bank rises high above its neighbors. As is customary around the world, this bank is owned by the government. As is also customary, the bank is in deep financial trouble. Many of its largest borrowers have defaulted, often after a noisy public scandal. A would-be movie mogul, for example, has defaulted on a huge loan and has since been found guilty on criminal charges in the United States, jumped bail, and disappeared without a trace. Another major borrower jumped off his boat and drowned after a massive fraud was uncovered at one of his companies. Both of these customers of the bank had ties to the country's governing party at the time the loans were made. The bank's overall losses added up to $30 billion. Although many of these losses are explainable by poor lending decisions made as the bank tried to become the biggest on its continent, a large share of the losses has been attributed to fraud.

The bank's attempts to restore itself to financial health have not succeeded. The bank owned a large stake in one of the country's most profitable companies. But when the management attempted to sell the stake to the highest bidder, it was advised by the government to sell the shares to the company's founder at a quarter of the market price instead. The founder turned out to be a close friend of the country's president.

Where is this bank? It happens to be Crédit Lyonnais in France, a bank that has lost $30 billion while attempting to become the largest in Europe.[1] But this bank could be almost anywhere. Similar stories can be told about government-owned banks in dozens of other countries in Western and Eastern Europe, Asia, Latin America, and Africa.

One need not look only at banks. Enormous losses from bad decisions as well as fraud have bedeviled public enterprises around the world, whether they operate in industry, services, or transportation. A World Bank (1995) publication describes a Turkish state-owned coal-mining company that runs annual losses per worker equal to six times the per capita national income, a state-owned power utility in the Philippines that shuts off electricity for seven hours a day in many parts of the country, a state sugar-milling monopoly in Bangladesh that employs 8,000 unneeded workers while forcing the price of sugar in the country to stay at twice the international level, and a Tanzanian state-owned shoe factory which, with the World Bank's help, could not get its production to rise above 4 percent of capacity before eventually shutting down.[2] Nor does one need to stop at public enterprises when discussing the inefficiency of government performance. One can instead focus on overstaffed and inefficient agencies, fraudulent redistribution schemes, and corrupt judges and officials. Again, the universe of countries to draw on for examples encompasses most of the globe.

These ubiquitous public sector performance failures have called into question economists' conventional views of the state. Most significant, they have challenged the post–World War II advocacy of massive state intervention in markets to cure so-called market failures, based on what can be best described as the helping hand model of government (e.g., Musgrave 1959 or Stiglitz 1989). According to this model, unbridled free markets lead to monopoly pricing, to externalities such as pollution, to unemployment, to defective credit supply to firms, and to failures of regional development, among other ills. Solutions ranging from corrective taxes, regulations, and aggregate demand management to price controls, government ownership, and planning are then proposed to cure these market failures.

Although the helping hand model of government was initially conceived as a prescriptive model, describing what a welfare-maximizing government should do, it increasingly came to be used as a descriptive model, allegedly describing what actual governments do. Economists began to describe government regulations, government ownership, price controls, and other widely practiced interventions as actual responses to alleged market failures. Unfortunately, the helping hand model has failed as both a descriptive and a prescriptive model of government. It has failed as a descriptive model because governments pursue interventions such as state ownership and agricultural supports that serve their political goals and only occasionally coincide with social welfare. The helping hand model also fails as a guide to policy because it presumes that the government will maximize social welfare. Because of the falsity of its premise, this model's advice is often the opposite of what serves the public.

The traditional alternative to the helping hand model is the laissez-faire view of the state—the invisible hand model. This model begins with the idea that markets work very well without any government. The government may perform basic functions needed to support a market economy, such as the provision of law, order, and national defense. Other than delivering these few public goods, the less the government does, the better. The adherents of the invisible hand model rarely inquire what the reasons for massive government intervention in real economies are, or focus on the reforms that would contain the government.

Like the helping hand model, the invisible hand model of government was initially conceived as a prescription for an ideal, limited government. Its irrelevance as a descriptive model is quite obvious, since the government intervenes in economic life much more than any version of an invisible hand model would allow. This failure to deal with reality also renders the invisible hand model unhelpful for generating policy advice. Because it ignores politics, the invisible hand model does not come up with viable strategies for achieving its advocates' ultimate goal of limited government. In the more complex cases where the route to more limited government is indirect, the invisible hand model can offer genuinely harmful policy advice.

The third view of government—what we describe here as the grabbing hand model—focuses squarely on politics as the determinant of government behavior. The grabbing hand model shares with the invisible hand model a skeptical view of government, but describes more accurately what governments actually do and therefore focuses more constructively on the design of reforms. The grabbing and helping hand models share their activist interest in reforming government, although since their conceptions of government are so different, their ideas of good reforms rarely coincide. The grabbing hand analysis typically looks for ways of limiting government as opposed to expanding its scope.

At the root of the grabbing hand analysis are models of political behavior that argue that politicians do not maximize social welfare and instead pursue their own selfish objectives. Dictators use their powers to keep themselves in office, to direct resources to political supporters, to destroy political challengers, and to enrich themselves, often at the expense of public welfare. Democracies often imbue politicians with more public-spirited incentives, in part because they need to be reelected, but democratically elected politicians typically do not maximize social welfare either. As stressed by Buchanan and Tullock (1962) as well as by the authors of the *Federalist Papers* (1788), the winning majorities in democracies tend to pursue highly wasteful policies of redistribution from their losing minorities. Sometimes, for instance, the winning majorities impose extremely high—nearly confiscatory—taxes on the rich and transfer their wealth to themselves, even at the cost of stunting entrepreneurial activity and growth in a country. Sweden over the last thirty years is a good example (Lindbeck 1997).

Another reason why democratic politics give politicians objectives very different from social welfare is the influence of interest groups and lobbies on political choices (Olson 1965; Becker 1983). Lobbies influence political decisions because politicians need votes and contributions from their members. Lobbies use this influence to redistribute resources from the public to themselves, sometimes at a high social cost. Labor union lobbying for labor market restrictions and for massive social redistribution schemes under the Labour governments in Britain is probably an important reason for that country's stagnation prior to Thatcher's reforms.

The political models tell us that both despotic and democratic governments are likely to pursue goals that are very different from social welfare—the alleged objective of the helping hand government. The analysis here is therefore radically different from that of the helping hand model, in which the government maximizes social welfare. The analysis is also different from that of the invisible hand model, which does not have much of a theory of government at all. Because the grabbing hand model starts with politics, it can supply a descriptive theory of government choices and thus coherently analyze the pathologies—as well as the good uses—of the public sector. The analysis yields theories of government ownership and privatization, corruption, legal institutions, the growth of government, and so on. The grabbing hand analysis also serves as a useful guide to policy because it helps to formulate practical advice that recognizes the limitations of government. It can help design institutions that insulate economic agents from the political attempts to prey on them (something the helping hand model does not do) without assuming away the influence of government altogether (as is common in the invisible hand model).

This activism of the grabbing hand model raises a crucial question, namely, who is going to execute the reforms? After all, if the government is selfish, is it not a contradiction for its leaders to deliver political reform, particularly the kind of reform that makes the government weaker? The grabbing hand analysis surely does not presume that the reformers who improve social welfare necessarily have the sole objective of maximizing it. However, democratically elected leaders such as Margaret Thatcher in Britain, Carlos Salinas in Mexico, Boris Yeltsin in Russia, or Vaclav Klaus in the Czech Republic, among many others, often pursue policies of rolling back the state. They do so, at least in part, because their principal political supporters—both lobbies and voters—benefit from these policies. These benefits may include tax cuts, disinflation, improvement of opportunities for starting new businesses, increases in growth and productivity resulting from depoliticization, growth in financial markets, and so on. Indeed, the best opportunities for reforms favored by the grabbing hand model occur precisely when the political interests of the government coincide with social welfare. And one of the central, and most interesting, elements of the grabbing hand analysis is precisely how to build political coalitions in support of reforms.

As a preliminary illustration of the differences among the three views of government, return to the debacle of Crédit Lyonnais. What would be the three analyses of the bank's problems? A helping hand economist is unlikely to admit that Crédit Lyonnais's problem is one of political control. In fact, while this economist may recognize that the bank is in trouble and that the status quo is likely to lead to further losses and inefficiencies, he is likely to see the problem as one of corporate governance, that is, of market failure, rather than as one of political governance, that is, of government failure. For this reason, the helping hand economist would see a number of complexities and tradeoffs in the decision regarding what to do with the bank.[3]

To begin, the helping hand economist would see many advantages in state ownership of a large bank, including the possibility of subsidized loans to nationally and regionally important projects, the maintenance of large employment at the bank itself, the opportunity to use the bank to correct assorted failures in private capital markets, and so on. To pursue these social goals, political control is generally a plus. As a consequence, the helping hand economist is likely to resist a rapid privatization of Crédit Lyonnais, especially since the bank is so large that it might have market power.

At the same time, the helping hand economist might agree that corporate governance at Crédit Lyonnais has failed, and that therefore improvements in this area are in order. To this end, he might suggest offering the bank's management a performance-based incentive contract or appointing an independent board of directors. Of course, it would be better if these changes did not limit the control that the government needs to pursue its social goals. The helping hand economist might also suggest restructuring the bank's assets and maybe breaking it up, preferably under the supervision of a public commission. In the end, he is likely to support more government work with the bank rather than privatization.

Both the invisible hand and the grabbing hand economists would see many fewer benefits of state ownership. They would generally agree that the trouble with the bank is not corporate governance per se, but rather the fact that it is controlled by the government. As long as government control remains intact—either directly, through a government-appointed board, or indirectly, through a new commission—the bank's resources will continue to be wasted on poor projects at a large cost to the taxpayers. Corporate governance of Crédit Lyonnais may well be a problem, but it is a problem precisely because the ultimate control is political. As a consequence, both the invisible hand and the grabbing hand economist would recommend rapid privatization of Crédit Lyonnais. However, while the two economists would agree that private ownership of the bank is better, their views would differ in important details.

The invisible hand economist would generally be bored with the details of privatization. She would take the position that the less government intervention in the banking sector there is, the better, and that competition in the marketplace would take care of whatever problems the bank has. She might object to any government regulation of banking at all, including deposit insurance.

The grabbing hand economist would be more focused on the questions of why the bank is still publicly owned, and how privatization can isolate it from future government intervention in its activities. He might argue, for example, that to reduce the risk of future nationalization, the government should transfer to its own books some of the bank's bad loans. He might also argue that the shares of the bank should be sold as widely as possible, to make such renationalization politically costlier. If there is political opposition to privatization, say from the employees of the bank accustomed to having well-paid government jobs, the grabbing hand economist might consider ways of convincing these employees to go along, perhaps by bribing them with cheap equity. In this particular instance, then, while the invisible and the grabbing hand economists agree on the basic idea, the latter might get further in proposing a feasible strategy precisely because his analysis is much more focused on politics.

This discussion begins to make our case that the choice of the model is not just a matter of completeness, analytical elegance, or emphasis. Rather, we believe that both the helping hand and the invisible hand models often give incomplete or even incorrect answers to crucial economic questions, and that the grabbing hand model is much more likely to give the right answer. We establish this proposition more definitively in the rest of this chapter. In subsequent chapters we develop our grabbing hand analysis of particular problems, but do not specifically advocate it. Yet the principal benefit of the grabbing hand analysis is precisely this: it gives the right answers to problems of great importance.

1.2 Perspectives Matter

To begin, the grabbing hand perspective is helpful in understanding the existing institutions in different countries, the reasons for the ways in which they have been put together, and the benefits and costs of these institutions for economic development and growth. When writing about institutions in a country, such as ownership patterns, regulatory structures, and legal mechanisms, economists used to focus on the benefits of institutional development (e.g., North and Thomas 1973). More recently it has become clear that many institutions retard rather than accelerate growth (e.g., North 1990). Regulatory agencies prevent entry, courts resolve disputes arbitrarily and sometimes dishonestly, politicians use government property to benefit their supporters rather than the population at large. To understand how such dysfunctional institutions come about and stay around for decades or centuries, we need to understand the political objectives and powers of their designers and operators.

But an equally important reason for pursuing the study of the grabbing hand government is institutional reform. What strategies can reduce corruption in government bureaucracies? What reforms will prevent the state from using its companies to pursue political goals incompatible with economic efficiency? How should capital markets be regulated? What constitutes a good system of laws? Can foreign aid be useful? As already mentioned, the grabbing hand agenda is fundamentally activist, in contrast to the invisible hand's pessimism. The goal of this research is not to bash the government or to advocate pure laissez-faire. Rather, the goal is to understand how alternative institutions function under skeptical assumptions about the interests of the politicians, and to examine the strategies for replacing truly dysfunctional institutions with better ones, recognizing that reform itself must cope with political interests and constraints.

Our work on the grabbing hand government falls naturally into the public choice tradition initiated by Buchanan and Tullock (1962), Olson (1965), and Becker (1983). Our emphasis on institutional reform, however, is quite different from the skepticism of the public choice scholars. Buchanan, for example, is sufficiently skeptical about government in general and the tyranny of the majority in particular to oppose most policy reforms, and prefers once-and-for-all constitution building behind the veil of ignorance. Olson is similarly skeptical about government activism because he believes that policies are determined by lobbies, and lobbies promote inefficiency, leading to ever-increasing sclerosis of societies over time. Our view instead is that both popular majorities and lobbies can sometimes be used by political entrepreneurs to promote efficiency-improving reforms.]Indeed, the grabbing hand perspective on government often suggests where a reformer can go looking for these helpful majorities and lobbies.

Many—though not all—of the essays in this book have been motivated by our advisory work in Russia on privatization, capital market development, and legal reform. This work convinced us that the perspective one takes on a problem matters enormously for the solutions that one accepts, advocates, or helps carry out. Starting with an inappropriate perspective, a beautiful theory, which yields the most logical set of policy prescriptions, will deliver an entirely wrong answer to the policy question at hand. To see this point—which is the most fundamental reason for this book—consider three examples of reforms that Russia and other emerging countries have faced.

Take first the example of privatization. Privatization is a striking example of how differently the three types of economists confront the dramatic performance failure of state firms. Helping hand economists are generally ambivalent about privatization, even when they accept as factual the pervasiveness of performance failures of state firms. In some cases, the helping hand analysis focuses on corporate governance and maintains that the problem with government-owned firms is poor selection and motivation of managers (e.g., Laffont 1994). Such analysis emphasizes the selection of the best management teams and proper corporate governance as the critical goals of reforming state firms. Privatization itself often becomes unnecessary if the government can find good managers and provide them with appropriate incentives. The helping hand analysis is also focused on market failure in the product as well as the capital market. Excessive monopoly power is then regarded as the fundamental problem of large state firms. The breakup and restructuring of these firms by the government, and the creation of new regulatory institutions, are needed before any privatization takes place (e.g., Tirole 1991). The beliefs in the centrality of management incentives and of monopoly follow naturally from the helping hand model of government and its emphasis on market, as opposed to government, failure. In this model, the government itself must guard against market failure, and therefore the analysis of privatization typically leads to extremely cautious, if not negative, recommendations. The consequence of this caution, as with Crédit Lyonnais, is the continued stagnation of firms under state ownership while deliberations about the tradeoffs go on.

The invisible hand perspective on privatization, particularly in emerging markets, is sometimes even less helpful. Recall that one of the few legitimate functions that invisible hand economists assign to government is the defense of property rights and the provision of law and order. Without these public goods, a market economy cannot function. In developed economies, where these institutions function well, invisible hand economists favor privatization, as the case of Crédit Lyonnais illustrates. But what if the market-supporting institutions are extremely undeveloped, as they are in many emerging markets? The recommendation of the invisible hand economists is to establish them. In fact, many invisible hand economists are adamant that the creation of institutions defending property rights should precede privatization, since without these institutions, the economic benefits of private property are likely to be small. For this reason, many free market economists opposed privatization in Russia in the early stages of reform.

The trouble with this invisible hand analysis of privatization is that it ignores politics. In particular, it ignores the fundamental fact that institutions supporting property rights are created not by the fiat of a public-spirited government but, rather, in response to political pressure on the government exerted by owners of private property. Privatization then offers an enormous political benefit for the creation of institutions supporting private property because it creates the very private owners who then begin lobbying the government. Without privatization, such private owners do not exist, and hence the political sentiment for creating institutions that support property rights is terribly weak. The Russian experience, in a striking way, confirmed the pitfalls of the invisible hand analysis. It is precisely because of privatization, and the creation of groups with a vested interest in protecting their own property, that the Russian government began to take steps to create market-supporting institutions. Without the political dimension to their analysis, the invisible hand economists missed a crucial dynamic of a transition economy.

The grabbing hand perspective on privatization is different from the other perspectives. Unlike the helping hand perspective, it suggests that the key problem of state firms is government interference in their activities to direct them to pursue political rather than economic goals, such as excess employment. As a consequence, the design of privatization must focus on restricting the possible future influence of the state on privatized firms, through subsidies, regulations, or even minority ownership. Indeed, assigning to the government the role of actively finding better managers or of restructuring monopolies contradicts the essential premise of the grabbing hand approach: that government control is itself the fundamental problem. The change in focus leads to a privatization strategy that aims at depoliticization rather than a mere reorientation of the allegedly benevolent government intervention in firms. The Russian privatization stressed such ideas as speedy and broad distribution of share ownership and cooptation of corporate insiders into supporting privatization. The program deemphasized corporate governance precisely because the intent was to reduce the damage from government failure rather than from market failure. The architects of the Russian privatization were aware of the dangers of poor enforcement of property rights. Yet because of the emphasis on politics, the reformers predicted that institutions would follow private property rather than the other way around.[4] Again, the difference in the economic model led to a very different approach to policy.

As a second example, consider the problem of fighting corruption by government officials. The helping hand diagnosis of corruption is that government bureaucracies select officials of poor quality (and morals) and that moreover the incentives facing these officials are not conducive to honesty. The officials have secure jobs, they are underpaid, and they are rarely penalized for corruption or rewarded for honesty. The helping hand model recommends a number of strategies for fighting corruption, including finding better people for government jobs and improving their incentives (e.g., Klitgaard 1988). Perhaps the bureaucrats should be paid more to reduce their temptation to take bribes, perhaps the penalties for corruption should be made heavier, perhaps there should be prizes and promotions for honesty. Most important, the helping hand model presumes that the government restrictions and regulations that create the opportunities to collect bribes are necessary in the first place. The reason for this assumption is obvious: since the helping hand economists see market failures everywhere, they also see much need for the government to restrict and regulate markets.

The invisible hand economist generally does not focus on corruption. To such an economist, corruption is one of many government failures, and not necessarily the worst one. Indeed, taking government regulations as given, an invisible hand economist sees many benefits of corruption, since it allows private agents to get around the regulations (Leff 1964).

The grabbing hand model, in contrast, begins with the idea that many regulations are introduced in order to enrich and empower politicians. As a consequence, the model immediately implies that deregulation and liberalization are far more important for fighting corruption than the improvement of incentives and personnel selection inside the bureaucracy. To the extent that some regulation is unavoidable, the grabbing hand approach suggests that individual bureaucrats must have as little discretion as possible in exercising their powers. We stress that this is a radically different approach to fighting corruption from that suggested by the helping hand economists. Indeed, the traditional helping hand studies of corruption are nearly unanimous in focusing on personnel policies inside bureaucracies rather than on what these bureaucracies actually do.

Our final, and perhaps most telling, example illustrates how the grabbing hand and invisible hand models sometimes offer radically different advice. The example focuses on the controversial question of foreign aid. Helping hand economists typically approve of most foreign aid. This is not surprising: since they see so many market failures in wealthy economies, they see even more in the developing ones (Stiglitz 1989). Since the government is supposedly curing market failures, and since foreign aid transfers resources to governments that have more market failures to cure, helping hand economists naturally support virtually all foreign aid. Useful aid covers macroeconomic assistance, health, education, industry, infrastructure, financial markets, the energy sector, and everything else that the World Bank supports.

The invisible hand economist, in contrast, is extremely hostile to all foreign aid (Bauer 1976). After all, it is a form of government spending, and one where the donor government might be especially ignorant of the effective ways to spend taxpayers' money.

In this particular instance, the grabbing hand view of foreign aid is sharply different from both of the others (Boycko, Shleifer, and Vishny 1995). The grabbing hand analysis would agree with the invisible hand view that most foreign aid is wasted, in part because the projects it supports are poorly selected and in part because the recipient governments steal or waste the money. However, the grabbing hand analysis recognizes that,[while the economic role of aid is probably minor, the political role of aid can be huge.] Economic reformers and liberalizers in poor economies are often politically weak, and sometimes cannot command even meager resources from their national budgets to pursue their reform agenda. Foreign aid, if used politically, can come to the aid of these reformers, and offer them resources that help them to stay in power and pursue their goals. Such aid is often limited in scope, and directed quite surgically toward assisting certain political groups in their battle against other groups. As a consequence of its extreme politicization, such aid is often criticized even by the helping hand economists. But such aid can play an enormous role in fostering the cause of economic reform and liberalization, as it has, for example, in Russia during the first five years of the Yeltsin administration. The fact that the invisible hand economists do not see the benefits of politically directed aid—even though it promotes the goals they favor—is testimony to the incompleteness of their views and to the importance of the political perspective in getting to the right policies.

These three examples illustrate the crucial message of this book, namely that the perspective one adopts on the nature of government decision making often matters enormously for the conclusions. Whether one starts with the helping hand, the invisible hand, or the grabbing hand approach matters not only for the details of the model one writes down, but also for the conclusions one reaches on critical policy matters. The design of privatization, strategies for fighting corruption, and attitudes toward foreign aid are just three of many examples. In this book we elaborate this basic point of view in a variety of ways.

1.3 Organization of the Book

Economists do not have nearly as impressive a body of analytical work describing the workings of the grabbing hand as they do for the workings of the invisible hand or, for that matter, of the helping hand, for which a beautiful theory has been developed (e.g., Atkinson and Stiglitz 1980). The key questions of the grabbing hand model are, first, what the interests of the political actors are, and second, how these interests translate into policies and institutions that further the objectives of the political actors. Much of the research in economics and political science has focused on the first question, and attempted to model the political system, including elections, legislatures, parties, interest groups, and so on. The seminal contributions of Buchanan and Tullock (1962) and Olson (1965) are precisely in this tradition.

Our work is not focused on modeling the political process, and we generally take political interests as given. Instead we try to provide quite detailed, almost anatomical, answers to the second question, that is, how interests translate into policies and institutions. We describe how phenomena such as growth-stunting taxation, state ownership, predatory regulation, corruption, shortages, and so on emerge when political actors use their power for personal gain.[5]

This book collects ten studies of the grabbing hand model of government. We approach this problem from a variety of directions, and try both to construct theories and to assemble evidence. We deal with some of the issues arising in socialist economies, capitalist economies, precapitalist economies, economies in transition from socialism to capitalism, and developing economies. But the essays have a unifying goal: to examine the consequences for resource allocation of the choices of policies and institutions made by the political actors, and to consider the cures for the adverse consequences of excessive political power.

The chapters in this book fall into four groups. The first focuses on the adverse consequences of the political power to "grab" economic development. The theme of these essays is that grabbing is not just redistribution, but can have enormous efficiency costs. Chapter 2, written by Bradford DeLong and Shleifer, considers eight hundred years of European economic history prior to the industrial revolution, and finds that economic progress, as measured by the formation of cities, was faster in the regions of Europe that had more limited government. Chapter 3, written with Kevin M. Murphy, looks at a particular mechanism through which the grabbing hand works, namely the allocation of talented people to rent-seeking rather than productive occupations. One such occupation, perhaps the most important one in many countries, is government service. The fact that the best and the brightest in these countries become politicians and bureaucrats rather than entrepreneurs, and so devote their talents to taking wealth from others rather than creating it, is often very costly to the rest of the citizens. Chapter 4, also written with Murphy, illustrates theoretically how the allocation of people to rent-seeking occupations can so discourage the producers on whom they prey that, under some circumstances, the economy is stuck in a poverty trap from which it cannot escape. These chapters show the large cost of the grabbing hand government to society, and thus provide a reason for examining further the particular institutional maladies that we are hoping to understand and cure.

In the next section we begin to probe. Chapter 5, central to our discussion, presents a model of corruption. Corruption is interpreted as the consequence of government officials' intentionally creating regulations that entrepreneurs will pay bribes to get around. Corruption is thus a mechanism whereby power is converted into income for politicians. Because corruption raises the cost of productive economic activity, it reduces efficiency. The damage from corruption is particularly large when several politicians, acting independently, create separate barriers to private economic activity so that each can collect a bribe in return for removing his own barrier. When entrepreneurs need to jump over all these independently erected barriers, they eventually give up and stop trying, or else move into the underground economy to avoid regulations altogether. The key message of Chapter 5, however, is more general. Corruption emerges not as some moral aberration, but as a general and natural consequence of the operations of the grabbing hand government.

In the following two chapters we examine two closely related issues arising in discussions of socialism. In Chapter 6 we argue that price controls create bribe-taking opportunities for the officials, since people are prepared to pay bribes to obtain scarce goods. The chapter suggests that shortages—one of the defining features of a socialist economy—are themselves a result of rational economic choices made by the politicians rather than of some miscalculation or of benevolent social policy. In Chapter 7 we take up the issue of market socialism—a never realized economic system combining markets for goods with central planning of production. Market socialism was advocated by leftist intellectuals in the 1930s, when capitalist economies suffered through severe depressions, and is being revived by their successors today as a strategy of transition from socialism. We show that most arguments about market socialism by both its proponents and its opponents assume that the government is benevolent and focus on the relatively minor issue of what resource allocation such a government can achieve under alternative systems. These arguments ignore the much more central problem of empowering a grabbing hand government to run the economy, and the mischief that would befall any community where such a government has the instruments to implement market socialism. Again the focus on the private objectives of politicians leads to an entirely different analysis of the problem than the one generated by the helping and the invisible hand perspectives.

In the third group of chapters, we focus on a key form of the exercise of political power: the use of government-controlled property to pursue political objectives, such as employment. In Chapter 8, written with Maxim Boycko, we outline a theory of political control of firms, and examine privatization as a strategy of dealing with the adverse consequences of such control. We show that soft budget constraints of state firms are a reflection of politicians' buying influence through subsidies, and that hardening of the budget constraints is essential for privatization to enhance efficiency. Depoliticization, the reduction of opportunities for political control of firms, emerges as the central objective of privatization.

In Chapter 9 we take this argument further, and consider a variety of forms of political control, including regulation, and their consequences for economic efficiency. We also examine reform strategies that are complementary to privatization. One of them, macroeconomic stabilization, has the beneficial effect of reducing subsidies and thus hardening budget constraints. Finally, in Chapter 10, written with Florencio Lopez-de-Silanes, we present an empirical analysis of privatization of local government services by counties in the United States. Consistent with our theoretical arguments, the analysis reveals that political variables such as the softness of local governments' budget constraints and the power of labor unions are the critical determinants of the privatization decision.

The last portion of the book contains only one chapter. It is also the only chapter that deals explicitly with Eastern Europe and Russia. The chapter, by Shleifer, asks the question why, as of 1996, some of the countries in Eastern Europe, such as Poland, have been more successful in their transition to capitalism than the countries of the former Soviet Union, such as Russia. The answer, we believe, has little to do with the speed and nature of conventional reforms such as price liberalization and stabilization, which have been rather similar in these places. Rather, the political transition away from the unbridled grabbing hand government and toward a more limited government has been a good deal more successful in Eastern Europe than in Russia. Survey and other evidence from 1996 points clearly to an extreme version of grabbing hand government as the source of Russia's problems, including relatively slow growth, corruption, and crime.

But here as before, the benefit of a clear diagnosis and an appropriate approach is that one can begin thinking rationally about the cures. In Russia's case, as in that of other economies with a severe case of grabbing hand government, reforms of the legal and regulatory systems, of taxation, of federalism, and of some particularly egregious central government institutions are essential. These reforms can bring significant benefits of reducing the predatory role of the bureaucracy, creating incentives for local and regional governments to raise their own taxes and provide local public goods such as elementary education, health, and police protection, improving the incentives for small business formation, and so on. These reforms call for an expansion of the government's role in some activities, most notably the provision of public goods such as police protection, and a diminution of government intervention in others, such as the control of land. The grabbing hand perspective is allowing reformers to think about these institutional changes as a mechanism for making the government more responsive to the needs of the public. Perhaps ironically, the grabbing hand perspective is the one that allows us to understand how a government can offer the public a helping, and not just a grabbing, hand.

Princes and Merchants: European City Growth before the Industrial Revolution

2

2.1 Introduction

One of the oldest themes in economics is the incompatibility of despotism and development. Economies in which security of property is lacking—because of either the possibility of arrest, ruin, or execution at the command of the ruling prince or the possibility of ruinous taxation—should experience relative stagnation. By contrast, economies in which property is secure—either because of strong constitutional restrictions on the prince or because the ruling elite is made up of merchants rather than princes—should prosper and grow. Adam Smith argued that "in all countries where there is tolerable security [of property], every man of common understanding will endeavor to employ whatever [capital] stock he can command . . . A man must be perfectly crazy who, where there is tolerable security [of property], does not employ all the [capital] stock which he commands . . . In those unfortunate countries . . . where men are continually afraid of the violence of their superiors, they frequently bury and conceal a great part of their [capital] stock . . . in case of their being threatened with any of those disasters to which they consider themselves as at all times exposed. This is said to be a common practice in Turkey, in Indostan, and, I believe, in most other governments of Asia. It seems to have been a common practice among our [feudal] ancestors."[1]

By J. Bradford DeLong and Andrei Shleifer; originally published in *Journal of Law and Economics*, 36, no. 2 (October 1993): 671–702.

This theme had been used more than a quarter century before Smith by Montesquieu to make sense of the contrast between the booming commercial economies of republican Holland and constitutional England and the stagnant economy of absolutist eighteenth-century France: "Great enterprises in commerce are not found in monarchical, but republican governments . . . [A]n opinion of greater certainty as to the possession of property in these [republican] states makes [merchants] undertake everything . . . [T]hinking themselves sure of what they have already acquired, they boldly expose it in order to acquire more . . . A general rule: A nation in slavery labors more to preserve than to acquire; a free nation, more to acquire than to preserve."[2]

This theme is also echoed in the standard narrative histories of European nations, which often describe in one chapter the rise of strong dynasties with powerful armies, and in the next subsequent urban and mercantile decline. The Norman d'Hauteville dynasty, for example, conquered Sicily and southern Italy in the eleventh century when it was the most prosperous and urbanized region in Europe. The government the d'Hautevilles founded was the most centralized and powerful in Europe.[3] But after its Norman conquest, southern Italy's prosperity declined, especially when measured relative to the prosperity of the city-states of northern Italy. Imperial Spain was the core of the immense empire ruled by absolutist Habsburg princes in the sixteenth and seventeenth centuries. They imposed heavy taxes on the prosperous towns of Catalonia and Andalusia to fight the wars of the Counter-Reformation. Spain's imperial golden age somehow also saw its cities lose wealth and population. By 1800 Spain had become a relative backwater.

European history also presents cases where cities grew rapidly and commerce flourished in the absence of strong princes in regions where political power was held by merchant oligarchies or checked by constitutional limitations and representative assemblies. The city-states of northern Italy, of the Low Countries, and of Burgundy prospered and grew in the later Middle Ages and the Renaissance before they came under autocratic Habsburg control in the sixteenth century. Before the industrial revolution the Netherlands and Great Britain flourished under constitutional governments: the Netherlands after its successful revolt against Spain, and Great Britain after its Great Rebellion of 1640–1660 and Glorious Revolution of 1688 that together established the absolute supremacy of Parliament in matters of taxation.[4]

Here we take up the theoretical and narrative contrast between growth under princes and merchants using more systematic data. Between 1050 and 1800 some areas of western Europe were governed by strong princely rulers, whom we call "absolutist,"[5] who saw the legal order as an instrument of control rather than as a constraint on their actions. Other areas were free from such princes. Some had maintained feudal customs or won charters of liberties that limited princely authority—"societies of estates" in which groups like landowners, guild masters, and burghers had long-standing rights and the monarch was but one "estate" among others. Other regions were dominated by merchant-ruled city-states.[6]

Jan de Vries divides western Europe into regions that follow 1914 boundaries.[7] We find that, on average, for each century that such a region is free of government by an absolute prince, its total population living in cities of 30,000 or more inhabitants grew by 120,000, relative to a century of absolutist rule. This difference is larger than the average growth rate of urban populations in European regions between 1000 and 1800. In a purely statistical sense, therefore, the association between absolutism and slow city growth can more than account for why some western European regions had relatively low rates of urbanization in 1800, while others had flourishing cities and abundant commerce. Strong princely rule is systematically associated with retarded urban commerce. By contrast, more restricted governments that give a voice or a constitutional veto to merchants or assemblies of landed magnates are systematically associated with much faster urban growth. The pattern that Smith and Montesquieu noted does not hold merely between constitutional Europe and despotic Asia, or between constitutional Britain and despotic France, but more generally across the western half of the European continent in the millennium before the industrial revolution.[8]

Montesquieu and Smith, but also more recent reformulations by Geoffrey Brennan and James Buchanan, Douglass North, North and Robert Thomas, and Mancur Olson, account for this regularity by drawing a contrast between the economic effects of despotic and of limited government.[9] In their view, absolutist princes are concerned primarily with the tax revenues that their domains yield; they tax in order to maximize revenue and thus cripple the economies they govern. By contrast, limited governments are more concerned with private economic prosperity: either they are led by merchant oligarchs who have a stronger interest in maintaining and expanding the flow of commerce than in promoting the power of the state and the splendor of the court, or they give a veto to parliaments or estates-general that bear the weight of heavy taxes. Such limited governments would set lower tax rates that minimize the disruptive effect on the economy—at least on the economy considered as a source of rents for landed gentry and of commercial profits for merchant oligarchs. Limited governments should therefore be more favorable to economic growth.

2.2 Data on Preindustrial Cities

The larger preindustrial cities of Europe were nodes of information, industry, and exchange in areas where the growth of agricultural productivity and economic specialization had advanced far enough to support them. They could not exist without a productive countryside and a flourishing trade network. The population of Europe's preindustrial cities is a rough indicator of economic prosperity.[10]

This correlation between economic prosperity and city size may not hold in general for the preindustrial world. The population of Tenochtitlan, or Peking, or imperial Rome had more to do with the power of the networks of tribute and redistribution that underlay their respective empires than with mercantile prosperity. Such consumption-intensive "parasite cities," to use Paul Bairoch's term,[11] were centers of neither trade nor urban industry but were instead the homes of bureaucrats and landlords. But the primarily rural orientation of Europe's medieval ruling class meant that Europe's cities did not develop as centers of landlord consumption or of territorial administration. We can use the sizes of European cities as indicators of commercial prosperity because the typical post-classical European city was primarily a center of commerce, and not of bureaucracy, administration, or landlord consumption.[12]

For our purposes, Europe's larger cities are also important indicators of economic prosperity because they are highly visible: contemporary historians and travelers and modern-day urban archaeologists all give estimates of city size and prosperity. Other aggregate quantitative indicators of economic prosperity before the industrial revolution are very scarce. We use the numbers and sizes of large preindustrial cities as an index of economic activity, and changes in the numbers of cities and the sizes of urban populations as indicators of economic growth.

To measure the growth of western European cities, we use two databases. The first was constructed by taking estimates of city sizes over the period 1500–1800 from de Vries. De Vries constructs population estimates from archives: church attendance lists, baptisms and burials, censuses, tax records, and so on. He accepts as sources "secondary works, usually town histories, where the historian makes population estimates based on his general knowledge about the city."[13]

Estimates for the period before 1500 are derived from Josiah Russell, as amended by subsequent work. Russell puts more stress on estimates of the size of the inhabited area at a given time as a way to estimate population. He argues that the average density of a medieval city was about 120 persons per hectare, with the most densely populated cities approaching 200 persons per hectare. Russell thus rejects high estimates in the several hundreds of thousands for the circa A.D. 1000 population of Mediterranean cities like Cordova, Palermo, and Constantinople, because according to his calculations the built-up areas of these cities were too small to support such populations.[14]

The second database was constructed by Bairoch, Jean Batou, and Pierre Chèvre, also from both primary and secondary sources. They began with the estimates of city size provided by Tertius Chandler and Gerald Fox and extended them using G. Sundbard's 1908 statistics and the international retrospective sections of the official French *Annuaire Statistique*.[15] They continued to add to and correct their database for more than a decade, following what they call a "craftsman-like" approach: "[T]he system was . . . 1) [to] replace a figure each time a more recent source revealed an alternative, but without systematically noting the reference . . . [and] 2) [to] add . . . previously unavailable figures . . . following the same procedure."[16]

Some confidence in the reliability, or at least the consistency, of the databases can be gained by noting that Bairoch's data fit closely with the independently derived database of de Vries toward the end of the preindustrial period. Their estimates for the sum of the populations of the ninety-one cities with populations over 20,000 in 1700 differ by only 0.6 percent. Their estimates for the sum of the populations of the sixty-two cities with populations more than 20,000 and less than 50,000 differ by only 2.5 percent. Such close agreement of two independently constructed databases is remarkable.

Earlier years show more divergence between the two databases. The Bairoch database estimates somewhat larger urban populations than does the Russell–de Vries database for the years before the Renaissance. The greatest difference arises because Bairoch accepted higher estimates for the population of early medieval cities than Russell believed plausible, given his assessments of the settled urban area. The divergences are most serious in the cases of early medieval Muslim Mediterranean cities, like Cordova and Palermo, that were both mercantile and governmental centers.

Table 2.1 shows the population of western Europe's thirty largest cities, according to the Bairoch database, at six points in time—in the first half of the eleventh century, at the end of the twelfth, on the eve of the bubonic plague in the early fourteenth century, at the beginning of the sixteenth, at the middle of the seventeenth, and at the end of the eighteenth centuries. Table 2.1 presents, and in the analysis we use, fourteenth-century population estimates as of c. 1330 rather than 1350. By 1350 some cities had been severely hit by the first wave of the Black Death, while others were still untouched. To use 1350 population estimates would give a false picture of urban development in the thirteenth and early fourteenth centuries.

In the year 1000 western Europe was a backwater. North of the urban Muslim centers of Cordova in southern Spain and Palermo in Sicily (of large but uncertain populations), there were at most four cities with populations of 40,000 or more: Venice, Naples, perhaps Rome, and perhaps Regensberg in Germany. By contrast, the Mediterranean fringe of Europe under Muslim rule had at least four cities with populations over 40,000: Palermo and the three Muslim Spanish cities of Granada, Seville, and Cordova. The largest of these cities may have been larger at that time than any other European city was to be until the seventeenth century.

The five centuries from 1000 to 1500 saw a shift in the center of gravity of the European economy northward. Only Naples on the Mediterranean ranked among the largest cities. The largest cities were on the northern edge of the Mediterranean, or even further north. Other, smaller centers of urban commerce and industry included Bruges and

Table 2.1 The thirty largest cities in Europe by population (in thousands), 1050–1800

c. 1050		c. 1200		c. 1330	
Cordova*	450	Palermo	150	Granada	150
Palermo*	350	Paris	110	Paris	150
Seville	90	Seville	80	Venice	110
Salerno	50	Venice	70	Genoa	100
Venice	45	Florence	60	Milan	100
Regensburg	40	Granada	60	Florence	95
Toledo	37	Cordova	60	Seville	90
Rome	35	Cologne	50	Cordova	60
Barbastro	35	Leon	40	Naples	60
Cartagena	33	Ypres	40	Cologne	54
Naples	30	Rome	35	Palermo	51
Mainz	30	Bologna	35	Siena	50
Merida	30	Toledo	35	Barcelona	48
Almeria	27	Verona	33	Valencia	44
Granada	26	Narbonne	31	Toledo	42
Speyer	25	Salerno	30	Bruges	40
Palma	25	Pavia	30	Malaga	40
Laon	25	Messina	30	Aquila	40
London	25	Naples	30	Bologna	40
Elvira	22	Genoa	30	Cremona	40
Cologne	21	Angers	30	Pisa	38
Trier	20	Palma	30	Ferrara	36
Caen	20	Speyer	30	London	35
Lyon	20	Worms	28	Montpelier	35
Paris	20	Ferrara	27	Rouen	35
Tours	20	Orleans	27	St.-Omer	35
Verona	20	Metz	27	Lisbon	35
Worms	20	Valencia	26	Angers	33
Lisbon	15	Cremona	25	Marseille	31
Florence	15	London	25	Toulouse	30

Table 2.1 (continued)

c. 1500		c. 1650		c. 1800	
Paris	225	Paris	400	London	948
Naples	125	London	350	Paris	550
Milan	100	Naples	300	Naples	430
Venice	100	Lisbon	150	Vienna	247
Granada	70	Venice	140	Amsterdam	217
Prague	70	Milan	120	Dublin	200
Lisbon	65	Amsterdam	120	Lisbon	195
Tours	60	Rome	110	Berlin	172
Genoa	58	Madrid	100	Madrid	168
Ghent	55	Palermo	100	Rome	153
Florence	55	Seville	80	Palermo	140
Palermo	55	Florence	74	Venice	138
Rome	55	Vienna	70	Milan	135
Bordeaux	50	Granada	70	Hamburg	130
Lyon	50	Marseille	70	Lyon	109
Orleans	50	Copenhagen	65	Copenhagen	101
London	50	Genoa	64	Marseille	101
Bologna	50	Bologna	63	Barcelona	100
Verona	50	Antwerp	60	Seville	96
Brescia	49	Brussels	60	Bordeaux	96
Cologne	45	Lyon	60	Genoa	90
Seville	45	Rouen	60	Manchester	84
Marseille	45	Danzig	60	Edinburgh	83
Malaga	42	Leiden	55	Turin	82
Valencia	42	Valencia	50	Florence	81
Ferrara	42	Prague	50	Valencia	80
Rouen	40	Hamburg	40	Rouen	80
Cremona	40	Cologne	40	Nantes	77
Nuremberg	38	Nuremberg	40	Stockholm	76
Bruges	35	Ghent	40	Prague	76

Source: The Bairoch database; see Paul Bairoch, Jean Bateau, and Pierre Chèvre, *La Population des villes européenes de 800–1850* (1988).

* Russell's estimates of the populations of Cordova and Palermo are only one-third as large.

Antwerp in what was to become Belgium, Rouen and Lyon in France, and Brescia, Genoa, Padua, Bologna, Florence, and perhaps one or two more in northern Italy. The center of gravity of urban life had shifted from the southernmost edge of Europe to an axis from the Low Countries to Lombardy.

By 1800 western Europe had become the most prosperous and economically advanced region in the world. South of the Baltic Sea, north of the Mediterranean, and west of Wroclaw and Konigsberg were perhaps fifty-six cities of 40,000 or more, of which perhaps sixteen had more than 100,000 people. London and Paris had populations greater than 500,000. Cities of more than 100,000 population included Dublin, Amsterdam, Hamburg, and Berlin in northern Europe; Vienna, Lyon, Milan, Venice, Rome, Naples, Palermo, Barcelona, Madrid, and Lisbon in southern Europe.

The center of gravity of European urban life had shifted even further northward. Perhaps most startling was the growth of large urban population centers in Britain and Ireland. Twelve of the fifty-six largest cities in western Europe were located in the British Isles. Only one of these— London—had ranked among the fifty largest cities of western Europe even two centuries earlier.

2.3 Political Regimes

2.3.1 ABSOLUTIST REGIMES

We classify western European governments into two broadly defined classes of regimes: absolutist states and all others. Absolutist states are characterized by the subjection of the legal framework to the prince's will. As Cardinal Richelieu, the creator of French absolutism, explained to his master Louis XIII, his policies were aimed at ensuring that his majesty was absolutely obeyed by great and small and at eliminating all rival centers of power and resistance: "to reduce and restrict those bodies which, because of their pretensions to sovereignty, always oppose the good of the realm." And "the good of the realm" meant "the will of the king": it was Louis XIII's son Louis XIV who brought Bourbon dynasty absolutism to its peak and said, "L'état c'est moi."[17]

In absolutist regimes "property"—defined broadly to encompass everything from estates, to rank, to monopolies, to means of production—is always potentially insecure. Subjects do not have rights; they have privileges, which endure only as long as the prince wishes. An absolutist government thus comes close to Olson's pure type of a stationary bandit or Brennan and Buchanan's constitutionally unconstrained Leviathan.[18] Such a government has a monopoly on theft—called "taxation"—in a territorial domain. A stationary bandit squeezes the territory until he extracts the maximum revenue: his incentive to extract resources is restricted only in that he has an interest in keeping the people prosperous enough for him to extract more resources in the future, and is augmented by the possibility of using taxes from his current domain to conquer other lands.

Canonical examples of such absolutist states are the seventeenth-century France of the Bourbon Louis XIV "the Sun King" and sixteenth-century imperial Spain under the Habsburg Philip II "the Prudent." Borderline cases include the thirteenth-century Kingdom of Naples under the Hohenstaufen Frederick II "the Wonder of the World" and the English kingdom as established after the Norman Conquest destroyed subordinate territorial lordships.[19]

2.3.2 NONABSOLUTIST REGIMES

Governments that lacked a single strong prince exhibited wide variation. Some regions see the establishment of constitutional monarchies—"governments of estates," in which the prince is bound by the law. Gianfranco Poggi comments, "[T]he law was the distinctive package of rights and privileges traditionally claimed . . . it existed in the form of differentiated legal entitlements. Such law could be modified by the Estates when entering into or renewing compacts with the ruler . . . but . . . could not be modified at the will of any one party."[20]

Under such regimes the legal framework was not an instrument of the prince's rule, but more of a semifeudal contract between different powers establishing the framework of their interactions. Legal judgments could be enforced only with the consent of parliaments. Taxes could be raised only with the consent of feudal estates. Both of these bodies had a feudal duty to implement the prince's judgments and to advise him on the law. Their interpretation of the duty to advise the prince was often close to an assertion that they had the authority to veto: their major threat was to refuse to assist in tax assessment and collection until their substantive demands were met.

The canonical example of such a limited and constitutional monarchy is Britain under the houses of Orange and Hanover, after the Glorious Revolution of 1688. Other examples are the Low Countries (Belgium and Holland) when ruled by the dukes of Burgundy and Catalonia before Ferdinand married Isabella and established absolutism in Spain. Such governments found it much more difficult to increase tax revenues than did absolutist states.

A second type of nonabsolutist government was city-state-based rule by merchant oligarchies. Self-governing city-states directed their own affairs and often controlled substantial tracts of the rural countryside as well. In merchant- and burgher-ruled city-states, the government was close to a committee for managing affairs in the common interest of the bourgeoisie—a class that has always had a very strong interest in rapid economic growth. The Venetian and Florentine republics are the most often-cited examples.[21] The Amsterdam-led United Provinces of the Netherlands after the successful revolt by Prince William "the Silent" of Orange is another canonical example.

A third group of regions were under "feudal" governments. In theory, feudal government is centralized: each duke or count owes loyalty to the king, each castellan owes loyalty to his count, and each knight owes loyalty to his castellan. In practice, the system lacked authority. Dukes and counts would not necessarily obey the king. Thus Duke Henry "the Lion" of Saxony refused a summons from the Hohenstaufen Emperor Frederick I "Red-Beard" to join the imperial army, and the emperor was unable to impose his authority on the northern Italian city-states.

Classifying this third group in which the political regime is one of "feudal anarchy" is the most difficult part of the exercise. In some cases each local feudal despot acted like a miniature absolutist prince, imposing confiscatory taxation in order to enhance military power and maintain a properly princely style of life. In other cases jurisdictions were so small that merchants could flee to feudal domains that provided protection, and competition between petty despots to attract merchants and their commerce constrained arbitrary exactions. In still other cases, the most powerful political units in feudal anarchy turned out to be mercantile republics, which owed their self-government to the inability of feudal authorities to enforce commands.[22]

One approach to classifying this widely disparate set of political regimes would be to construct a finely tuned sliding scale. Security of property would vary according to the constitutional constraints on the ruler preventing him from imposing arbitrary taxation, the mechanisms of selection influencing his desired policies, and the ability of the nascent state to protect its subjects from the depredations of local thieves or of other rulers. The major difficulty with using such a scale is that the classification is inevitably arbitrary. For most of this chapter, we take instead the brutal road of dividing western European regimes into only two categories—absolutist and nonabsolutist. The simplicity of this classification minimizes discretion and also focuses attention on the power of the ruler to appropriate private wealth for his own benefit, whether through arbitrary confiscation or ruinous taxation. Constraints on this power appear to us to be the most important determinants of what Adam Smith calls "security of property."[23] To identify the absence of these constraints, we focus on the presence or absence of absolutist princes. To check the robustness of our results, however, we will also use more finely graded but also more arbitrary classifications.

2.3.3 CLASSIFICATION OF REGIMES

To classify regimes for our analysis using the Russell–de Vries database, we divide western Europe into the same regions used by de Vries,[24] which by and large follow 1914 political boundaries. We split de Vries's Italian region into two: northern Italy and southern Italy have very different political histories. Southern Italy was taken from the Muslims and the Byzantines by the d'Hauteville dynasty from Normandy in the first half of the eleventh century. The *regno* then established has been called the first modern state, with a single system of royal justice and an integrated system of tax collection from the middle of the eleventh century. Southern Italy was thus under centralized princely rule for the entire period.

Northern Italy, by contrast, secured its effective independence during the Investiture struggle.[25] It remained independent from kings and divided into quarreling merchant-ruled city-states until the French and Habsburg invasions of the sixteenth century that brought an end to the Renaissance.

Thus our analysis of the Russell–de Vries database covers nine regions: Spain, France, northern Italy, southern Italy, Germany, Britain, Belgium, the Netherlands, and Austria-Bohemia. We examine city growth since 1050 over five periods: 1050–1200, 1200–1330, 1330–1500, 1500–1650, and 1650–1800. These periods are chosen for convenience given the data available. They minimize the amount of interpolation required to construct the Russell–de Vries database.

We associate a dominant regime type with each region in each era. Table 2.2 summarizes the classification we adopt.[26] The table also reveals the gradual growth of absolutism in Europe. At the beginning of the sample, the Norman *regno* of southern Italy, the Norman-conquered kingdom of England, and the anarchy of medieval Germany count as "absolutist" regimes. Nowhere else did kings or princes have even the beginnings of the administrative mechanisms, military power, and authority to establish centralized states, nor did they have the freedom from control by higher authorities or representative assemblies that German princelings had in the middle of the Investiture struggle.

By the middle of the sample, absolutist princes had become more common. This was in large part due to the rise of the Habsburg dynasty, which at its peak controlled Spain, southern Italy, northern Italy, Austria-Bohemia, Belgium, and Holland. But the extension of absolutism was not solely a Habsburg creation. France and Prussia, in eastern Germany, adopted similar systems of rule. Southern Italy had possessed a powerful and centralized monarchy since its Norman conquest. England and the Netherlands made revolutions, threw off protoabsolutisms, and under their constitutional and limited governments dominated the European economy in the century before the industrial revolution.

To check whether the division into regions and the dates demarcating periods were in any important way distorting our results, we analyze the Bairoch database using a different grid. Periods are individual centuries.

Table 2.2 Classification of western Europe regimes, Russell–de Vries database

Region	1050–1200	1200–1330	1330–1500	1500–1650	1650–1800
Southern Italy	Prince (Norman d'Hautevilles)	Prince (Hohen-staufens and Angevins)	Prince (Aragonese)	Prince (Habsburgs)	Prince (Habsburgs)
Northern Italy	Free (Investiture struggle)	Free (Republics)	Free (Republics)	Prince (Habsburg domination)	Prince (Habsburg domination)
Austria-Bohemia	Free (feudal)	Free (constitution)	Free (constitution)	Prince (Habsburgs)	Prince (Habsburgs)
Germany	Prince (Medieval empire)	Prince (anar-chy: Great Interregnum)	Prince (petty despots)	Prince (petty despots)	Prince (petty despots)
Netherlands	Free (feudal)	Free (constitution)	Free (constitution)	Free (Dutch republic)	Free (Dutch republic)
Belgium	Free (feudal)	Free (constitution)	Free (constitution)	Prince (Habsburgs)	Prince (Habsburgs)
England	Prince (Normans)	Prince (Angevin empire)	Prince (Wars of Roses)	Prince (Tudors)	Free (constitution)
France	Free (feudal)	Free (feudal)	Free (Hundred Years' War)	Free (religious strife)	Prince (Bourbons)
Spain	Free (feudal)	Free (constitution)	Free (constitution)	Prince (Habsburgs)	Prince (Bourbons)

Regions are further subdivided: Italy into three—northern, central, and southern; France into two—northern and southern; and Spain into three subregions—roughly Castile, Aragon, and Granada. These differences in definitions of eras and regions have no significant effect on the statistical results.

2.4 Absolutist Princes and City Growth

2.4.1 DEPENDENT VARIABLES

In this section we examine the relationship between political regimes and city growth. The Russell–de Vries database consists of a panel with nine regions over five time periods, or 45 observations in total. The Bairoch database consists of a larger panel: fourteen regions over eight time periods, or 112 observations.

For the Russell–de Vries database we use three different urbanization measures as dependent variables. The first is the growth over a period in the number of people living in cities of more than 30,000. This measure is equal to (a) population growth (or decline) in cities that begin and end the period with populations of 30,000 or more, plus (b) the end-of-period populations of cities that begin the period with less and end the period with more than 30,000, minus (c) the beginning-of-period populations of cities that fall below 30,000 inhabitants over the period. The second dependent variable is the growth in the number of cities with a population greater than 30,000. This measure is equal to the number of cities that cross the 30,000 population limit during any particular period. The third is the proportional growth in large city population during the period, where the base by which the change is divided in order to obtain proportional growth is the average of the beginning and end of the period levels.

These are not ideal measures. The cities included are selected ex post, not ex ante. Moreover, only the largest cities in any region are included. Nevertheless, these measures do reflect changes in market activity, urban commerce, and economic prosperity.

For the Bairoch database we use four different urbanization measures: the change in the number of cities larger than 30,000 and the growth of population living in cities of more than 30,000 as for the Russell–de Vries database; and the change in the number of cities of population greater than 10,000 and the growth of population living in cities of more than 10,000.

The more complete coverage available from the Bairoch than from the Russell–de Vries database allows for use of the lower 10,000 population cutoff. This diminishes the potential small-numbers problem and makes the measures of urban population changes better indicators of changes in mercantile and urban prosperity. Of course there is considerably less information underlying the population estimates for the smaller cities. So the gain from using a larger sample and a lower city-size cutoff may not be great.

An additional urbanization measure that we experimented with is the growth in population living in cities of more than 30,000 that are not royal capital "parasite cities." Growth of such royal capitals is arguably not so much a result of increasing commerce and industry as of an increasing ability to tax the countryside. According to standard interpretations of Italian history, Naples' very large size in the seventeenth century was the result not of prosperous industry and commerce but of the extraction of large rents and taxes from the countryside. Madrid, Vienna, and Berlin are other preindustrial large cities that were more centers of redistribution and consumption than production. The inclusion of royal capitals in our city growth measure might confuse inference, for absolutist regimes hostile to commerce might be effective at exploiting the countryside and increasing the size of their capital cities. Use of this alternative dependent variable allows us to check for such a possibility.

The principal independent variable we focus on is an indicator: is a given region in a given period ruled by an absolutist prince, or not?

Regions have different populations, soil fertilities, access to transport, and resource endowments. These factors would lead to systematic differences in rates of urbanization even if political regimes were identical. In most specifications, we control for persistent regional differences by including regional dummies as independent variables. Different eras also saw different overall trends in population and economic growth. For example, the bubonic plague was continentwide. It and subsequent plagues devastated Europe over 1330–1500. The "little ice age" of the seventeenth century adversely affected agricultural productivity throughout much of Europe. In all specifications we include period dummies to control for differences in the overall pace of economic growth in Europe.

2.4.2 BASIC RESULTS: RUSSELL–DE VRIES DATA BASE

Tables 2.3 and 2.4 present basic results using the Russell–de Vries database. Coefficients reported are measured in units of people (or cities, or proportion of the population) per century. The first column of Table 2.3 reports the dependent variable in the regression. The second column reports the estimated effect of the presence of an absolutist prince on city growth and the standard error of this estimated effect. The third and fourth columns report summary statistics: what fraction of the total variation in city growth is accounted for by the independent variables, and what is the standard error of the regression line? The fifth and sixth columns report whether the particular regression specification controls for region- and era-specific influences.

According to the regression in row 1 of Table 2.3, the presence of an absolutist prince reduces the growth of population in cities of more than 30,000 by nearly 180,000 people per century, with a standard error of 50,000 people per century.[27] According to the regression in row 3, the presence of an absolutist prince for a century reduces the number of cities of 30,000 or more inhabitants in the region by slightly over two, with a standard error of about five-sixths of a city per century.[28]

The results controlling for differences among regions are stronger than the results without such controls, which are reported in rows 2, 4, and 6 of Table 2.3. The estimated damage done to an urban population by an absolutist prince is only two-fifths as large, and the estimated damage done to the number of urban cities is only two-thirds as large when the regression does not control for regional differences.[29]

The less good performance of the regressions omitting controls for regional differences is not surprising. The different regions do not divide Europe into segments equally capable of supporting city growth. Some regions have good harbors, many navigable rivers, and abundant and rich agricultural land. We would expect such regions to support the growth of relatively many cities. Other regions, like Belgium or Holland, are very small in area. We would not expect them to have as many cities as France or Italy. Different cultures, as well, may also have influenced city growth. The regions were in fact chosen by de Vries with an eye toward grouping areas that shared common cultures and languages.

In an attempt to control for differences between regions without introducing a host of regional dummy variables, the fifth and sixth rows

Table 2.3 Regression results for the Russell–de Vries database

Dependent variable	Prince coefficient (thousands of people or number of cities lost per century of absolutism)	R^2	Standard error of the estimate	Region controls?	Era controls?
Growth in population of cities over 30,000	−178.47 (48.53)	.70	156.70	Yes	Yes
Growth in population of cities over 30,000	−79.65 (40.40)	.48	185.13	No	Yes
Growth in number of cities over 30,000	−2.28 (.82)	.54	2.63	Yes	Yes
Growth in number of cities over 30,000	−1.52 (.60)	.36	2.75	No	Yes
Proportional growth in population of cities over 30,000	−.30 (.24)	.49	.76	Yes	Yes
Proportional growth in population of cities over 30,000	−.15 (.16)	.37	.76	No	Yes

of Table 2.3 report regressions using the proportional change in the population of cities in a region as the dependent variable. Even if a region's geography makes it relatively hospitable—or inhospitable—to city growth, the presence or absence of an absolutist prince may have the same proportional effect on urban populations. Unfortunately, in early periods the stock of cities in many regions is so low that small random changes in their populations lead to enormous differences in proportional growth. The regressions using proportional change as the dependent variable hint at very large negative effects of princely rule—that a century of princely rule reduces urban populations by a third, for example. But the wide swings in the dependent variable leave the regression with little power, and the coefficient is very imprecisely estimated in rows 5 and 6 of Table 2.3.

The regressions indicate that the presence or absence of absolutism may have been substantively very important for setting the pace and location of urban growth in Europe. Under one possible interpretation of our regression results, rule by absolutist princes in a region simply diverts commerce and urban life to other neighboring regions. In this case, the extent of absolutist regimes would have little effect on the pace of overall western European development. Under another possible interpretation, rule by absolutist princes does not displace merchants and artisans to neighboring regions but simply displaces them back to the countryside. In this case, the extent of absolutist regimes had an enormous effect on overall European urbanization.

The total population living in western European cities of 30,000 or more in 1650 was 4.7 million. Had each of the nine regions experienced an additional century and a half of absolutist rule before 1650, this urban population would have been reduced by two million according to the regression in row 1 of Table 2.3. In such a scenario Europe in 1650 might well have played the same role in world history that it had played in 1000: a poor and barbarous backwater compared to the high civilizations of Islam, India, and China, rather than a continent on the verge of three centuries of world domination.

Conversely, had all of western Europe been free of absolutist rule over 1050–1650, then the regression in row 1 of Table 2.3 predicts that Europe in 1650 would have had a total urban population of nearly 8 million and would have had forty additional cities with more than

30,000 inhabitants. Such a heightened level of commerce and urban civilization might have triggered the industrial revolution considerably earlier.

No matter whether one believes that absolutist regimes displace or eliminate urban activity, the rise of absolutism in regions like Italy and Spain, and absolutism's failure to entrench itself in Holland and early modern England, were according to our regressions decisive factors in making Europe in 1800 a civilization focused on the English Channel and the Atlantic rather than on the Mediterranean. Without the rise of absolutism in southern Europe, the southern half of the continent might have continued to surpass the northern half in commerce and civilization throughout the preindustrial era—as it had surpassed the northern half during the Roman Empire and even during the High Middle Ages before the bubonic plague.

2.4.3 REGION AND ERA EFFECTS

Table 2.4 reports the region and era effects for the same regressions reported in rows 1 and 2 of Table 2.3. Table 2.4 reports what the regression calculates the average values of city growth would be in each region and for each era if other variables in the regression were equal to their sample averages. The western Europe-wide patterns of city growth are clearly visible from the values of the era effects in Table 2.4. City growth—both in the population in large cities and in the number of cities—is on average negative during the crisis and plague period of 1330–1500. Thereafter city growth rebounds, with the growth in the number of large cities recovering to its high medieval average and with the population in large cities expanding much more rapidly. And 1650–1800 sees the explosion in European commerce and urban life across the continent that set the stage for the industrial revolution.

Strong regional patterns in city growth can be discerned in Table 2.4. The low region effect coefficients for Belgium and the Netherlands are as expected: though rich, the Low Countries are small. They could not support urban populations as large as those of regions like France. The high value of the regional dummy coefficient for England is largely a consequence of the extraordinary explosion in British city growth over the 1650–1800 period, at the very end of our sample. Our model does not explain why England industrialized first in the eighteenth century.

Table 2.4   Region and era means for the Russell–de Vries database, controlling for the effect of an absolutist prince

Dependent variable	Growth in population (thousands per century), mean value	Standard error	Growth in number (cities per century), mean value	Standard error
Era				
1050–1200	2.0	36.2	1.25	.61
1200–1330	11.7	36.2	1.25	.61
1330–1500	−56.1	35.1	−1.27	.59
1500–1650	209.1	36.8	1.38	.62
1650–1800	289.3	36.8	2.42	.62
Region				
Austria	30.6	47.2	−.22	.80
Belgium	20.4	47.2	.72	.80
England	254.4	48.5	1.90	.81
France	129.0	49.4	.72	.83
Germany	163.0	52.0	2.04	.87
Netherlands	−46.5	53.0	−.87	.90
Northern Italy	85.9	47.2	2.45	.80
Southern Italy	160.6	52.0	1.63	.87
Spain	30.7	46.8	.71	.79

2.4.4   BASIC RESULTS: INFLUENTIAL OBSERVATIONS

Figure 2.1 graphically displays the source of the correlations that produce the large negative estimated absolutist prince coefficient. The figure corresponds to the regression in the third row of Table 2.3. It plots the partial scatter of the change in the number of large cities in a region on the vertical axis (controlling for nation and era effects) against the presence or absence of an absolutist prince (once again controlling for nation and era effects).

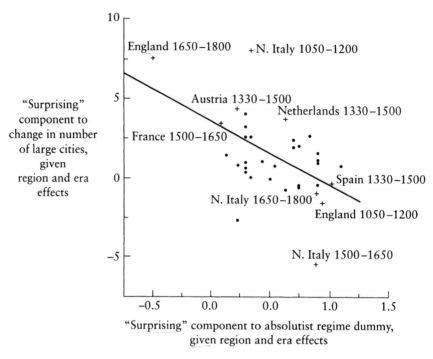

Figure 2.1 Partial scatter of change in number of cities against absolutist regime

A large positive value along the horizontal axis for a region/era data point reveals that this particular data point sees an absolutist regime— and that, given the region and the era, an absolutist regime is surprising. Northern Italy from 1500 to 1650, for example, has a high value along the horizontal axis in Figure 2.1 because it sees absolutism in a region and an era in which absolutism is relatively rare. Conversely, a large negative value along the horizontal axis reveals that the absence of absolutism in this particular case is surprising—England in 1650–1800, for example, is both a country and an era predisposed to absolutism.

Figure 2.1 shows which particular data points have the most "leverage" in generating the strong negative absolutist prince coefficient. The point with the most leverage is England over the years 1650–1800. Other influential points in the high growth/no absolutism corner of the figure include France over 1500–1650 and northern Italy over 1050–1200. At the other end of the least-squares fit line are the influential observations with relative urban decline and absolutist regimes: northern Italy after the arrival of the Habsburgs and their dependents, England under the Norman kings, Spain during the later Middle Ages as its early absolutism gathers strength, and Belgium after the arrival of the Habsburgs.

Thus the influential observations in the database are those one would expect to be important from the standard narratives of European history. In northern Italy, according to the Russell–de Vries database, city population growth during 1200–1330 exceeded by 208,000 people the predicted value from the regression of Table 2.3. In the century and a half following the assertion of Habsburg authority over northern Italy, the population of large cities fell by 335,000 more over 1500–1650 than would be expected from the Table 2.3 regression. Second comes the urban boom in England following the establishment of constitutional monarchy: the excess of English city growth in 1650–1800 over what would have been expected from the Table 2.3 regression amounts to 325,000 people. Third comes the collapse of the cities of the Belgian region in the sixteenth century: a loss of 166,000 from the populations of large cities in excess of what the Table 2.3 regression predicts following the institution of Spanish absolutism by the Habsburg dynasty's viceroy, the Duke of Alva.

The most substantial influence on the regression coefficient is exerted by seventeenth- and eighteenth-century England. The removal of England from the Russell–de Vries database cuts the estimated effect of an absolutist prince on city growth by almost 30 percent. Nevertheless, the effect remains statistically significant at standard confidence levels. England is the only country that significantly shifts the estimated coefficient when it is removed from the sample. The individual removal of other regions from the sample does not significantly shift the estimate of the effect of an absolutist prince on city growth. Nor does the removal of data from any individual era significantly affect the estimates.

An alternative way of looking at the evidence in the Russell–de Vries database is to examine the changes in city growth rates when a region shifts from one type of regime to another. Table 2.5 lists the regions that undergo a regime change, the average rate of population growth in cities of 30,000 or more in that region while it is governed by a non-absolutist regime (controlling for era effects), the average rate of pop-

Table 2.5 City population growth (in thousands) under absolutist and nonabsolutist regimes

Region	Average growth under a nonabsolutist regime	Average growth under an absolutist regime	Difference
Austria	−20	−110	90
Belgium	28	−222	250
England	695	41	654
France	124	226	−102
Spain	−72	−103	31
Northern Italy	123	−134	257

ulation growth under an absolutist regime (once again controlling for era effects), and the difference. In five of the six cases, the populations of large cities grow faster (controlling for era effects) under nonabsolutist regimes. In three cases—northern Italy, Belgium, and England—the differences in rates of city growth are very large. And in only one case—that of France under Bourbon absolutism—does a shift to an absolutist regime fail to be followed by subsequent city growth at a slower pace relative to the average for European regions.

2.4.5 ALTERNATIVE SPECIFICATIONS: FINELY GRADED CLASSIFICATIONS

Does our simple absolutist/nonabsolutist classification of European regimes bias our results? Statistical theory would suggest not: use of a crude classification introduces additional sources of error into statistical relationships, but if a relationship nevertheless shows itself strongly it should be even more apparent using a finer classification.

Nevertheless, to see whether our use of a crude classification has led us astray, we reclassified regimes using an eight-point scale suggested to us by Robert Putnam.[30] At one extreme of the classification is the full constitutional monarchy or republic (1). In order, the other categories are weak-prince standestaats (2), independent city-republics (3), princes checked extraconstitutionally by powerful magnates (4), feudal anarchy (5), strong-prince protoabsolutism (6), nonbureaucratic absolutism (7),

Table 2.6 Finely graded classification of regimes, Russell–de Vries database

Region	1050–1200	1200–1330	1330–1500	1500–1650	1650–1800
Southern Italy	8	7	7	8	8
Northern Italy	3	3	3	8	8
Austria	5	4	7	8	8
Germany	4	4	5	5	5
Netherlands	3	2	2	1	1
Belgium	4	2	2	8	8
England	7	7	6	8	1
France	5	4	4	4	8
Spain	5	2	6	8	8

and, at the other extreme, full bureaucratic absolutism or rule by military conquerors (8). Table 2.6 presents this finely graded classification.

Another possible classification scheme would use Charles Tilly's categories of the relative strength of "capital" as opposed to "coercion."[31] In some regions (like pre-1500 northern Italy), the development of commerce and the accumulation of capital had advanced proportionately further than the mechanisms of large-scale organized coercion, and in these property was relatively more secure (−1 on the scale). In other regions the development of coercion had outrun the development of capital (+1). In still others the development of the two forms of social organization were more equally matched (0). Table 2.7 presents a three-point scale based on Tilly's categories.

Table 2.8 shows our two basic Table 2.3 regressions for the Russell–de Vries database using these two alternative classification schemes. The "regime scale" coefficient estimates the effect on city growth of a shift by one classification, either on the eight-point Putnam scale—for example, from nonbureaucratic to bureaucratic absolutism or from a full constitutional monarchy to a weak-prince standestaat—or on the three-point Tilly scale. Table 2.8 shows that the relationship between city growth and the absence of absolutism is at least as strong using the more finely graded classifications.

Table 2.7 Classification of western Europe regimes by relative development of "coercion" as opposed to "capital," Russell–de Vries database

Region	1050–1200	1200–1330	1330–1500	1500–1650	1650–1800
Southern Italy	1	1	1	1	1
Northern Italy	−1	−1	−1	1	1
Austria	0	0	0	0	1
Germany	0	0	0	0	1
Netherlands	0	0	−1	−1	−1
Belgium	−1	−1	−1	1	1
England	1	1	1	0	−1
France	0	0	0	0	1
Spain	0	−1	0	1	1

2.4.6 ALTERNATIVE SPECIFICATIONS: THE BAIROCH DATABASE

Table 2.9 presents basic results for our second database, drawn from the work of Bairoch and his collaborators, to check that our results are not due to peculiarities in the Russell–de Vries database.[32] Once again the incidence of absolutist rule is significantly and negatively related to urban growth. Coefficients estimated in Table 2.9 are close to the coefficients estimated in Table 2.3: a century of absolutist princely rule reduces populations in cities (of more than 30,000) by 139,000 according to Table 2.9 and by 158,000 according to Table 2.3.[33] Table 2.9 also reports results for a broader sample covering all cities of 10,000 or greater.

2.4.7 DIRECTION OF CAUSALITY

The association between absolutist princes and the retardation of city growth might arise not because strong princes are bad for city growth, but because prosperous cities resist absolutist rule more successfully than the poorer and thinly scattered rural populations of the countryside.[34]

Contrary to this hypothesis, rich regions in our sample are often conquered by princes, with the result that growth deteriorates. Aided by the

Table 2.8 Regression results for the Russell–de Vries database using alternative classification scheme: Effect of a one-point shift in the classification scale

Dependent variable	Coefficient on regime scale (thousand people or number of cities lost per century)	R^2	Standard error of the estimate	Region controls?	Era controls?
Growth in population of cities over 30,000 (Putnam)	−48.44 (13.71)	.70	106	Yes	Yes
Growth in number of cities over 30,000 (Putnam)	−.79 (.22)	.57	1.51	Yes	Yes
Growth in population of cities over 30,000 (Tilly)	−87.06 (29.96)	.68	107	Yes	Yes
Growth in number of cities over 30,000 (Tilly)	−1.52 (.43)	.56	1.52	Yes	Yes

Table 2.9 Absolutist princes and city growth, Bairoch database

Dependent variable	Prince coefficient (thousands of people or number of cities per century)	R^2	Standard error of the estimate	Controlling for
Growth in number of cities of more than 10,000 population	−5.802 (2.157)	.425	7.37	Region, era effects
Growth in population living in cities of more than 10,000 population	−225.70 (53.34)	.434	182.29	Region, era effects
Growth in number of cities of more than 30,000 population	−1.516 (.535)	.245	1.83	Region, era effects
Growth in number of cities of more than 30,000 population	−.423 (.371)	.133	1.83	Era effects only
Growth in population of cities of more than 30,000 population	−149.06 (38.08)	.322	130.11	Region, era effects
Growth in population of cities of more than 30,000 population	−40.82 (28.08)	.125	138.23	Era effects only
Growth in population of cities of more than 30,000—excluding royal capitals	−88.70 (28.24)	.227	96	Region, era effects

popes, the d'Hauteville family conquered and centralized southern Italy and, aided by the popes, northern Italian city-states defended themselves against Salian and Hohenstaufen dynasty attempts to conquer and centralize them. Southern Italy was the richer and more commercial half of the peninsula in 1050. But northern Italy was far richer by 1500.

Habsburg success in establishing absolutism in the southern Low Countries (that were to become Belgium) and failure in establishing absolutism in the northern Low Countries (that were to become the Netherlands) is perhaps the clearest example of the general principle that political and military fortune determines the governing regime, which in turn shapes economic growth. The Dutch Revolt of the sixteenth century preceded the explosion of economic growth in the Netherlands in the seventeenth century. Here the cause and effect is clear, for a substantial fraction of the population of Antwerp fled to Amsterdam over the period 1570–1620 to escape Spanish taxation and the Inquisition.[35] These examples suggest that the correlation between economic decline and absolutist princes says more about the effect of absolutist princely rule on economic life than about the effect of economic prosperity on political order.

2.4.8 THE NEW WORLD

The rise of absolutism in southern Europe—the centralization of Spain and the Habsburg conquest of Milan—roughly coincides with the European discovery of the Americas. The age of exploration that followed saw a shift in the center of gravity of the European economy to the Atlantic coast. Much of what our statistical procedures attribute to the baneful influence of absolutism should, perhaps, be instead attributed to shifts in the base of overseas resources on which Europe could draw. The closing of the Indian Ocean to much Arab trade by the Portuguese and the availability of gold, sugar, and eventually other staple commodities from America all served to make a Mediterranean location less, and an Atlantic location more, advantageous.

This argument is probably true to some degree, but it cannot be the whole story. Although some of the variation in city growth that our models attribute to the presence or absence of absolutism is associated with the general shift of Europe's commercial center of gravity to the Atlantic coast, a substantial proportion is not. Consider northern and southern Italy before 1500, the United Provinces and the Spanish (and then Austrian) Netherlands after 1570, and Britain and France after 1649. In these cases the more absolutist region saw relative decline. But in none of them can this decline be attributed to inferior access to resources from overseas.

Thus we do not believe that we have taken the shifts in European commerce that arose from the age of discovery and mistakenly attributed them to the rise of absolutism. In fact, our failure to take account of the age of discovery in our statistical models works against us: Spain shows only a small decline in the pace of city growth after the coming of Habsburg absolutism, and France shows a rise in the pace of city growth after the coming of Bourbon absolutism. In both cases access to New World resources and a favorable location on the Atlantic coast may have cushioned what would otherwise have been a steeper decline.

2.5   Short Princely Horizons

Our basic interpretation of the evidence suggests that limited governments allow faster city growth because they tend to impose lower and less destructive taxes. One effect, however, might point in the direction of suggesting that lower taxes would be found under absolutist princes. Absolutists might have a longer time horizon than merchants if their businesses have relatively short lives while princes' realms are passed on to their children. As a result, absolutist princes who belong to stable dynasties might care about present and future economic prosperity because it increases the future tax base. If absolutists care more about the long run than do merchants or estates, they would tend to impose lower taxes and nurture economic growth.[36] While attractive theoretically, this argument appears to be wrong empirically. It is a mistake to think that princes establish stable dynasties. In Europe, the time horizons of princes are short.

Consider the monarchy of England, the strongest in Europe for the five hundred years 1000–1500, and still strong up until the Glorious Revolution of 1688. Table 2.10 lists kings, queens, and the dictator (Oliver Cromwell) of England. A check marks each monarch who was followed by a usurped or disputed succession, who—like Elizabeth I—

Table 2.10 The English succession, 1066–1702

Dynasty and monarch	Disputed succession?	Reason
Godwin		
Harold	✓	Harold overthrown by William the Bastard
Norman		
William I "the Bastard"		
William II "the Red"	✓	William II assassinated while hunting: an "accident"
Henry I	✓	Heir Maud displaced by her cousin, Stephen
Blois		
Stephen	✓	Stephen displaced by Maud's son, Henry II
Plantagenet		
Henry II	✓	Dies fleeing the armies of his son, Richard
Richard I "the Lionhearted"	✓	Brother John bribes Austrians to imprison Richard
John "the Landless"		
Henry III		
Edward I		
Edward II	✓	Murdered by queen and her lover
Edward III		
Richard II	✓	Overthrown by his cousin, Henry IV
Lancaster		
Henry IV		
Henry V		
Henry VI	✓	Overthrown by his cousin, Edward IV

Table 2.10 (continued)

Dynasty and monarch	Disputed succession?	Reason
York		
Edward IV	✓	Throne usurped by his brother, Richard III
Richard III	✓	Overthrown by Henry VII
Tudor		
Henry VII		
Henry VIII		
Edward VI	✓	Coup by Dudley faction upon his death
Dudley		
Lady Jane Grey	✓	Ten-day reign, then "bloody" Mary gains power
Tudor		
Mary ("Bloody")		
Elizabeth I	✓	Executed her heir, Mary Queen of Scots
Stuart		
James I		
Charles I	✓	Executed by Parliament
Republic		
Oliver Cromwell	✓	Republic ends when General Monck defects to Charles II
Stuart		
Charles II		
James II	✓	Glorious Revolution: army defects to William III of Orange
Orange		
William III of Orange and Mary	✓	William holds the throne even after Mary's death despite the stronger claim of Mary's sister, Anne

executed her heir, or who—like Richard I "the Lionhearted"—found that his younger brother, the regent John, had bribed the duke of Austria to keep him imprisoned. The succession of eighteen out of thirty-one monarchs went seriously awry before or upon their death. Usually, the threat came from within the extended family of the king: of the rulers only Oliver Cromwell and William "the Bastard" himself came from outside the previous royal family.[37] There was only a 22 percent chance that the English throne would pass peacefully down to the legitimate grandson (or other heir of the second generation) of any monarch.

Instability in the succession keeps princes from taking a long view: how could they afford to worry about the state of the economy under their great-grandsons when they first had to worry about whether their sons would rule and whether they would even have grandsons? England was not exceptional. Most European thrones were insecure.[38] War demanded current rather than future revenue if a dynasty was to benefit from the economy under the ruler's successors.

2.6 Conclusion

We have presented statistical evidence showing that absolutist governments are associated with low economic growth, as measured by city growth, during the eight hundred years prior to the industrial revolution. We have interpreted this evidence as suggesting that "tax policies," broadly interpreted, are less favorable under autocrats than under nonautocratic, often merchant-controlled, governments. This result has implications both for the historical analysis of Europe and for the analysis of modern economic growth. European historians have often written to celebrate the firm establishment of princely authority: princes like Louis XIV "the Sun King" of France, Frederick II "the Great" of Prussia, and Ferdinand and Isabella of Spain are heroes to many because of their successful construction of the absolutist states that provided the cores around which the nation-states of the nineteenth century were to grow.

But from the perspective of the welfare of the people alive at the time, or of the long-term growth of the economy, princely success is economic failure. For the people of southern Italy, the creation of the d'Hauteville *regno* was no blessing; for the people of Belgium, their incorporation into the Habsburg Empire was no benefit; for the people of Iberia, the marriage of Ferdinand and Isabella was no cause for rejoicing. The rise of an absolutist government and the establishment of princely authority are, from a perspective that values economic growth, events to be mourned and not celebrated.

The Allocation of Talent: Implications for Growth

3

3.1 Introduction

When they are free to do so, people choose occupations that offer them the highest returns on their abilities. The ablest people then choose occupations that exhibit increasing returns to ability, since increasing returns allow "superstars" to earn extraordinary returns on their talent (Rosen 1981). In these occupations, being slightly more talented enables a person to win a tournament, to capture a prize, to be promoted, or otherwise to gain a lot by being slightly better than the next person. For example, since everyone wants to listen to the best singer, she can earn a lot more than a marginally inferior singer, especially through compact disc and tape recordings. In occupations with increasing returns to ability, absolute advantage is the critical determinant of pay.

Some people have strong comparative advantage from natural talent for particular activities, such as singing, painting, or playing basketball. These people can earn vastly more by practicing these occupations than any others. But other people do not have great specialized abilities, yet at the same time possess great intelligence, energy, or other generally valuable traits. Such people can become one of the best in many occupations, unlike the best singer or basketball player. They can become

By Kevin M. Murphy, Andrei Shleifer, and Robert W. Vishny; originally published in *Quarterly Journal of Economics*, 106, no. 2 (May 1991): 503–530. © 1991 by the President and Fellows of Harvard College and the Massachusetts Institute of Technology.

entrepreneurs, government officials, lawyers, speculators, clerics, and so on. All these occupations exhibit increasing returns to ability, in that having marginally greater talent leads to a significantly higher payoff. The ablest people then choose occupations where returns to being a superstar are the highest. Here we discuss what determines their choices, and then argue theoretically and empirically that the allocation of talent has significant effects on the growth rate of an economy.

What determines the attractiveness of an occupation to talent? First, the size of the market is crucial: being a superstar in a large market pays more than being a superstar in a small market and so will draw general talent. A person of great general athletic ability, for example, would rather be the tenth best tennis player than the first best volleyball player, since far fewer people would pay to watch him play volleyball. Second, attractive activities have weak diminishing returns to scale. A superstar would want to spread her ability advantage over as large a share of the market as possible, but is limited by constraints on her time, physical ability, and more generally the size of the firm she can run. A surgeon can operate, at most, sixteen hours a day, unless of course she can teach others to use the procedure and reap a return on their time. In contrast, an inventor who can embody her idea in a product overcomes the constraints on her physical time, but is still limited by the size of the firm she can run. Because of stronger diminishing returns to scale, even the most successful doctors do not make as much money as successful entrepreneurs. The faster returns to scale in an activity diminish, the less attractive it is to a person of high ability.

Finally, the compensation contract—how much of the rents on their talent the superstars can capture—determines the sector's attractiveness to talent. For example, if returns to innovation are not protected by patents and cannot be captured by an entrepreneur, entrepreneurship becomes less attractive. When individual output is difficult to measure or is not sufficiently rewarded when measured, talented people are underpaid. Teamwork without attribution is unattractive to superstars, as is horizontal equity. The more of the rents on her talent a superstar can keep, the more likely she is to join a sector.

In different countries and time periods, talented people have chosen occupations in which it was the most attractive to be a superstar. When markets in a country are large and when people can easily organize firms and keep their profits, many talented people become entrepreneurs. Examples of such countries might be Great Britain during the industrial revolution, the United States in the late nineteenth and early twentieth centuries, and some East Asian countries today. In many other countries talented people do not become entrepreneurs, but join the government bureaucracy, army, organized religion, and other rent-seeking (Tullock 1967; Krueger 1974) activities because these sectors offer the highest prizes. In mandarin China, medieval Europe, and many African countries in this century, government service, with the attendant ability to solicit bribes and dispose of tax revenue for the benefit of one's family and friends, was the principal career for the ablest people in the society (Baumol 1990). In Latin America and parts of Africa today as well as in many other countries through history, the most talented people often joined the army as a way to gain access to resources from their own countries (as well as from foreign conquests). In eighteenth-century France, the best and the brightest also became rent seekers. The great chemist Lavoisier's main occupation was tax collecting, and Talleyrand was a bishop with a large tax income despite his prodigious entrepreneurial skills (demonstrated when he escaped to the United States after the French Revolution). These examples show that talent is often general rather than occupation-specific, and that its allocation is therefore governed not just by comparative advantage but also by returns to absolute advantage in different sectors.

Which activities the most talented people choose can have significant effects on the allocation of resources. When talented people become entrepreneurs, they improve the technology in the line of business they pursue, and productivity and income grow. In contrast, when they become rent seekers, most of their private returns come from redistribution of wealth from others and not from wealth creation. As a result, talented people do not improve technological opportunities, and the economy stagnates. Landes (1969) believes that the differential allocation of talent is one of the reasons why the industrial revolution occurred in England in the eighteenth century and not in France. In more recent times the allocation of talent to the rent-seeking sectors may be the reason for stagnation in much of Africa and Latin America, for slow growth in Europe, and for the success of newly industrializing countries where these sectors are smaller.

The allocation of talent to rent seeking is damaging for several reasons. First, as the rent-seeking sectors expand, they absorb labor and other resources and so reduce income. The enormous size of government bureaucracies in some less developed countries illustrates this effect. Second, the tax imposed by the rent-seeking sector on the productive sector reduces incentives to produce, and therefore also reduces income. A striking example of this is the difficulty of starting a firm in Peru, described in De Soto's (1989) *The Other Path*. Finally, if the most talented people become rent seekers, the ability of entrepreneurs is lower, and therefore the rate of technological progress and of growth is likely to be lower. The flow of some of the most talented people in the United States today into law and financial services might then be one of the sources of its low productivity growth. When rent-seeking sectors offer the ablest people higher returns than productive sectors offer, income and growth can be much lower than possible.

The sharp distinction we draw between productive and rent-seeking activities is exaggerated. Pure entrepreneurial activities raise current income as resources are used more efficiently, contribute to growth as technology is improved, and take profits away from competitors. Or take the case of traders in financial markets. Trading probably raises efficiency, since it brings security prices closer to their fundamental values. It might even indirectly contribute to growth if more efficient financial markets reduce the cost of capital. But the main gains from trading come from the transfer of wealth to the smart traders from the less astute who trade with them out of institutional needs or outright stupidity. Even though efficiency improves, transfers are the main source of returns in trading. The same is true for some kinds of law, such as divorce and contract law, the army and the police in some countries, and to some extent organized religion. Although few activities are purely rent seeking or purely efficiency improving, the general point remains: talent goes into activities with the highest private returns, which need not have the highest social returns.

Olson (1982) also addresses the relationship between rent seeking and growth. His idea is that "cumulative distortions" due to rent seeking reduce growth. Olson does not deal with the allocation of talent. Magee, Brock, and Young (1989) discuss rent seeking in great detail and present a model of the allocation of labor between rent seeking and production. Like us, they present some evidence that lawyers have a detrimental effect on growth, using different data. They do not focus on the allocation of talent. Baumol (1990) makes the same basic point as we do that entrepreneurship can be "productive" or "unproductive," and the allocation of people between the two activities depends on the relative returns and provides many interesting historical examples. But Baumol does not discuss the role of increasing returns to ability in explaining why rent seeking and productive entrepreneurship are in fact competing for the very same people, who are the ablest in the society.

3.2 Entrepreneurship and Growth: A One-Sector Model

This section presents a model of entrepreneurship and growth. The model is based on Lucas (1978) and has been previously used by Kuhn (1988). In the model, high-ability people become entrepreneurs and hire low-ability people in their firms. When they do, they improve the current productive techniques. As the improvement of the technique is imitated, everyone's productivity rises, and income grows. The rate of technological progress and of income growth is determined by the ability of the ablest person engaged in entrepreneurship. The model illustrates the importance for growth of allocating the ablest people to the productive sector of the economy.

We assume that there is a distribution of abilities in the population, with the support of $(1, a)$ and the density function $f(A)$. We measure a person's ability by how much he can improve the technology he operates. Ability in our model is unidimensional: we do not address the allocation of people to jobs because of particular aptitude in those jobs. Each person is alive for one period, and the distribution of abilities is the same each period.

We assume that there is only one good in the economy, which is produced by many firms. Each firm is organized by an entrepreneur. If a firm is organized by an entrepreneur with ability A, its profits are given by

$$y = s \cdot A \cdot F(H) - w \cdot H,$$

.1)

where s is the common state of technology, F is the constant over time production function, H is the aggregate human capital (ability) of all the workers employed by this entrepreneur, w is the workers' wage, and the price of the good is normalized to be 1. We can think of $s \cdot A$ as the productivity parameter of the firm, where s is the public level of technology and A is the entrepreneur's contribution. The entrepreneur takes the current state of technology s and the wage w as given. F is a standard concave production function.

The profit function (3.1) builds in our key assumptions. The abler entrepreneurs can earn more than proportionately to their ability higher profits from operating the same technology as the less able entrepreneurs. This is because their output and therefore revenues rise with their ability but their costs do not. There is, therefore, an increasing return to ability. This assumption makes it more attractive for the ablest people to become entrepreneurs, for two reasons. First, they can earn more than proportionately higher profits for a fixed size of the firm H. Second, the abler expand the size of the firm so that they can spread their ability advantage over a larger scale. The concavity of the production function F determines how strongly the returns diminish with scale, and so measures how much one can benefit from high ability.

The first-order condition with respect to H is given by

$$(3.2) \qquad\qquad s \cdot A \cdot F'(H) = w, \qquad A \uparrow H \uparrow$$

so the abler people, obviously, run larger firms. In the extreme case of constant returns to scale, the ablest entrepreneur captures the whole market. In the case of diminishing returns, his ability to expand is limited, but he still runs a larger firm.

Each person in the model lives for one period. He decides whether to become an entrepreneur or a worker. If he becomes an entrepreneur, he picks the size of his firm $H(A)$ according to (3.2) and then earns a profit as in (3.1). If he becomes a worker, he earns $w \cdot A$. We have the increasing return to ability in entrepreneurship since someone with double the ability earns double the income as a worker, but more than double the income as an entrepreneur for a fixed firm size. In fact, what matters here is that returns to ability in entrepreneurship relative to other work be increasing.

A person becomes an entrepreneur when

3)

$$s \cdot A \cdot F(H(A)) - w \cdot H(A) > w \cdot A,$$

and a worker otherwise. The abler people become entrepreneurs in equilibrium, and the less able ones become workers. There is a cutoff ability $A*$ such that those with higher ability become entrepreneurs and those with lower ability become workers.

The demand for workers by entrepreneurs must equal the supply of workers:

.4)

$$\underbrace{\int_1^{A*} Af(A)dA}_{\text{Supply}} = \underbrace{\int_{A*}^{a} H(A)f(A)dA}_{\text{Demand}}$$

Equation (3.4) describes how the real wage adjusts. If there are too many workers and too few entrepreneurs, there is excess supply of labor, and so the best workers want to switch to entrepreneurship. Conversely, if there are too few workers, the wage is high, and the marginal entrepreneurs would rather become workers.

To specify the growth model, we need to describe the evolution of technology s. We assume that the state of technology today is the state of the last period times the ability of the ablest entrepreneur in the last period:

.5) $$s(t) = s(t - 1) \cdot (\text{maximum ability of an entrepreneur at } t - 1).$$

This assumption says that last period's best practice becomes common knowledge this period and is therefore accessible to any entrepreneur, who can then improve on it. The constantly improving technology generates permanent growth in our model. In addition, the assumption that the entrepreneur does not capture the future returns from his innovation builds in the standard externality, as in Arrow (1962). As in Arrow, this assumption generates inefficiency in some versions of the model.

The model we present does not distinguish between innovation and running firms. In reality, they are distinct activities and in principle can be done by different people. In this case, how the returns from innovation and managing are divided can influence the willingness of people to become innovators. This is one of the examples of the way in which contracting can influence the allocation of talent. Historical experience, especially from the British industrial revolution, shows that the two functions (innovation and management) have very often been combined in the same person, suggesting that the problem of splitting the rewards is substantial enough to overcome the forces of comparative advantage.

This model is essentially static, since agents take the state of technology as given. The equilibrium is easy to describe. Each period all agents with ability above $A*$ become entrepreneurs, and those below $A*$ become workers. The profit function and the income of workers are homogeneous in s and w, which means that $A*$ is constant over time. The same part of the distribution becomes entrepreneurs each period. Technology, wages, profits, and income per capita all grow at the constant rate $a - 1$ given by the ability of the best entrepreneur. This person determines the rate of growth of this economy.

The allocation of resources in this economy is first-best efficient. This means both that the growth rate is efficient, and that the cutoff ability level $A*$ between entrepreneurs and workers is efficient. The latter result obtains because both the social and the private product of the least able entrepreneur is exactly equal to his wage as a worker. The efficiency of the growth rate is very special: it is a consequence of having only one sector and not having any labor supply decisions by entrepreneurs that might be distorted. At the same time the flavor of the result that more talented people are allocated to entrepreneurial activities with beneficial consequences for growth is going to be preserved in more general specifications.

This simple model illustrates several general principles. First, the ablest people in the society enter occupations where they can take advantage of increasing returns to ability. In this model there is only one such activity—entrepreneurship—and so the question of *which* sector with increasing returns to ability to enter does not arise. When the ablest people become entrepreneurs, they organize production and improve the available techniques. Second, the growth rate of the economy is determined by the ability of the entrepreneurs. It is therefore essential for growth that the ablest people turn to entrepreneurship. Next we examine the implications of introducing an alternative sector that competes for the talents of the entrepreneurs.

3.3 A Two-Sector Model

In this section we discuss the allocation of talent between sectors. The determinant of attractiveness of a sector that we model formally is the extent of diminishing returns to scale. Nonetheless, in interpreting the results, it is important to remember that market size and contracts also affect the allocation of talent.

Suppose that there are two sectors rather than one. Each sector has its own concave production function, but sectors are identical in all the other respects. Suppose also that preferences are Cobb-Douglas, so that the same fixed share of income is spent on a given good each period. Denote the share of income spent on good 1 by b. For this model we can prove the following:

Proposition 3.1 If the production function for good 1 is more elastic than that for good 2, then each period the ablest people down to some constant over time threshold ability level A_1 become entrepreneurs in sector 1, the next range of ability down to a constant over time A_2 become entrepreneurs in sector 2, and the least able people become workers.

The ablest people are all drawn into the sector with less diminishing returns (higher elasticity of output with respect to labor), because they run larger firms there and so can spread their ability advantage over a larger scale. The quasi-rents accruing to talent are higher in that sector. Productivity in each sector grows at the rate given by the ability of the ablest entrepreneur in that sector, which of course is higher in sector 1. The real wage grows at the rate $g = a^b \cdot A_1^{1-b}$, which is the weighted average of productivity growth rates in the two sectors. At the same time the price of good 1 falls over time relative to that of good 2, since technological progress is faster in sector 1. The fall in the relative price of good 1 exactly offsets the increase in the relative productivity, so that in equilibrium revenues and profits in each sector grow at the same rate g as do wages. Because revenues, profits, and wages all grow at the rate g, the cutoff ability levels A_1 and A_2 between sectors remain constant over time.

There is a stark inefficiency in this model. At the social optimum the ablest person becomes an entrepreneur in one sector, and the second ablest person in the other sector. That way both sectors' productivity grows at the maximum possible rate. In equilibrium, however, the second ablest person would rather be in the sector with less rapidly diminishing returns, since the first one captures only a small part of that sector, and there is still more money for the ablest person to make in this rather than in the other sector. Each person is quasi–rent seeking, and quasi-rents on ability are higher in sector 1. As a result, all the ablest people become entrepreneurs in sector 1, where the externality from all of them other than the ablest is zero. In contrast, the person generating the externality in sector 2 is much less able, and as a result that sector's productivity grows at a much lower rate. The pursuit of quasi-rents by the able people unbalances growth of the two sectors, with the result that one grows inefficiently slowly.

This inefficiency is much more general than our model, in which only the ablest person determines the rate of technological progress, would suggest. Obviously, the result that people of comparable ability bunch into the same sector does not depend on the form of externality. So unless such bunching generates the maximum externality, there will be an inefficiency. We see no reason why bunching of people of comparable ability into the same sector is optimal, so many types of externality generate an inefficiency. For example, if the externality depends on the *average* or *total* ability of entrepreneurs in a given sector, it may still be efficient to have very similar distributions of abilities in the two sectors. One can argue perhaps that there is an agglomeration economy of people with comparable abilities working in the same sector, and that the pace of innovation depends on that. In this case, one would want many innovators of comparable ability working together. But again, there is no reason to think that the number of people needed to take advantage of the agglomeration economy is as large as this model would put into the same sector, or that the agglomeration economy is the highest in the sector where the most talented people go. The equilibrium we have is inefficient, except by coincidence. The inefficiency is smaller, of course, when individuals have comparative advantage at working in particular sectors or when there are increasing returns to agglomeration of talent.

The ablest people tend to flow into a sector where they can spread their ability advantage over the largest scale. In the model this means that they run the largest firms in the economy, a prediction that seems patently false. We have assumed in this model that the compensation arrangements enable the ablest people to collect full quasi-rents from their talents (though none of the future rents because of perfect imitation). If this is not the case in some sectors, the ablest people would move into sectors where they collect the most even if firms are smaller. The reasons that people cannot collect full quasi-rents have to do with imperfect contracting and problems of allocating output to individuals. The allocation is then determined by the compensation contract and not just by technology.

In fact, differences in contracts between industries are probably as important or more important than physical diminishing returns to scale. In industries where it is easy to identify and reward talent, it might be possible to pay the able people the true quasi-rents on their ability and so to attract them. This is probably true in industries at the early stages of their development, where able people can start and run firms rather than work as part of a team. Perhaps the reason the auto industry attracted enormous talent when it started but attracts much less talent now is that talent was easier to identify and reward earlier. Starting one's own company is obviously the most direct way to capitalize on one's talent without sharing the quasi-rents. Talent will then flow into industries where it is easy to start a firm, and these will be the newer and less capital-intensive industries. Also, talent will flow into sectors with less joint production, so it is easier to assign credit and reward contributions. Finally, the most talented people will not go into activities where horizontal equity and other ethical considerations prevent them from capturing the quasi-rents on their ability. Meritocracy is an obvious attractor of talent.

We emphasize that what matters for the allocation of talent is the relative rewards in different sectors. If all sectors tax quasi-rents to ability equally, then obviously the compensation contract will not make any of them more attractive. This logic also suggests that there are two ways for a particular sector to be attractive to high-ability people. The first is for this sector to have attractive compensation contracts; the second is for the other sectors to have unattractive contracts. Alternative opportunities are thus a key determinant of the allocation of talent.

The Cobb-Douglas assumption on preferences gives the result that the allocation of talent across sectors is constant over time. If we relaxed this assumption, the allocation of talent would change over time, and the analysis would become more complicated. The Cobb-Douglas assumption also has the unfortunate implication that the level of technology in a sector does not affect who goes into it. There is thus no sense in which the most talented people are attracted to "hot" sectors that experience a technology shock or a price rise (although of course the sector to which the best people go grows faster). To analyze how the allocation of talent might change in response to such shocks—in order to explain, for example, the U.S. experience in the 1970s and 1980s—we need to depart from the simple framework. Below we consider one plausible framework and look at the static allocation problem rather than a growth model.

Consider a one-period model with two sectors with prices p_1 and $p_2 < p_1$, and identical production functions. In our current model this could not be an equilibrium, because all entrepreneurs would rather be in sector 1 than in sector 2. But suppose that there are only a fixed number of firms, n_1 in sector 1 and n_2 in sector 2, and there is no free entry. Then entrepreneurs bid for the opportunity to run the firms, and the owners of these firms earn quasi-rents on their fixed factor. The equilibrium is easy to describe. The ablest n_1 people go into sector 1, the next n_2 go into sector 2, and the rest become workers. Let the ability of the least able entrepreneur in sector 1 be A_1, and that of the least able entrepreneur in sector 2 be A_2. The entrepreneur with ability A_2 earns $w \cdot A_2$, and the rest of his profits go to the fixed factor in sector 2. Similarly, the least able entrepreneur in sector 1 earns what the ablest entrepreneur in sector 2 does, and the rest of his profits go to the fixed factor in sector 1.

In this equilibrium the abler people enter the hotter sector with the higher price, and free entry does not make them indifferent between sectors. The reason that the abler people end up in the hotter sector is that they bid more for the fixed factors because it is worth more to them to gain access to these factors. The fixed factors get the rents of the least able people gaining access to them, just as in Ricardo, and the abler people earn quasi-rents on their ability as well.

We describe this extension for two reasons. First, it explains why the implausible feature of our basic model, namely that the level of technology does not affect the allocation of talent, is not really a problem. More important, this extension helps explain why changes in particular sectors can attract a different type of talent into that sector. Suppose that there is a technological improvement in some sector, say financial services, and so the output per unit of ability in that sector rises sharply. Suppose also that demand is elastic and that the number of firms in that sector is fixed in the short run. In this case, we might see that the ability of people moving into this sector rises, since they are able to profit the most working in a scarce number of firms. By doing so, they would pay the most to the owners of those firms for the privilege of working there. Without free entry we would see that some of the benefits of the productivity increase would go to the firm owners, and some to the new employees who can produce the most.

When the ability of the most talented employees joining a sector rises, so does technological progress in that sector. This illustrates an important positive feedback in this model: when a sector with elastic demand experiences a positive technology shock, it attracts better talent, and so technology improves further. Such continuation of the original innovation or other rent-creating shock through attraction of talent describes the growth of many industries (Porter 1990). This model might explain, for example, the enormous technological progress in the U.S. financial services in the 1980s after deregulation.

3.4   Rent Seeking and Growth

In this section we introduce rent seeking into the one-sector growth model. We have described rent seeking in detail in the introduction; here we simply take it to be a tax on the profits of the productive sector. Specifically, we assume that when an entrepreneur earns a profit y, $T \cdot y$ is taken away by rent seekers through bribes, taxes, fees, and other costs of doing business in a rent-seeking society. We assume that T is exogenous. One might argue in contrast that the amount of rent seeking is a function of the level of development, so that T is a function of the level of income or the stability of government (Olson 1982). For simplicity, we assume that there is no productive component to rent seeking; it is therefore not a completely accurate description of financial services, law, or organized religion. We assume that rent seekers tax profits rather than all income, including wages, to simplify the analysis. This assumption leads to a distortion of allocation of people between entrepreneurship and work, but to no distortion in the size of the firm once a person becomes an entrepreneur. Of course some taxes, such as the famous growth tax in India which imposes a penalty on revenue increases beyond a certain rate, distort the size of the firm as well (Little, Mazumdar, and Page 1987).

The rent-seeking technology is also subject to increasing returns to ability and diminishing returns to scale. We assume that the rents collected by a person with ability A are given by

(3.6)
$$R = \underbrace{\frac{A \cdot G(H) \cdot T \cdot Y}{\int AG(H)f(A)dA}}_{\text{rent seekers}} - w \cdot H,$$

where H is the total human capital or ability of others that this rent seeker employs, Y is the aggregate profits of the entrepreneurs, and $G(H)$ is the concave production function in the rent-seeking sector. In this specification the share of total gross rents $T \cdot Y$ collected by the rent seeker of ability A is proportional to $A \cdot G(H)$. Total gross rents collected by the rent seekers thus automatically add up to the total revenues lost by the entrepreneurs. We assume for simplicity that there is no technological progress in rent seeking. This assumption allows us to keep the model homogeneous in the state of technology s. The rent-seeking technology, like the productive technology, allows abler people to earn higher profits at a fixed size H as well as to expand H to maximize profits. In this respect, rent seeking is similar to entrepreneurship.

Each person now has three choices: entrepreneurship, work, and rent seeking, and he picks the most attractive option. If it is one of the former two, he also sets the size of the firm. In equilibrium the wage adjusts until the combined demand for workers by the productive and the rent-seeking sector is equal to the supply of workers:

(3.7)
$$\underbrace{\int H(A)f(A)dA}_{\text{rent seekers}} + \underbrace{\int H(A)f(A)dA}_{\text{entrepreneurs}} = \underbrace{\int Af(A)dA.}_{\text{workers}}$$

We consider two cases. In the first the production function (F) for output is more elastic with respect to H than the production function (G) for rent seeking; in the second it is the other way around. The results are similar to those of the two-sector model. In the first case the ablest people go into the productive sector where firms are the largest, the next group goes into rent seeking, and the least able become workers. The cutoff ability levels are constant because the model is homogeneous in the level of technology s and so the allocation decision is the same each period. In this case the level of technology s, productivity, wages, profits, and aggregate returns to rent seekers all grow at rate a—the ability of the ablest person in the economy. The growth rate is optimal since this person is an entrepreneur. However, the level of income is lower than it would be without rent seeking. First, some workers are allocated to the rent-seeking rather than to the productive sector, and as a result output is forgone. Put differently, demand for workers in the rent-seeking sector drives up wages and so reduces equilibrium employment in the productive sector. Second, the less able entrepreneurs become rent seekers, and so do not organize production. Although this does not lead to a reduction in the growth rate, it leads to a once-and-for-all reduction in the level of income.

The situation is worse when the production function for rent seeking is more elastic and so the ablest people become rent seekers because firms (correcting for compensation contracts) are the largest in that sector. The next group becomes entrepreneurs, and the least able are workers. Now output grows at a lower rate than a, since the ablest entrepreneur is no longer the ablest person available. Here we have three distortions from rent seeking. It absorbs labor; it distorts the choice of least able entrepreneurs who now become workers; and finally, it turns the ablest people, who are pivotal for growth, into rent seekers. The model thus captures the crucial point that rent seeking can reduce growth (and not just the level of income) because it attracts potential innovators and entrepreneurs. As the ability of the ablest person who becomes an entrepreneur falls, so does the growth rate.

This model makes several interesting predictions. First, suppose that the tax rate T on entrepreneurial profits falls. This fall can correspond to the improvement in the property rights suggested by North and Thomas (1973), and also to a reduction in corruption or in taxes. The first direct effect of this fall is to reduce the size of the rent-seeking sector. Workers move out of this sector and into production. Also, in the case where the ablest people are entrepreneurs, the ablest rent seekers move out and become entrepreneurs since incentives for this activity have improved. Although the growth rate in this case remains at a, the level of income jumps as resources move from rent seeking into entrepreneurship and production.

The case where the ablest persons were rent seekers is different. As the tax rate T falls, the least able rent seekers become entrepreneurs, and so the ability of the best entrepreneur rises. As a result, not only does the level of income jump, but the growth rate also increases as the person determining the growth rate of technology is now more talented. This result demonstrates perhaps the most important cost of a large rent-seeking sector (high T). By drawing people out of entrepreneurship and into rent seeking, it reduces the growth rate of the economy permanently. The result also demonstrates how a one-time reduction in the extent of rent seeking can permanently raise the growth rate of the economy. Barro (1991) finds that countries with smaller government consumption relative to GDP grow faster, which is what our theory would predict if government consumption were a measure of the tax rate T.

In this model, changes in the tax rate T do not affect whether the ablest person is an entrepreneur or a rent seeker. The reason is that the ablest person has the strongest comparative advantage at being in the sector that he is in, and so is the last to switch. For example, as T rises, there is more entry into the rent-seeking sector, but the entry is by people who have the least attachment to other sectors. This entry drives down the returns without affecting the allocation of inframarginal people. Where the ablest person goes is determined in the model only by the relative elasticity of the two production functions, or how fast the diminishing returns set in, in the two activities. Since the career choice of the ablest people determines the growth rate, how fast returns to scale diminish in entrepreneurship and in rent seeking is one of the key determinants of growth.

More generally, the allocation of talent between entrepreneurship and rent seeking is determined by market size and by the nature of contracts as well as by firm size (diminishing returns to scale) in the two types of activities. The puzzle that must be addressed is why, in most countries and times, talented individuals choose rent-seeking activities, and the entrepreneurial choice is a fairly rare exception. Rent seeking seems to have an inherent advantage as a career choice. Table 3.1 summarizes characteristics of countries and markets that influence the allocation of talent; in the following we discuss why the choice is so often rent seeking.

Rent-seeking activities are attractive when the potential amounts to be taken are large. When the "official" rent-seeking sectors such as the

Table 3.1   Factors favoring rent seeking and entrepreneurship

	Factors making rent seeking an attractive choice	Factors making entrepreneurship an attractive choice
Market size	Large resources go to "official" rent-seeking sectors, such as the government, army, or religion. Poorly defined property rights make wealth accessible to "unofficial" rent seekers. Large wealth is up for grabs, especially relative to smaller goods markets.	Large market for goods. Good communication and transportation that facilitate trade.
Firm size	Substantial authority and discretion of rent seekers (such as government officials, army, etc.) enable them to collect large sums unhindered by law or custom.	Easy entry and expansion, few diminishing returns in operations, access to capital markets.
Contracts	Ability to keep a large portion of collected rents. In firms, observability of output that yields appropriate rewards.	Clear property rights, patent protection. No expropriation of rents by rent seekers. Ability to start firms to collect quasi-rents on talent.

government, religion, or the army are big and powerful, the resources (and power) that a talented person gets by joining them and succeeding are large. As a result, these sectors attract talent. In such countries the official institutions have well-defined property rights over private wealth. Because the "official" rent-seeking institutions are and have been extremely powerful in most countries, this type of rent seeking often attracts talent.

Countries with poorly defined property rights also attract talent into rent seeking, since success at redefining these property rights brings high rewards. Rent seeking pays because a great deal of wealth is up for grabs. In these cases, rent seeking is "unofficial" and takes the form of bribery, theft, or litigation. In the United States today, lobbying to influence the Congress and some kinds of litigation are examples of this activity, which is so attractive because the redistributed wealth is enormous. In many countries such "unofficial" rent seekers are official agents of the government, who use their official positions to collect unofficial rents. Customs officials in Equatorial Guinea take a cut of meat and liquor imports allegedly to "inspect" them. Like the "official" rent seeking, "unofficial" rent seeking out-competes entrepreneurship for talent when wealth available for taking is larger.

Importantly, rent seeking unlike entrepreneurship usually deals with capital and other forms of wealth, which rent seekers fight over. Entrepreneurship typically allows the innovator to capture a portion of a market for some period of time, which is in most cases much less lucrative than getting one's hands on a piece of the country's wealth. Moreover, a country with large wealth but slow growth is especially attractive for rent seeking. The reason is that new goods often have more than unitary income elasticity of demand, and therefore future growth is essential for the profitability of innovation. Slow growth then reduces the attractiveness of innovation and entrepreneurship. This logic suggests that the productivity growth slowdown can be self-sustaining: as talent leaves entrepreneurship and growth slows, the returns to entrepreneurship fall further, relative to those to rent seeking. We thus expect rent seeking to prosper in countries with substantial wealth and slow growth, such as the United States or Argentina.

Feasible firm size, broadly interpreted, also often benefits rent seeking at the expense of entrepreneurship. When rent seekers such as government officials or the military have substantial authority and discretion, they can expand their operations and collect larger sums unhindered by law or custom. In this respect, poorly defined property rights are responsible not just for large potential markets for rent seeking, but also for the ability of rent seekers to run larger "firms."

In entrepreneurship, physical diminishing returns to scale are only one limitation on firm size. In many less developed countries legal restrictions on entry and on expansion, such as industrial capacity licensing, are a government-imposed limitation on firm size that makes entrepreneurship less attractive. Access to credit is also a crucial determinant of feasible firm size, and therefore of the attractiveness of entrepreneurship. Because rent seekers themselves often limit the ability of entrepreneurial firms to expand, high returns to rent seeking often go with low returns to entrepreneurship. Entry and capacity restrictions, for example, invite bribes. In contrast, in countries where firms can easily organize and expand with few constraints from the state and from the capital markets, entrepreneurship will be attractive to the most talented relative to rent seeking. When rent seekers tax entrepreneurs by limiting firm expansion, the ablest entrepreneurs suffer and the best potential entrepreneurs become rent seekers.

Perhaps the single most important determinant of the allocation of talent is the compensation contract. The ability of rent seekers to keep a large portion of the rents on their talents, whether legally or illicitly, raises the attractiveness of rent seeking. In many countries official positions come with a territory that allows the collection of bribes. People pay hundreds of thousands of dollars for positions with the power to allocate supposedly free water to farmers in India, since these jobs give them monopoly rights to charge for water. Tax farmers throughout history bid fortunes for positions. Illegal rent seeking is most attractive when it is protected by the state. What distinguishes these rent-seeking activities is that, at the margin, rent seekers can keep all or most of the return from their ability.

In market rather than official rent seeking, such as some forms of law and speculation, the output of rent seeking is often easily verifiable and therefore can be rewarded. This might not be true in entrepreneurial jobs where the inventor cannot start his own firm but must work as part of a team in a large firm. In mature manufacturing industries in the United States, for example, it is extremely hard to identify individual contributions and to reward them accordingly even if they are identified. The difficulty of verifying output might drive the potential entrepreneurs out of such industries and into rent seeking.

To summarize, talent in the rent-seeking sectors in many countries benefits from property rights that enable rent seekers to claim a substantial part of the productive output through official and unofficial expropriation. As talent joins the rent-seeking sectors, it expands and improves them. The higher taxes on productive activities reduce the returns to entrepreneurship, and drive even more talent into rent seeking. Large rent-seeking institutions and weak rent-protecting institutions draw talent out of entrepreneurship. One benefit of the shrinking rent-seeking institutions, such as the decline of central government, is that talent moves into productive activities. As the *New York Times* described Hungary's move to capitalism, "Government now has to compete with business for talented workers."

In some countries entrepreneurs have managed at least in part to avoid the tax from rent seekers by becoming rent seekers themselves. In these countries it is common for government officials to own businesses run either by themselves or by their relatives, and to protect these businesses from competition or from bribes by virtue of their government positions. Misallocation of talent nonetheless persists, since a large portion of these people's time is spent in rent-seeking activities designed to foster their own businesses at the expense of those of their competitors.

Our model has one additional interesting implication. Suppose that the most lucrative sector for the most talented is rent seeking and that there is a dominant group in the population that has access to that sector. Suppose that this group now excludes some ethnic or racial minority from access to the rent-seeking sector, such as the army or the government. In this case, the ablest people from the excluded group must go into other sectors, one of which might very well be entrepreneurship. If the exclusion is effective, and if the overall distribution of abilities is the same for each group, this means that the ability of the ablest entrepreneurs rises. The growth rate of the economy then also rises as a result of this exclusion. Moreover, exclusion of others benefits the dominant group, both because it leaves them a greater share of the rent-seeking pie and because the size of that pie rises as the quality of entrepreneurship improves. Competition for the rent-seeking positions may in part explain why Jews have been excluded from many rent-seeking occupations in Europe, the Chinese have similarly been excluded in Malaysia, and the Indians and Lebanese in Africa. Faster growth can be one of the few inadvertent benefits of discrimination in rent seeking. Of course, discrimination against minorities in entrepreneurship hurts both them and the majority.

3.5 Evidence

A major implication of this discussion is that the allocation of talented people to entrepreneurship is good for growth and their allocation to rent seeking is bad for growth. Unfortunately, it is hard to directly measure the allocation of talent to these two types of activities. Barro (1991) provides some evidence that high government consumption and a high number of coups, both of which might measure the extent of rent seeking, have a negative effect on growth, but this finding is too indirect. An alternative approach is to associate individual occupations with entrepreneurship and rent seeking. Magee, Brock, and Young (1989) have in fact assembled data on the number of lawyers in thirty-five countries, and found that countries with more lawyers grow more slowly. We have not found data on the numbers of people in different occupations in different countries, but have instead used data collected by UNESCO on college enrollments in different fields for a large cross-section of countries. We use the data on college enrollment in law as a measure of a talent allocated to rent seeking, and on college enrollment in engineering as a measure of talent allocated to entrepreneurship. Although lawyers do different things in different countries, and undergraduate enrollments might not be a good proxy for the extent of each activity, these are the best measures of rent seeking and entrepreneurship we could find.

We use Barro's (1991) data set augmenting the Summers and Heston (1988) data base. We frame our analysis as an extension of Barro's regressions. The variables we use for each country are the growth rate of real GDP per capita between 1970 and 1985, real GDP per capita in 1960, average from 1970 to 1985 of the ratio of real government consumption (exclusive of defense and education) to real GDP, primary school enrollment rate in 1960, average from 1970 to 1985 of the ratio of real private investment to real GDP, and the number of revolutions and coups. Although these are not all of Barro's variables, they are the most important ones, and include measures of general investment in human capital (primary education), in physical capital (private investment), and of government consumption.

We add to Barro's list the ratio of college enrollments in law to total college enrollments in 1970, and the same ratio for engineering. The reason that we choose total enrollments rather than population or population of a given age as a denominator is that we are interested in the allocation of the ablest people among fields. Fractions of college enrollment in law and engineering in fact measure the incentives to be in these fields as opposed to being in college more generally. Looking at the ratios to population would tell us less about the allocation of the ablest

Table 3.2 Summary statistics for engineering and law majors as percentage of college students

	Full sample		Countries with 10,000 or more students	
	Engineering	Law	Engineering	Law
Mean	10.39	8.89	12.03	7.25
Median	9.08	5.52	10.25	5.61
25th percentile	3.83	2.65	7.26	3.10
75th percentile	14.31	11.20	15.92	10.05

people and more about incentives to go to college. The intersection of the sample of countries for which data on college enrollments by field are available for 1970 with Barro's 98-country sample for which data on investment and government consumption are available yields 91 observations.

We run the regressions first for all 91 countries in the sample, and then for the 55 countries that have more than 10,000 college students. We look at countries with more than 10,000 students in order to reduce the problem of college attendance abroad. We found this approach preferable to running population-weighted regressions, since some large population countries have a significant commitment to education abroad. In addition, the subsample with large college enrollments gets rid of some smaller countries that probably have less reliable data, and might be preferred for this reason as well. Table 3.2 presents the summary statistics for the engineering and law variables in the total and the restricted sample.

Table 3.3 presents the basic results of the regression of 1970 to 1985 growth rate on law and engineering enrollments, controlling only for the 1960 GDP. In the regression for all countries, we find a positive and significant effect of engineers on growth, and a negative and basically insignificant ($t = 1.2$) effect of lawyers on growth. The signs of the coefficients are consistent with the theory that rent seeking reduces growth, while entrepreneurship and innovation raise it. If an extra 10 percent of

Table 3.3 Regressions of growth of growth-read GDP per capita between 1970 and 1985 on proportions of majors in engineering and law (in 1970)

Model	All countries (1)	>10,000 Students (2)
Constant	0.013	0.015
	(0.005)	(0.004)
Engineering	0.054	0.125
	(0.027)	(0.037)
Law *insignificant*	−0.031	−0.065
	(0.025)	(0.049)
GDP 1960	0.000	−0.002
	(0.001)	(0.001)
N	91	55
R^2	0.09	0.23

enrollment were in engineering, which corresponds roughly to doubling average engineering enrollments, the growth rate would rise 0.5 percent per year. If an extra 10 percent were in law, which also roughly corresponds to doubling enrollments, growth would fall 0.3 percent per year. If we look at countries with large student populations, the effect of engineers more than doubles and becomes more significant. The negative effect of lawyers also doubles, but remains insignificant. The R^2 of the second regression is much higher as well.

We cannot interpret these relationships as structural, of course, since law and engineering enrollments might be correlated with other sources of growth. Accordingly, we next consider the Barro regression augmented by our law and engineering variables, and then decompose the reduced-form effects of law and engineering on growth into direct effects and indirect effects operating through correlation with other variables.

Table 3.4 presents the results of the augmented Barro regression for the whole and the large college population samples. In both regressions investment in physical and in human capital increase growth, while government consumption and revolutions reduce growth. There is also some evidence of convergence as in Barro, although it is not clear that it makes sense to define convergence holding investment constant. The

Table 3.4   Determinants of growth rate of real GDP per capita between 1970 and 1985

Model	All countries (1)	>10,000 Students (2)
Constant	0.018 (0.010)	0.020 (0.011)
Investment	0.086 (0.032)	0.085 (0.039)
Primary school enrollment	0.022 (0.009)	0.012 (0.011)
Government consumption	−0.145 (0.040)	−0.064 (0.053)
Revolutions and coups	−0.028 (0.009)	−0.035 (0.009)
GDP 1960	−0.007 (0.001)	−0.006 (0.001)
Engineering	−0.010 (0.023)	0.054 (0.034)
Law	−0.024 (0.020)	−0.078 (0.040)
N	91	55
R^2	0.47	0.56

direct effects of lawyers and engineers are very insignificant in the whole sample, with the sign on engineers switching to negative. In contrast, the direct effect of engineering in the reduced sample is still positive and almost significant, although it falls to under half of the total effect in Table 3.3. More surprisingly, the direct effect of lawyers is negative and significant in the reduced sample, and its absolute value is higher than in the whole sample. Based on this sample, Table 3.4 confirms the direct negative relationship between rent seeking and growth, and the direct positive relationship between entrepreneurship and growth.

The positive direct effect of engineers and the negative direct effect of lawyers are consistent with our theory, which says that the rate of technological progress is determined by the allocation of talent. If engineering is an attractive major, the quality of talent in engineering is higher, therefore entrepreneurs are of higher quality, the rate of technological progress is greater, and the growth rate of GDP per capita is higher. This argument of course assumes a positive correlation between the fraction of college majors in engineering and the rate of technological progress that they will generate and does not deal with the abilities of engineers. Similarly, if law is an attractive major, the quality of rent seekers is higher, and hence, indirectly, the quality of entrepreneurs is lower, and technological progress and income growth are smaller. There may be other mechanisms that explain these direct effects, of course, and our theory also predicts that there may be indirect effects of the allocation of talent on growth. For example, less rent seeking and more technological progress are likely to raise physical investment.

To decompose the total effect of lawyers and engineers on growth from Table 3.3 into the direct and indirect effects, Table 3.5 presents the estimates from auxiliary regressions of Table 3.4 independent variables (investment, primary education, government consumption, and revolutions) on lawyers and engineers. In all these regressions, we control for 1960 real GDP. High engineering enrollments predict high investment in pure and physical capital, low government consumption, and low revolutions and coups. This suggests that some of the effect of engineers on growth comes from the fact that countries with many engineering majors also do other things that are good for growth, such as educate the young and accumulate capital. They also avoid things that are bad for growth, such as government consumption and revolutions. Our engineering variable may be a proxy for good incentives and the efficiency of allocation on a variety of margins.

In contrast to the finding for engineers, the correlations between Table 3.4 independent variables and law enrollments are weak and insignificant. To our surprise, lawyers do not have a significant negative effect on investment, which they would if rent seekers specialized in redistribution of physical capital. The results suggest that most of the effect of lawyers on growth is direct.

Table 3.6 decomposes the total effect into the direct and the indirect effects. For engineers the direct effect on growth is trivial for the whole sample, but about half of the total for the reduced sample. As we mentioned, this direct effect is consistent with the view that allocating good people to entrepreneurial activities is good for growth. In both samples the indirect effects are large because engineering enrollments

Table 3.5   Regressions of Table 3.2 independent variables on proportions of majors in engineering and law

Model	All countries (1)	>10,000 Students (2)
A. Estimated auxiliary regressions for engineering		
Investment	0.243 (0.081)	0.432 (0.119)
Primary schooling	0.904 (0.271)	1.02 (0.408)
Government consumption	−0.142 (0.056)	−0.181 (0.078)
Revolutions and coups	−0.090 (0.265)	−0.300 (0.445)
N	91	55
B. Estimated auxiliary regressions for law insignificant		
Investment	−0.093 (0.076)	0.055 (0.160)
Primary schooling	−0.093 (0.254)	0.576 (0.548)
Government consumption	0.006 (0.053)	−0.089 (0.105)
Revolutions and coups	−0.121 (0.248)	0.141 (0.597)
N	91	55

are strongly positively correlated with investment in physical and human capital, which are positively correlated with growth, and negatively correlated with government consumption, which is negatively correlated with growth. This result suggests that countries that invest and have a good labor force attract able people into engineering as well and that as a result of this allocation of resources they grow. They do all the right things at the same time. They also avoid high government consumption, which discourages engineering majors as well as reduces growth. Avoiding revolutions does not discourage engineering concentrators, and so there is no indirect effect there. Our results suggest, not surprisingly,

Table 3.6 Decomposition of the effect of engineering and law majors on growth into direct and indirect effects

Model	All countries (1)	>10,000 Students (2)
A. *Estimated effects for engineering*		
Investment	0.021	0.037
Primary schooling	0.020	0.012
Government consumption	0.021	0.012
Revolutions and coups	0.002	0.003
Direct	−0.010	0.054
Total	0.054	0.125
B. *Estimated effects for law*		
Investment	−0.008	0.005
Primary schooling	−0.002	0.007
Government consumption	−0.001	0.006
Revolutions and coups	0.004	−0.005
Direct	−0.024	−0.078
Total	−0.031	−0.065

that people choose the engineering major when other conditions in the economy make investment in industry-related human capital attractive.

The indirect effects of law enrollments on growth are all trivial. By far the main effect is direct, which in the reduced sample is even larger in magnitude than the total effect. This evidence from the reduced sample might mean that the most important effect of lawyers on growth is the opportunity cost of not having talented people as innovators. The small indirect effect suggests that lawyers reduce growth-creating activities but not through reducing the incentives to invest.

In summary, the sample with large college enrollments reveals a large direct and large indirect positive effect of engineers on growth, and a large direct negative effect of lawyers on growth. One, but not the only one, interpretation of these findings is that the allocation of talent is important for growth. The allocation of talent into engineering seems to occur in countries that also invest in human and physical capital, suggesting that some countries just do things right.

3.6 Conclusion

We have argued both theoretically and empirically that the allocation of talent is a potentially important channel through which the institutions of a society influence its economic performance. A society whose institutions allow talented people to reap the rewards of entrepreneurship and innovation is likely to prosper, but a society whose talent flows to government or private rent seeking is likely to stagnate. The flow of talent to rent seeking rather than entrepreneurship reduces the level of income, but its more damaging effect is to lower the rate of innovation, technological progress, and growth. Economic and other institutions that foster the allocation of talent to entrepreneurial activity, such as protection of property from government expropriation, would have large benefits for economic development.

Why Is Rent Seeking So Costly to Growth?   **4**

Economists from Adam Smith (1776) to Douglass C. North (1981) agree that poor protection of property rights is bad for growth. But why is this problem so severe? Why have Peru (De Soto 1989) and Equatorial Guinea (Klitgaard 1990) failed to grow at all when public and private rent seeking made property insecure? Here we explore two reasons why rent seeking, meaning any redistributive activity that takes up resources, is so costly to growth.

First, rent-seeking activities exhibit very natural increasing returns. That is, an increase in rent-seeking activity may make rent seeking more (rather than less) attractive relative to productive activity. This condition can lead to multiple equilibria in the economy, with "bad" equilibria exhibiting very high levels of rent seeking and low output.[1]

Second, rent seeking, particularly public rent seeking by government officials, is likely to hurt innovative activities more than everyday production. Since innovation drives economic growth, public rent seeking hampers growth even more severely than production.

4.1 Increasing Returns in Rent-Seeking Activities

The rent-seeking technology itself often exhibits increasing returns. Three mechanisms are relevant. First, there may be a fixed cost

By Kevin M. Murphy, Andrei Shleifer, and Robert W. Vishny; originally published in *American Economic Review Papers and Proceedings*, 83, no. 2 (May 1993): 409–414.

to setting up a rent-seeking system, such as laws facilitating private suits. Once it is set up, however, lawyers can cheaply sue one another's clients, which they could not do if the law did not exist. Second, rent seeking may be self-generating in that offense creates a demand for defense. If one feudal lord builds an army, his neighbor does so as well; if a customer hires a lawyer, his supplier must do likewise, and so on. This too is a form of increasing returns. Third, rent seekers have "strength in numbers." If only a few people steal or loot, they will get caught; but if many do, the probability that any one of them is caught is much lower, and hence the returns to stealing or looting are higher. All these mechanisms, which rely on increasing returns to the aggregate rent-seeking technology, can generate multiple equilibria, some of which have a very high level of rent seeking and a low level of income.

We focus on perhaps an even more generic form of increasing returns to rent seeking, which arises not from the structure of rent-seeking technology, but instead from interaction of rent seeking and productive activities. Specifically, as more resources are allocated to rent seeking, returns to production, as well as to rent seeking, fall. Over some range, as more resources move into rent seeking, returns to production may fall faster than returns to rent seeking do, and so the attractiveness of production relative to rent seeking falls as well, even though both production and rent seeking exhibit diminishing-returns neoclassical technologies. When this happens, rent seeking exhibits general equilibrium-increasing returns, in the sense that an increase in rent seeking lowers the cost of further rent seeking. Below we present a simple model that illustrates this idea.

Consider a farm economy, in which each person can engage in one of three activities. He can produce a cash crop for the market, in which case his output is α. He can also produce a subsistence crop, in which case his output is $\gamma < \alpha$. The subsistence output is not subject to rent seeking; it cannot be stolen or expropriated. In contrast, market output is subject to rent seeking. Rent seeking is the third activity that each person can pursue; if he does, the maximum amount of cash crop he can expropriate is β. Thus an individual's rent-seeking technology is subject to diminishing returns in the sense of an upper bound on how much he can grab with limited time and abilities. In this model, rent seeking drives farmers out of cash-crop production, which is subject to

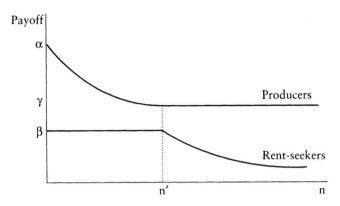

Figure 4.1 Payoffs to production and rent seeking, $\beta < \gamma$ case 1. $n=0$

expropriation, and into subsistence production, which is not, with the consequent substantial decline in productivity and living standards, as has happened in many African countries (Bates 1987).

An equilibrium in this economy is an allocation of the population among cash-crop production, subsistence production, and rent seeking. Denote the ratio of people engaged in rent seeking and market production by n and denote income per capita by y. To study equilibria in this economy, we consider the payoffs to production and rent seeking as a function of n. These payoffs are presented in Figure 4.1. At $n = 0$, the returns to market production are α since nothing is expropriated from the farmers, and the returns to rent seeking are β since the first rent seeker can take all he can get subject only to the diminishing returns on his technology. As n rises above 0, returns to market production fall to $\alpha - n\beta$, as farmers get a part of their output expropriated but are still better off than they would be with subsistence production. In this interval, the returns to rent seeking are still β, since rent seekers can still get all they are physically able to take.

At some critical level n', the after-transfer returns to market production fall all the way to the subsistence level γ. This is the highest ratio of rent seekers to cash-crop producers consistent with rent seekers getting their full potential output β. The critical level n' is given by $\alpha - n'\beta = \gamma$, or $n' = (\alpha - \gamma)/\beta$, where $\alpha - \gamma$ has the obvious interpretation of the maximum amount that can be taken from a market producer before he switches to subsistence. As the ratio of rent seekers to cash-crop producers rises above n', rent seekers begin to crowd one another, since cash-crop producers drop into subsistence production to keep their income level at γ. As a result, for $n > n'$, the return to both cash crop and subsistence producers is given by γ, and the return to each rent seeker is given by $(\alpha - y)/n < \beta$. In this regime of extreme rent seeking, rent seekers crowd one another and operate below their full potential, since they continue to divide a fixed pie among more and more of themselves.

Figure 4.1 illustrates the fundamental element of this model, namely that even though all aggregate technologies here exhibit constant returns, the relative returns to rent seeking (relative to entrepreneurship) may be increasing. Specifically, over the range where $0 < n < n'$, the aggregate returns to rent seeking are constant because the aggregate amount redistributed is limited only by the number of rent seekers, but aggregate returns to market production are diminishing as more rent seekers take more wealth away from market producers. As a result aggregate relative returns to rent seeking over this range are increasing, which, as we shall see, gives rise to multiple equilibria in some cases. To analyze equilibria, we must consider three cases that correspond to the relative positions of the two curves in Figure 4.1. In case 1, $\beta < \gamma$; in case 2, $\beta > \alpha$; and in case 3, $\gamma < \beta < \alpha$.

Case 1: $\beta < \gamma$. In this case, which actually corresponds literally to Figure 4.1, property rights are extremely well protected, and the rent-seeking return is even lower than the return to subsistence production. The equilibrium in this economy is unique: every person produces the cash crop, and there are no rent seekers or subsistence producers. In this sense, well-defined property rights lead to the highest possible output per capita, namely α.

Case 2: $\beta > \alpha$. This case corresponds to extremely poorly protected property rights, or equivalently, weak diminishing returns to individual rent seeking. In this case, a first rent seeker can grab more than a farmer can produce for the market. Figure 4.2 illustrates the relative position of the returns to rent seeking and to production in this case and shows that there is only one equilibrium. At this equilibrium, the return to production, driven all the way down to γ, must equal the return to rent seeking when rent seekers are crowding themselves [that is, $\gamma = (\alpha - \gamma)/n$]. That is, in equilibrium, $\underline{n'' = (\alpha - \gamma)/\gamma}$. (It follows

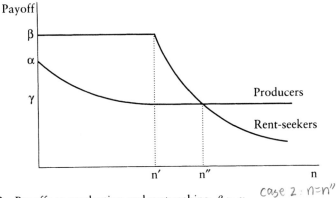

Figure 4.2   Payoffs to production and rent seeking, $\beta > \alpha$ case 2 : n=n''

immediately that $n'' > n'$.) In this equilibrium, everyone's income is equal to subsistence productivity γ rather than market productivity α.[2]

Case 3: $\gamma < \beta < \alpha$. In this intermediate case, there are two equilibria, as shown in Figure 4.3. The first equilibrium corresponds to that in case 1, where everyone is a cash-crop producer and income per capita is α. The second corresponds to that in case 2, where rent seeking is savage, people are split among market production, subsistence production, and rent seeking, and per capita income is driven down all the way

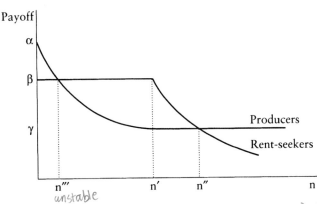

Figure 4.3   Payoffs to production and rent seeking, $\gamma < \beta < \alpha$ case 3: n=0, n''', n''

to γ. In the third equilibrium, people are split between market production and rent seeking (with no subsistence producers), and the return to each activity is β. In this equilibrium, $\alpha - \beta n = \beta$, or $n''' = (\alpha - \beta)/\beta$. (It follows immediately that $n''' < n'$.) Entry by rent seekers drives the returns of market producers down to a rent seeker's return, yet crowding by rent seekers has not yet set in. This, however, is not a stable equilibrium, since an incremental increase in n beyond n''' raises returns to rent seeking above those to market production, and hence invites further increases in resources devoted to rent seeking. The two stable equilibria, then, are the "good" one with $n = 0$, and the "bad" one with $n = n''$.

Having presented the equilibria in this model, we can briefly discuss what they mean, and examine how changes in parameter values affect the equilibrium outcome. First, consider the productivity of rent seeking, β, which captures the quality of property-rights protection in this model. As the analysis has shown, β does not affect the value of output in either equilibrium. However, β obviously affects which case obtains. In particular, a very high value of β, corresponding to very poor protection of property rights, eliminates the good equilibrium, whereas a very low level of β, corresponding to good protection of property rights, eliminates the bad equilibrium. This result accords well with intuition.

Holding other parameters constant, raising α increases income in the good equilibrium but also raises the likelihood that this equilibrium exists. A higher α also means a higher ratio of rent seekers to market producers in the bad equilibrium, since there are more rents to be dissipated per producer before income falls down to γ. Finally, an increase in γ can be interpreted either as the improvement in the subsistence technology or, better yet, as an alternative measure of protection of property rights, since $\alpha - \gamma$ is the maximum amount that could be taken from a producer. An increase in γ does not affect the good equilibrium but raises the income in the bad equilibrium, through two channels. First, raising γ cuts the pie available to rent seekers and hence drives people out of that activity. Second, raising γ raises the pay in the alternative occupation, namely subsistence production, which keeps down the amount of crowding in the rent-seeking activity. Reducing how much rent seekers can take thus raises the living standards in the bad equilibrium.

Of course, the essential point of this model is that the bad equilibrium exists and is characterized by extremely low living standards. If the economy begins in that equilibrium, it needs to be jump started out of it. To get to the best case, case 1, it is essential to provide enough property-rights protection so that β falls below γ (that is, that the returns to subsistence production exceed those to rent seeking). A legal system, a rigid culture, or some other form of anti–rent seeking ideology can play a role (North 1981); but some protection of subsistence production, as well as raising its productivity, may also work. Whatever strategy for property-rights protection is used, it must be quite radical, since the bad equilibrium is stable and will not be affected by minor improvements of property rights. This may explain why countries find it so costly to switch out of rent-seeking equilibria and often need a major government or institutional reform to do so.

As a final implication, the model suggests that an economy that starts out in a good equilibrium can slide into a bad equilibrium as a result of a war, a coup, or social unrest that reduces both productivity and protection of property rights. This may describe what has happened during military instability in Africa or during the collapse of communism in Russia. The model shows how difficult it is to snap out of such equilibria.

4.2 Rent Seeking and Innovation

In Section 4.1, rent seeking reduced output in the economy. Economic growth, however, often depends critically on investment and innovation. This raises the obvious question: is rent seeking likely to attack the innovation sector or the production sector more severely? That is, is rent seeking particularly bad for growth?

To address this question it is useful to distinguish between private and public rent seeking. Private rent seeking takes the form of theft, piracy, litigation, and other kinds of transfer between private parties. Public rent seeking is either redistribution from the private sector to the state, such as taxation, or alternatively from the private sector to the government bureaucrats who affect the fortunes of the private sector. The latter kind of public rent seeking takes the form of lobbying, corruption, and so on.

Private rent seeking, such as that described in our model, attacks the productive, rather than the innovative, sector of the economy. Private rent seekers go after existing stocks of wealth, such as land, output, capital, and so on. Bandits steal crops, lawyers sue deep-pocket corporations, and armies invade rich countries. In contrast, public rent seeking attacks innovation, since innovators need government-supplied goods, such as permits, licenses, import quotas, and so on, much more than established producers. To start a new firm, an innovator must obtain business, building, water, and fire permits, tax documents, import licenses if he needs new machinery, and often dozens of other documents (De Soto 1989). Innovators' demand for these government-produced goods is high and inelastic, and hence they become primary targets of corruption. In contrast, established producers usually do not need as many government goods, since they have bought them already.

Of course, the government can also try to blackmail the established producers into getting new licenses and permits. If the government makes no commitments, established and potential producers are in the same boat. Even so, more likely than not, new producers are more vulnerable to public rent seeking.

First, innovators have no established lobbies and are not part of the government "elite." Whereas the established producers are often part of the government, innovators are outsiders and hence are subject to particularly heavy bribes and expropriations. This problem becomes even worse when the interests of new and established producers are opposed, in which case the government may even stop innovators altogether.

Second, unlike the established producers, innovators are often credit-constrained and cannot as easily find the cash to pay bribes. Human capital is poor collateral. (This also explains why they are less vulnerable to private rent seeking.) When innovators do not have their own cash to pay bribes and cannot raise the funds to do so for lack of collateral, they can be completely deterred by public rent seeking from entering and innovating.

Third, innovative projects are typically long term and involve slow accumulation of capital. This provides rent seekers plenty of opportunities for future expropriation. In fact, in developing countries with weak protection of property rights, capital is often used in trade, rather than being committed to long-term investments, to avoid expropriation.

Fourth, innovative projects are typically risky, which makes them particularly vulnerable to rent seeking. For if a project succeeds, the returns are expropriated, whereas if it fails, the innovator bears the cost. Such ex post rent seeking raises the risk of innovation.

These problems can be mitigated if the rulers or the bureaucrats can take an equity stake in innovative activities, so that they can effectively accept a bribe without demanding cash, turn innovators into insiders, reduce their own incentives for subsequent expropriation, and bear some of the risk. In some countries, bureaucrats and even political leaders do exactly that, which presumably allows for some innovation. If the politicians had a long horizon, and could collect bribes efficiently, they would always back the innovator over the established producer if innovation increases the wealth in the economy. On the other hand, if innovators destroy more profits than they create (perhaps because they increase consumers' surplus), and if the bureaucrats cannot collect the bribes from consumers' surplus, they might side with established monopolies and stop innovation. Moreover, if corruption must be kept secret, politicians might prefer lower bribes from a clique of insiders to higher bribes from outsiders (see Chapter 5). Such ruling oligarchies often prevent innovation in Asia (for example, the government of Ferdinand Marcos in the Philippines), Latin America, and Africa. For these reasons, the possibility of equity holdings rarely cures the adverse effect of public rent seeking on entrepreneurship.

These arguments suggest that public rent seeking can put a severe tax on innovative activities and thereby move resources into established production or the public rent seeking sector. The result would be a sharp reduction in economic growth.

4.3 Conclusion

This chapter has suggested two reasons why countries with productive rent-seeking technologies, such as easy corruption and poor laws, can suffer economically. First, we argued that rent-seeking activity is subject to natural increasing returns, which means that very high levels of rent seeking may be self-sustaining. Second, we argued that public rent seeking in particular may afflict innovative activity the most and hence sharply reduce the rate of economic growth. These arguments add further substance to recently renewed concern about the effect of poor property rights on economic development.

Corruption

5

5.1 Introduction

We define government corruption as the[sale by government officials of government property for personal gain.] For example, government officials often collect bribes for issuing permits and licenses, for providing passage through customs, or for prohibiting the entry of competitors. In these cases they charge personally for goods that the state officially owns. In most cases the goods that the government officials sell are not demanded for their own sake, but rather enable private agents to pursue economic activity they could not pursue otherwise. Licenses, permits, passports, and visas are needed to comply with laws and regulations that restrict private economic activity. Insofar as government officials have discretion over the provision of these goods, they can collect bribes from private agents.

Corruption is both pervasive and significant around the world. In some developing countries, such as Zaire and Kenya, it probably amounts to a large proportion of the gross national product. Corruption is also common in developed countries: defense officials sometimes sell contracts for personal gain, and local zoning officials are bribed to rezone. Still, economic studies of corruption are rather limited. Following Becker and Stigler (1974), most studies (e.g., Banfield 1975; Rose-Ackerman 1975, 1978; Klitgaard 1988, 1991) focus on the

Originally published in *Quarterly Journal of Economics*, 108, no. 3 (August 1993): 599–617. © 1993 by the President and Fellows of Harvard College and the Massachusetts Institute of Technology.

principal-agent model of corruption. This model focuses on the relationship between the principal, that is, the top level of government, and the agent, that is, an official, who takes bribes from private individuals interested in some government-produced good. These studies examine ways of motivating the agent to be honest, ranging from efficiency wages (Becker and Stigler 1974) to indoctrination (Klitgaard 1991). Here we take the principal-agent problem as given—the corrupt official has some effective property rights over the government good he is allocating—and focus on consequences of corruption for resource allocation.

In particular, we address two issues. First, we discuss the implications of how the corruption network is organized. In some economies, such as Korea today and Russia under Communism, while corruption is pervasive, the person paying the bribe is assured that he will get the government good he is paying for, and does not need to pay further bribes in the future. In other economies many government goods can be obtained without bribes altogether. For example, a citizen can get a passport in the United States without paying a bribe. In yet other economies, such as those of many African countries and post-Communist Russia, numerous bureaucrats need to be bribed to get a government permit, and bribing one does not guarantee that some other bureaucrat or even the first one will not demand another bribe. We examine the implications of these three regimes for their level of corruption and for the effects of corruption on economic activity.

Second, we ask why even well-organized corruption appears to be more distortionary than taxation. Several authors have pointed out that some corruption might be desirable (Leff 1964). First, it works like a piece rate for government employees (a bureaucrat may be more helpful when paid directly). Second, it enables entrepreneurs to overcome cumbersome regulations. Yet most studies conclude that corruption slows down development (Gould and Amaro-Reyes 1983; United Nations 1989; Klitgaard, 1991). We ask why bribery might be much more costly than its sister activity, taxation, and argue that the imperative of secrecy makes bribes more distortionary than taxes.

5.2 Basic Model

We consider the simplest model of one government-produced good, such as a passport, or a right to use a government road, or an import license. We assume that this good is homogeneous, and that there is a demand curve for this good, $D(p)$, from the private agents. We assume that this good is sold for the government by an official who has the opportunity to restrict the quantity of the good that is sold. Specifically, he can deny a private agent the passport, access to a road, or an import license. In practice, this denial might mean a long delay or an imposition of many requirements. But it is easier to assume for now that the official can simply refuse to provide the good. An important reason why many of these permits and regulations exist is probably to give officials the power to deny them and to collect bribes in return for providing the permits (De Soto 1989).

We also assume that the official can in fact restrict supply without any risk of detection or punishment from above. Corrupt officials go unpunished because their bosses often share in the proceeds and because public pressure to stop corruption in most countries is weak. We shall also discuss the case in which corruption is penalized. But for now, the government official is a monopolist selling a good. His objective is to maximize the value of the bribes he collects from selling this government good.

Let the official government price of this good be p. We assume that the cost of producing this good is completely immaterial to the official, since the government is paying this cost. This assumption is a bit restrictive. Although it covers the sale of an import license, a passport, or a passage on a government road, a policeman who sells services that he is supposed to provide for free does exert personal effort and so does care about its cost. For simplicity, we focus on government goods that cost the official nothing personally to provide, so that he has no interest in how much it costs the government to produce these goods.

What then is the marginal cost to the official of providing this good? We distinguish two cases. First, in the case without theft, the official actually turns over the official price of the good to the government. In this case, the marginal cost of providing the good to the official is the government price p. For example, when an official sells a license for a government price plus a bribe, he keeps the bribe but the amount p stays with the government; hence p is his marginal cost. In contrast, in the case with theft, the official does not turn over anything to the government at all, and simply hides the sale. In this case, the price that the buyer pays is only equal to the bribe, and might even be lower than the official price.

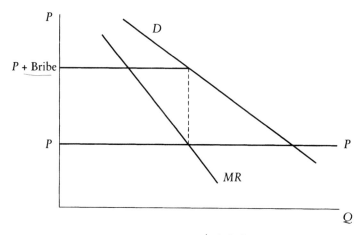

Figure 5.1   Corruption without theft   Case |: MC=P

For example, customs officials often let goods through the border for less than the official duty, but then give nothing at all to the government. In this case, the marginal cost to the official is zero. While conceptually the two cases are similar—they differ only in the level of the marginal cost to the official—in the first case corruption always raises the total price of the good, whereas in the second case it might reduce it. Corruption with theft is obviously more attractive to the buyers.

If the official cannot price discriminate between buyers, then as a monopolist he will simply set the marginal revenue equal to the marginal cost. In the case without theft, the total price with the bribe always exceeds the government price. It pays the official to create a shortage at the official price, and then to collect bribes as a way to clear the market for the government-supplied good (see Chapter 6). In the case with theft, the total price might be below the government price. Figures 5.1 and 5.2 present the solutions to this problem for the cases without and with theft, respectively.

This analysis suggests a similarity between bribes and commodity taxes. In the case without theft, the bribe is exactly equal to the revenue-maximizing commodity tax when marginal cost is equal to the state price *p*. Of course, taxes need not be set to maximize revenue. More important, taxes are typically kept by the government rather than the bureaucrats. In monarchial regimes, the distinction between taxes and

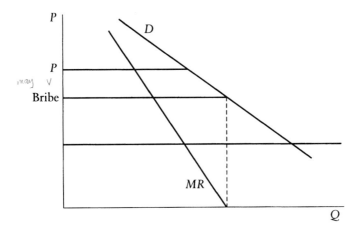

Figure 5.2   Corruption with theft   Case 2: MC=0

bribes is blurred by the fact that the treasury is indistinguishable from the sovereign's pocket. Yet for most governments, the distinction is material and shows how corruption substitutes for taxation.

Penalizing the official for corruption changes the level of the bribe he demands, but does not change the essence of the problem. If the probability of detection and the penalty are independent of the bribe and of the number of people who pay it, the official will charge the same bribe provided that the penalties are not so high that corruption is no longer profitable. If the expected penalty increases with the level of the bribe, he might reduce the bribe and raise output. On the other hand, if the expected penalty rises in the number of people he charges a bribe (for example, because of the higher probability of a complaint), then he will reduce the supply and raise the bribe. The official trades off the benefits given in Figures 5.1 and 5.2 against the expected penalties. For our purposes, we do not need to focus on this aspect of the problem (see Becker and Stigler 1974; Rose-Ackerman 1978; Klitgaard 1988).

This simple analysis suggests that corruption spreads because of competition both among the officials and among the consumers. If jobs are distributed among officials through an auction mechanism, whereby those who pay the most for a job get it, then the prospective officials who do not collect bribes simply cannot afford jobs. Conversely, those who will collect more (perhaps through more effective price discrimination) will offer the higher-level officials more for the jobs, and so will be able to get them.[Competition among officials will ensure that maximal bribes are collected.]

Even more important for the spread of corruption is competition among the buyers in the case with theft. If buyer A can buy the government service more cheaply than buyer B can, then he can out-compete buyer B in the product market. So if buyer A bribes an official to reduce his costs, his competitors must do so also. If all real estate owners in a city can bribe their way out of paying taxes, then those who pay them will not survive. If some trucks carry goods across a border after paying a small bribe instead of the official customs duty, the importers who pay the duty will not survive.[Competition among buyers of government services ensures the spread of cost-reducing corruption.]Interestingly, such competition does not help the spread of corruption without theft.

Corruption with theft spreads because observance of the law does not survive in a competitive environment. In addition, the buyer in this case has no incentive to inform on the official, and hence the likelihood that corruption will be detected is much smaller. This creates a further incentive for corruption with theft to rise. Because corruption with theft aligns the interests of the buyers and sellers, it will be more persistent than corruption without theft, which pits buyers against sellers. This result suggests that the first step to reduce corruption should be to create an accounting system that prevents theft from the government. In the collection of taxes and customs duties, such accounting systems might well reduce corruption, because without theft bribes raise the buyer's cost and hence give him an incentive to expose the corrupt official.

5.3 The Industrial Organization of Corruption

The model above makes two strong assumptions. First, a buyer needs only one government good to conduct his business. Second, the official is a monopolist in the supply of this good. Yet some critical issues in corruption arise when these assumptions do not hold. In many cases, a private agent needs several complementary government goods to conduct business. For example, an importer might need several government licenses and permits, to be obtained from several agencies, to bring in, unload, transport, and sell an imported good. A builder might need several permits from different departments, such as fire, water, and police. With multiple goods, the market structure in their provision becomes important. The different agencies that supply the complementary goods might collude, sell the different goods independently, or even compete in the provision of some goods. The focus on market structure in the provision of complementary government goods sheds light on the consequences of corruption.

The model of the previous section is most appropriate for understanding corruption in monarchies, such as the Bourbons in France or Marcos's Philippines, in the old-time Communist regimes, and in regions dominated by a single mafia. In such places, it is always clear who needs to be bribed and by how much. The bribe is then divided among all the relevant government bureaucrats, who agree not to demand further bribes from the buyer of the package of government goods, such as permits. In Russia, for example, bribes were channeled through local Communist Party offices. Any deviation from the agreed-upon pattern of corruption would be penalized by the party bureaucracy, so few deviations occurred. Once a bribe was paid, the buyer received full property rights over the set of government goods that he bought. Carino (1986) and Klitgaard (1988) describe similar monopolistic corruption structures in the Philippines.

There are two extreme alternatives to this monopoly corruption scheme. The first alternative is corruption in some African countries, in India, and in post-Communist Russia. Here the sellers of complementary government goods, such as permits and licenses, act independently. Different ministries, agencies, and levels of local government all set their own bribes independently in an attempt to maximize their own revenue, rather than the combined revenue of all the bribe collectors. In Russia in the early 1990s, for example, getting a business started often required bribing the local legislature, the central ministry, the local executive branch, the fire authorities, the water authorities, and so on. In some African countries, many quasi-independent government agencies have the ability to stop a project, and use this power to set bribes without collusion with other agencies (Klitgaard 1990). The army and the police also often demand a cut for protection—another needed government input. Unlike the single monopoly model, here complementary government goods are sold by independent monopolists.

Formally, consider first a joint monopolist agency that sets the cum bribe prices p_1 and p_2 of two government goods. Let x_1 and x_2 be the quantities of these goods sold. Let the official prices, equal to the monopolist's marginal costs, be denoted by MC_1 and MC_2. The per unit bribes then are $p_1 - MC_1$ and $p_2 - MC_2$. The joint monopolist agency sets p_1 at which

(5.1)
$$\rightarrow \quad MR_1 + MR_2 \frac{dx_2}{\underset{>0}{dx_1}} = MC_1,$$

where MR_1 and MR_2 denote marginal revenues from the sale of goods 1 and 2, respectively. When the two goods are complements, as government permits for the same project are, then $dx_2/dx_1 > 0$, and so at the optimum, $MR_1 < MC_1$. The monopolist agency keeps the bribe on good 1 down to expand the demand for the complementary good 2 and thus to raise its profits from bribes on good 2. For the same reason, this agency keeps down the price of good 2.

Suppose alternatively that permits 1 and 2 are allocated by independent agencies. Each agency then takes the other's output as given, and in particular, in equation (5.1), dx_2/dx_1 is set to zero. At the independent agency's optimum, $MR_1 = MC_1$. Hence the per unit bribe is higher, and the output lower, than at the joint monopolist optimum. Because the independent agency ignores the effect of its raising its bribe on demand for the complementary permits and hence the bribes to the other agency, it sets a higher bribe, which results in a lower output and a lower aggregate level of bribes. By acting independently, the two agencies actually hurt each other as well as the private buyers of the permits.

This problem is made much worse in many countries by free entry into the collection of bribes. New government organizations and officials often have the opportunity to create laws and regulations that enable them to become providers of additional required permits and licenses and charge for them accordingly. Having paid three bribes, the buyer of these inputs learns that he must buy yet another one if he wants his project to proceed. In some cases, the officials who collected the bribe previously come back to demand more (see Klitgaard 1990 for striking examples). In these cases, the property rights to his project are not really transferred to the buyer when he pays the bribe. Even the list of the complementary inputs is not fixed, and tends to expand when profitable corruption opportunities stimulate entry. When entry is completely free, the total bribe rises to infinity and the sales of the package of government goods, as well as bribe revenues, fall to zero.

In the third scenario, each one of the several complementary government goods can be supplied by at least two government agencies. For simplicity, begin with the case of one such good, such as a United States passport or a driver's license. A citizen can obtain a U.S. passport without paying a bribe. The likely reason for this is that if an official asks him for a bribe, he will go to another window or another city. Because collusion between several agents is difficult, bribe competition between the providers will drive the level of bribes down to zero. This example can be extended to the case of multiple complementary goods. If a builder needs several permits to erect a building, but any one of them can be obtained from one of several noncolluding government agents, Bertrand competition in bribes will force the equilibrium bribe on each permit down to zero. Unlike the first model, where a unified monopoly provides all the goods, and the second model, in which monopoly suppliers of different goods act independently, here the market for each government-supplied good is competitive.

As in other industrial organization contexts, even having two competitors is not necessary if the market is subject to potential competition or entry (Demsetz 1968). Consider, for example, a single government official in a small U.S. city who controls building permits, dog permits, permits to dispose of old appliances, and so on. If this official attempts to charge a bribe, or to price his services above marginal cost, another individual will offer the public the same service at a lower price, and the corrupt official will be recalled or fail to get reelected. The threat of such competition would then keep corruption down to zero, assuming that the official price covers the marginal cost of providing the permits.

The level of bribes is the lowest in the third case, intermediate in the first, and the highest in the second. But the total amount of revenues collected is higher in the first case than in the second, since the independent monopolist suppliers drive the quantity sold so far down that the total revenues from corruption fall. This result is obvious: in the first case the suppliers of the complementary inputs collude to maximize the total value of bribes, but in the second they do not.

efficiency cases 3 > 1 > 2

This problem is formally identical to a standard problem in industrial organization. Suppose that a car maker needs two complementary inputs, glass and steel. If one monopolist provides both, he will realize that raising the price of glass reduces the demand for his own steel, and hence his profits on the steel sales, and similarly with raising the price of steel. Accordingly, he will price steel and glass taking account of the demand complementarities. In contrast, if glass and steel are sold by two independent monopolists, each will ignore the effect of his raising his price on the demand for the product of the other. As a result, each would charge a higher price than a joint monopolist would, and both the quantity of steel and glass sold and the combined profits from these sales would be lower. In the last scenario, if each of these independent monopolists can sell both steel and glass, and they compete on price, they will drive the price of both steel and glass down to the marginal cost. The profits will be the lowest, and output the highest, of the three cases. Competition is the best; joint monopoly is the second best; and independent monopoly is the worst for efficiency. Moreover, the more inputs car production requires, the lower the output with independent monopolists.

Another helpful analogy is tollbooths on a road. The joint monopoly solution corresponds to the case of one toll that gives the payer the right to use the entire road. The independent monopolists solution means that different towns through which the road passes independently erect their own tollbooths and charge their own tolls. The volume of traffic and aggregate toll collections fall. In fact, they fall to zero when *any* party can erect its own tollbooth on this road. The competitive case corresponds to multiple booths competing with one another for the right to collect the toll or, alternatively, to the case of multiple roads. In this case, the volume of traffic is obviously the highest, and toll collections are the lowest.

This, in fact, is a very close analogy. In India, taking a road between two towns indeed requires paying a bribe in every village through which the road passes. Taking goods inland in Zaire is more expensive because of corruption than bringing them from Europe by ship to a port. In 1400 there were sixty independently run tolls along the Rhine. Along the Seine there were so many tolls that to ship a good twenty miles cost as much as its price. In contrast, rivers in England were free of such tolls, which in part explains the ability of England to develop specialized, commercial agriculture feeding London, the world's center of commerce (Heilbroner 1962). These examples suggest how costly free entry into bribe collection might be to development.

This industrial organization perspective on corruption sheds light on the consequences of corruption in different countries and places. It also raises the far deeper question: What determines the industrial organization of different corruption markets? How did Brezhnev and Marcos manage to enforce joint profit maximization? Why has this system fallen apart in Russia, and never existed in Africa? How has the U.S. government managed to eradicate corruption in the provision of at least some, though by no means all, government goods?

Enforcement of joint profit maximization in bribe collection is closely related to the problem of enforcing collusion in oligopoly. Stigler (1964) shows that collusion is more likely to be enforced when price cutting can be easily detected, and punishment for price cutting can be severe. In the corruption context the parallel argument is that collusive bribe maximization can be enforced more easily when bribe increases can be more easily detected and more severely punished.

Bribe increases can be easily detected in several circumstances. First, when the government has an effective policing machine to monitor the actions of bureaucrats, such as the KGB in the Soviet Union or the first Mayor Daley's Democratic Party machine in Chicago, it is hard to charge excessive bribes without being found out. Second, when the ruling elite is small, as in the Philippines or in Communist Russia, deviations from normal bribes will be easy to see. Third, when the society is homogeneous and closely knit, as in East Asia, deviations from normal bribes are likely to become known to friends and family, and such knowledge is likely to spread. Police states, small oligarchies, and homogeneous societies are thus likely to come closer to joint bribe maximization than more open, less tightly governed and more heterogeneous societies.

The ability of the cartel to punish those who charge excessive bribes is also essential to enforcing collusion. The ability of the leadership to exclude deviators from the rents associated with being an insider is essential. When large rents come from being a Communist in Russia, a Democratic politician in Chicago, a part of the ruling clique, or a member of the military elite, and when the sovereign can take these rents away from the deviators, deviations are unlikely. On the other hand, if the rents are small, and, more important, the sovereign is in no position to take them away, joint bribe maximization cannot be sustained. For example, in feudal Europe, in post-Communist Russia, and in many African countries, the central government is so weak that it cannot fire or penalize officials in the provinces, or even bureaucrats sitting in the capital, for running their own corruption rackets. In this situation the "independent monopolists" model, with its devastating economic consequences, describes reality best.

Huntington (1968) observes that political modernization, defined as a transition from an autocratic to a more democratic government, is usually accompanied by increases in corruption. He attributes this problem to underdeveloped institutions under the newly formed governments. If underdeveloped institutions mean a weak state machine, then Huntington's story fits well with our model. New governments lose their monopoly over bribe collection, and as a result, multiple agencies take bribes where only one did before, leading to a much less efficient allocation. Russia under Communism had a monolithic bribe collection system. With the Communists gone, central government officials, local officials, ministry officials, and many others were taking bribes, leading to much higher bribes in equilibrium though perhaps lower corruption revenues, just as the model predicts. Similar stories are told about Africa after independence, when the colonial corruption machines disintegrated (Ekpo 1979). The evidence is strikingly consistent in showing the superiority of monopolistic bribe taking over that by independent monopolists.

The two cases we examined share basically authoritarian government with little responsiveness to public pressure against corruption. As a result, both produce high levels of corruption, although they differ in how inefficient this corruption is. Countries with more political competition have stronger public pressure against corruption—through laws, democratic elections, and even the independent press—and so are more likely to use government organizations that contain rather than maximize corruption proceeds. It is implausible to think, for example, that the U.S. president maximizes corruption proceeds, since such a president is likely to be exposed and thrown out of office. Even in Japan and

Korea, where corruption is very common, the level of bribes tends to be significantly lower than in Russia or the Philippines. This difference stems from the political competition within the ruling parties as well as from the opposition parties in Japan and Korea. Because low bribes keep potential competitors out, political competition keeps corruption down (see Demsetz 1968).

Our industrial organization perspective suggests that a good way to reduce corruption without theft is to produce competition between bureaucrats in the provision of government goods, which will drive bribes down to zero. The passport office, and many other agencies of the U.S. government, have actually introduced such arrangements. The Pentagon has not, and it is probably more corrupt. The general idea behind federalism is precisely such competition in the provision of public goods, although it is usually stated in terms of taxes rather than bribes. Of course, in the case of corruption with theft, competitive pressure might increase theft from the government at the same time as it reduces bribes. The appropriate policy, then, is to create competition in the provision of government goods while intensively monitoring theft.

5.4 Corruption and Secrecy

Although some political scientists have argued that the optimal level of corruption is positive (Leff 1964; Huntington 1968), most studies suggest that existing corruption levels are detrimental to development (Gould and Amaro-Reyes 1983; United Nations 1989; Klitgaard 1991). Africa is reputed to be a very corrupt continent; it is also the poorest one. Central and South America are also known for their extreme corruption and poverty. In contrast, developed countries appear to be less corrupt.

Mauro (1993) presents the first systematic empirical analysis of corruption by focusing on the relationship between investment and corruption. Mauro uses an index of corruption from *Business International* (1984), a publication of the Economist Intelligence Unit, which supplies subjective assessments of fifty-six risk factors for sixty-eight countries to private investors. The corruption variable is defined as "the degree to which business transactions involve corruption and questionable payments," and is used for 1980. The average ratio of total and private investment to GDP for the period between 1970 and 1985 is drawn from Barro (1991), as is real GDP per capita for 1980. Mauro finds that, holding 1980 real GDP constant, [countries with higher corruption have a lower ratio of both total and private investment to GDP.] The estimates are statistically significant. These results are consistent with the view that corruption is bad for development.

The independent monopolists model, which shows that under the free entry of bribe takers supplying complementary inputs the total bribe rises to infinity and productive output falls to zero, may help explain why the most corrupt countries are so poor. Yet even more modest corruption seems to have detrimental effects. In this section we discuss these detrimental effects of corruption.

In the case of an economywide bribe-collecting monopolist, such as Marcos, corruption is similar to revenue-maximizing taxation. Like the sovereign who optimally taxes different goods and activities, the monopolist sets bribes to maximize revenue. In this world it is difficult to distinguish between bribes and taxes. Taxes are the markup on the price that goes into the treasury, and bribes are the markup that goes into the pocket of the monopolist. When the treasury and the pocket are one and the same, as in the case of kings and Marcos, taxes and bribes are exactly the same. With multiple monopolists, bribes are also similar to taxes, except that tax rates on different activities are set by independent agencies. In setting tax rates in this way, the agencies maximize their own tax revenues rather than the aggregate tax revenue. Because they ignore the cross-elasticities of demand, the aggregate tax revenues are lower in this case. Finally, the case of competing monopolists corresponds to the federalist ideal of competing jurisdictions. In this case as well, bribes are similar to taxes.[1]

Despite these similarities, bribes differ from taxes in one crucial way, namely, unlike taxation, corruption is usually illegal and must be kept secret. Efforts to avoid detection and punishment cause corruption to be more distortionary than taxation. On some goods, taking bribes without being detected is much easier than on others. Government officials will then use their powers to [induce substitution into the goods on which bribes can be more easily collected without detection.] For example, officials might ban some imports to induce substitution into others. Or they might prohibit entry of some firms to raise bribe revenue from existing monopolies. Historically, sovereigns used such mercantilist policies to increase tax collections because monopoly profits are easier to tax than income (Ekelund and Tollison 1981). But such policies can also be used to increase bribes. Using our roadblock analogy, bureaucrats shut down some roads to increase the tolls on the passage through others, especially if the tolls on the shut-down roads are more difficult to collect.

A real-world example of a bottle-making factory in Mozambique illustrates these distortions from corruption. In 1991 that factory had modern Western equipment for making bottles, but used a traditional process for putting paper labels on these bottles. Three old machines were used: one cut the labels from paper; one then glued the white label on the bottle; and finally one printed a red picture on the label. The bottles were moved manually between these machines. In roughly 30 percent of the cases, the picture was not centered on the label. When this happened, the bottles were handed over to approximately twelve women who sat on the floor near the machines and scraped off the labels with knives, so that the bottles could be put through this process again.

Apparently the process of labeling bottles could be mechanized with a fairly simple machine that cost about $10,000 and could be readily bought with aid money from any of a number of Western or even third world suppliers. The manager of the factory, however, did not want to buy such a machine, but instead wanted a $100,000 machine that not only mechanized the existing process, but also printed labels in sixteen colors and different shapes, and put them on different types of bottles. Only one producer in the world made this machine, and the Mozambiquan government applied to the producer's home country for an aid package to buy it. Since that aid was not immediately forthcoming, the factory kept using the traditional technology.

The demand for equipment much fancier than the factory appeared to need seems irrational until one realizes that buying a fancier machine offered the manager (and the ministry officials) much better opportunities for corruption. If the factory bought a generic machine, the manager would probably have to use international donors' guidelines and consider several offers. There would be very little in this deal for him personally. On the other hand, if he got a unique machine, he would not have to solicit alternative bids. The supplier in turn would be happy to overinvoice for the machine, and kick back some of the profits to the manager (and his ministerial counterpart). The corruption opportunities in buying a unique and expensive machine are much better than such opportunities in buying cheaper generic products.

The social cost of corruption in this example may be large. If the social value of the $100,000 machine is only $20,000, and the bribe that the manager can collect from overinvoicing is $3,000, then the social cost of corruption is $80,000. In other words, social costs of misdirection of resources toward activities that offer better corruption opportunities can vastly exceed bribe revenues.

Western observers often wonder about the preference for unnecessarily advanced rather than "appropriate" technology by third world governments. Overinvoicing provides the obvious explanation for this preference for advanced technology. The rational managers and bureaucrats in poor countries want to import goods on which bribes are the easiest to take, not the goods that are most profitable for the state firms. To do that, they discourage or even prohibit the importation of appropriate technology and encourage the importation of unique goods on which overpayment and overinvoicing are more difficult to detect. As a result, very poor countries end up with equipment that is way beyond their needs.

This example fits neatly into our framework. To maximize the value of their personal revenues, bureaucrats prohibit the import of goods on which bribes cannot be collected without detection, and encourage the import of goods on which they can collect bribes. As a consequence, the menu of both consumer and producer goods available in the country is determined by corruption opportunities rather than by tastes or technological needs. This argument might suggest why so many poor countries would rather spend their limited resources on infrastructure projects and defense, where corruption opportunities are abundant, than on education and health, where they are much more limited. In light of the enormous returns on these forgone health and education projects, the social costs of corruption might be enormous. Without the need to keep corruption secret, officials could collect their bounty in much less distortionary ways.

The imperative of secrecy entails another potentially important cost of corruption, namely its hostility to change and innovation. Keeping corruption secret requires keeping down the number of people involved in giving and receiving bribes. The elite must then include only a small oligarchy of politicians and businessmen, and refuse entry to newcomers. This situation may well describe the Philippines under Marcos, Russia under the Communists, or some African dictatorships. But innovation and change are often precipitated by outsiders. To the extent that the elite prevents them from entering, to maintain its profits or simply to keep down its numbers to preserve secrecy, growth will suffer.

5.5 Conclusion

We have explored two broad reasons why corruption may be costly to economic development. The first reason is the weakness of central government, which allows various governmental agencies and bureaucracies to impose independent bribes on private agents seeking complementary permits from these agencies. When the entry of these agencies into regulation is free, they will drive the cumulative bribe burden on private agents to infinity. A good illustration of this problem is foreign investment in post-Communist Russia. To invest in a Russian company, a foreigner had to bribe every agency involved in foreign investment, including the foreign investment office, the relevant industrial ministry, the finance ministry, the executive branch of the local government, the legislative branch, the central bank, the state property bureau, and so on. The obvious result is that foreigners did not invest in Russia. Such competing bureaucracies, each of which can stop a project from proceeding, hamper investment and growth around the world, but especially in countries with weak governments.

Downs (1967) calls the expansion of bureaucracies into new regulations "territoriality," but does not elaborate on its consequences for resource allocation. We have shown how costly territoriality can be when different agencies are neither kept honest nor controlled by a central authority. We have explored the effects of territoriality when agencies impose regulations independently to maximize their individual bribe revenues. But even if bureaucrats are kept honest and introduce regulations only to expand their own domains without coordination from above, compliance with these regulations can be very costly to private agents.

The second broad reason that corruption is costly is the distortion entailed by the necessary secrecy of corruption. The demands of secrecy can shift a country's investments away from the highest value projects, such as health and education, into potentially useless projects, such as defense and infrastructure, if the latter offer better opportunities for secret corruption. The demands of secrecy can also cause leaders of a country to maintain monopolies, to prevent entry, and to discourage innovation by outsiders if expanding the ranks of the elite can expose existing corruption practices. Such distortions from corruption can discourage useful investment and growth.

We have argued that economic and political competition can reduce the level of corruption and its adverse effects. If different agencies compete in the provision of the same services, corruption will be driven down provided that agents cannot simply steal. Similarly, political competition opens up the government, reduces secrecy, and so can reduce corruption, provided that decentralization of power does not lead to agency fiefdom and anarchy.

Pervasive Shortages under Socialism

6.1 Introduction

The single most pervasive phenomenon in socialist countries is shortage of goods. Consumer goods ranging from necessities, such as food, to luxuries, such as cars and gold, as well as many intermediate inputs are typically in short supply. Kornai (1979) and Weitzman (1984) argue that shortages, as opposed to excess supply of goods, distinguish socialism from capitalism. Here we offer a new explanation of shortages under socialism.

Standard explanations of shortages of goods under socialism are not completely persuasive.[1] The classical explanation (Lange [1936–37] 1964) argues that shortages result from temporary difficulties in calculating equilibrium prices, which occur because convergence to equilibrium takes time. It is hard to take this account seriously. In the former Soviet Union, shortages of some goods, such as cars, have lasted for decades, without any price increases. The planners simply have not raised prices to come closer to the market-clearing equilibrium.

Second, it is often argued that distributional considerations lead socialist planners to keep down prices of such goods as food (Weitzman 1977). Although distributional considerations may explain shortages of some goods, such as food and housing, they are hardly a general explanation. Why, for example, has the former Soviet Union always had

Originally published in *RAND Journal of Economics,* 23, no. 2 (Summer 1992): 237–246.

a shortage of luxuries such as cars and owner-occupied apartments? The government has long been trying to extract the excess savings from the rich, and raising the prices of luxuries would have been a natural way of doing this. It does not appear, then, that fairness is the real issue.

A third influential explanation of shortages, offered by Kornai (1979), is that socialist firms face soft budget constraints and so always want to get any inputs they possibly can at any price. In Kornai's model, it is not so much that goods are underpriced, but that the income of the buyers is effectively infinite. This model may be appropriate for some intermediate goods. But households face hard budget constraints, and therefore the systematic shortages of many consumer goods remain a puzzle. Moreover, we claim below that the notion that the socialist firm always wants to expand output is incorrect. Our explanation of shortages applies to consumer luxuries and necessities as well as to intermediate goods.

We argue that an important reason for pervasive shortages is self-interested behavior by the ministry bureaucrats who set the planned prices and output. These bureaucrats intentionally plan shortages in order to invite bribes from rationed consumers. If markets cleared, firms in an industry could earn profits, but most of these profits would accrue to the state treasury, not to the managers or the ministries. The key feature of socialism is that the decision makers who determine the prices and output of firms do not, to a first approximation, keep any of these profits. In contrast, when there is a shortage of a good, potential customers try to obtain it by offering bribes and favors to the bureaucrats in the ministry (and to the managers of firms). These bribes tend to be much larger than the share of official profits that the bureaucrats and the managers are allowed to keep. And because the bribes are not official transactions, none of them goes to the treasury. As a result, the industry is better off creating a shortage of its product and collecting the bribes than making official profits it cannot keep. To collect bribes, socialist industries will always try to produce a level of output entailing a shortage at official prices.[2]

This chapter is an application of the general principles of rent seeking, introduced by Tullock (1967), Krueger (1974), Posner (1975), and Bhagwati (1982). The literature on central planning has long recognized that price distortions can lead to Tullock-like welfare losses as people waste time queuing for goods (Stahl and Alexeev 1985). This literature has taken underpricing as exogenous, however. We suggest that underpricing and shortages are the result of the rational choices made by key decision makers who collect the rents that result from shortages. Although we focus on shortages in socialist countries, the point that bureaucrats create artificial barriers to private transactions in order to collect bribes is more general. Many laws, regulations, and other quantity restrictions in less developed and even in developed countries are probably introduced largely to collect bribes (De Soto 1990). It is useful to bring out the implications of this general principle for the most pervasive feature of socialism: the shortage of goods.

6.2 The Objective Function of a Socialist Industry

To describe its objective function, we must first define what we mean by a "socialist industry." We define a socialist industry as a combination of the firms in an industry and the ministry that supervises them. We assume that this industry has some demand curve and some cost curve. The objective function of this industry is the objective function of the bureaucrats in the ministry and the managers of the firms. Importantly, we assume that the bureaucrats and the managers collude to pursue their common objective function. As a result we do not focus on the potential conflicts between bureaucrats and managers. Our view is that both have the same broad objective—to enrich themselves at the expense of their customers and the state treasury—and that they bargain efficiently on how to divide the surplus. One example of this is that the ministry gives the orders and the firms follow them as best they can.

Given this view of a socialist industry, it is not important whether it consists of just one or several firms. Even if there are several firms, the bureaucrats in the ministry will enforce collusion between them, and they will act as a monopolist. In particular, the bureaucrats will not allow firms to compete for bribes. This assumption is quite natural: the ministry has a great deal of control over the prices and outputs of the firms it supervises, and it is in the long-run interest of the managers as well to make sure that the monopoly allocation is sustained. In short, we are assuming that the industry consists of one decision maker, who expresses the combined interests of the bureaucrats and the managers, and whom we shall call the "industry."

What is the objective function of this industry? Typically, the industry does not keep any of the profits it earns from selling its output at official prices, since the tax rate levied by the central authorities is close to 100 percent. Even if the industry can keep some of the profits, virtually none of them accrues to the managers and to the ministry bureaucrats. Official profits are of no value to the decision makers. Such taxation of profits implies, in particular, that the industry has no interest in charging an official price equal to the monopoly price and supplying the monopoly output. Nor does the industry have any interest in producing a competitive output at a competitive price, since the profits on the inframarginal units, again, accrue to the state. A socialist industry gets no or virtually no benefits from earning legal profits.

The only way that the industry can get anything for itself is by having a shortage of the good it produces and then collecting rents in the form of bribes from quantity constrained buyers. When there is a shortage, the buyers' valuation of the good exceeds the official price, so they are willing to stand in line, lobby the firm and the ministry, and most important, pay bribes to get the good. Of course, to the extent they lobby and stand in line, the buyers do not benefit the industry. But to the extent that the shortage brings in bribes, the industry decision makers benefit from a shortage. The advantage of bribes over profits is, of course, that bribes are hidden and therefore are not turned over to the treasury. As long as the tax rate on official profits is high enough that managers and bureaucrats prefer to collect bribes, even despite all the waste associated with queuing and lobbying, they will try to create a shortage. The industry's objective, briefly stated, is to maximize the value of bribes.

If we denote the inverse demand curve of the industry by $D(Q)$ and the official price by P, the objective function of the industry is given by

$$(6.1) \qquad D(Q) * Q - P * Q.$$
$$R(Q)$$

This objective function, for an arbitrary P and Q, is given by the shaded rectangle in Figure 6.1. We are assuming that the true price the industry charges the buyers is $D(Q)$—the reservation price of the marginal buyer—and that this price consists of two parts. The first is the official

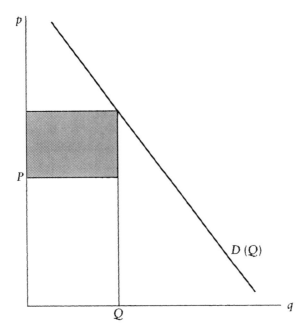

Figure 6.1   The objective function of a socialist industry

price P, and the second is the bribe $D(Q) - P$. The rents that this industry collects are the product of the bribe per unit of output times the output.

There is a simple way to think about this objective function. The first term, $D(Q) * Q$, is simply the revenue that any industry would collect if the market cleared at the output Q, which we will denote by $R(Q)$. However, the cost to a socialist industry is very different from the cost to a private industry. The real cost function does not even enter the objective function (6.1). As Kornai has pointed out, the socialist industry does not care at all about the cost of its inputs, since these inputs are paid for by the state, which usually covers the losses of the enterprises. With close to a 100 percent profits tax and full compensation for losses, the official cost of the inputs only trivially affects the fortunes of the industry's bureaucrats and managers. The assumption we make means that the official revenues of the firm, $P * Q$, are the only real cost to the managers and the bureaucrats. The higher the official price for its output, the lower the bribes the industry can collect per unit of output, and so the higher the effective cost of this output. To the bureaucrats and managers, the official revenues are a drain; they are just like the production cost or an excise tax to a private firm. Once this point is recognized, the objective function of the industry given by (6.1) is the revenue minus the total cost.[3]

In writing down this objective function, we make several specific assumptions. First, we assume that bribes are collected efficiently. Customers do not stand in line or inefficiently lobby the producers, they just pay the bribe $D(Q) - P$. This assumption is obviously unrealistic, since in socialist countries we observe queues, lobbying, and other inefficient behavior as well as bribes. We do not need such a strong assumption. We need only assume that the tax rate on official profits is high enough that the industry tries to collect bribes rather than official profits. Even if there are some restrictions on bribery that lead to queues in equilibrium, the objective function will be similar to (6.1), and we will still get the result that the industry wants to create a shortage.

Second, we assume that there is no price discrimination in bribes. Every customer who gets the good pays $D(Q) - P$. If price discrimination in bribes were perfect, every customer would pay his reservation price in the form of bribes, and there would be no shortage at the official price. But as long as price discrimination is not perfect, there will be a shortage.

Third, as we already mentioned, the ministry precludes bribe competition between producers, so in equilibrium, bribes are chosen monopolistically. If bribes were chosen competitively, producers would cut bribes competitively until they reached zero. But unlike market economies, in which price competition is intense, socialist economies have a natural collusion device, namely the ministries, that prevents competition in bribes.

Fourth, we assume that bribery is not penalized. For socialist and other severely regulated economies, this assumption is perhaps more realistic than it would be for a market economy. In part, bribery is so pervasive that it is difficult to detect more than a trivial fraction of it. In part, the authorities who are supposed to attack bribery typically get a cut of the proceeds and so protect corruption rather than attack it. Moreover, introducing a probability of detection and penalty into our model would not affect the qualitative results unless penalties were so severe as to stop bribes altogether. If the probability of detection or the size of the punishment is increasing in the size of the bribe, then bribes are lower than the level predicted by our model. But if the probability of

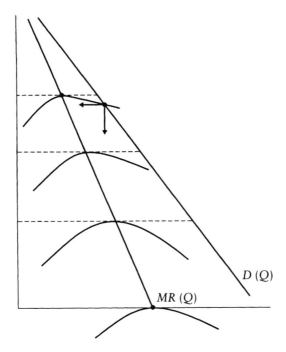

Figure 6.2   The decision problem of a socialist industry

detection increases in the number of people who bribe the monopolist, he might further reduce output and increase shortages to cut the number of customers and hence the probability of detection. These cases can be easily examined.

Once the objective function (6.1) is granted, our main point follows immediately. The industry maximizes the value of the bribes, and this value is zero if markets clear. The only way this industry can earn any income for its bureaucrats and managers is if quantity and official price are chosen to create a shortage. Only if there is a shortage will the value of bribes be positive. Shortage is thus not just the coincident consequence of the difficulty of socialist calculation; it is the most generic consequence of the true objective of people who run socialist industries.

Figure 6.2 illustrates what an unrestrained socialist industry would like to do. Differentiating (6.1) with respect to Q, holding the official price constant, we obtain the first-order condition for the industry for the case where the official price is given exogenously:

$$R'(Q) = P.$$

If the industry takes the price as exogenous, it will set the marginal revenue equal to the official price. This result is obvious once we recognize that the official price is the marginal cost of the socialist industry. Equation (6.2) explains the indifference curves of the socialist industry presented in Figure 6.2. These indifference curves peak at their intersection with the marginal revenue curve and decline on both sides of it. Figure 6.2 illustrates that if the industry could pick both its price and the quantity it produced, it would set the price equal to zero (to minimize what it perceives to be its marginal cost) and set the output at the point where the marginal revenue from producing more is equal to zero.

More generally, Figure 6.2 illustrates that, starting from any market-clearing price/output combination, the industry always wants to cut both its official price and its output. The industry wants to cut its price because lower official prices for a given output simply raise the market-clearing bribes. And the industry wants to cut its output at a given price for precisely the same reason that a monopoly wants to cut output from the competitive level at a given marginal cost: the marginal revenue curve is to the left of the demand curve. By cutting output from the market-clearing level, the socialist industry increases the value of the rents it collects. This socialist industry always wants to move southwest from the market-clearing position, that is, to create a shortage. If the plan imposed from the center were so tight as to force the industry to be on the demand curve, the market would clear, and no bribes would be collected. But if the socialist industry had any discretion whatsoever to renegotiate the plan, or to under-fulfill the plan, so as to move southwest from a point on the demand curve, it would do so and thereby create a shortage. This is our central proposition.

This result is quite different from the usual observation that socialist firms have low-powered incentives to produce, and therefore produce less than profit-maximizing firms would in the same circumstances. If the only problem were low output, the market would clear at a low output and a high price, and there would be no shortages. Instead, our result shows that socialist firms have an incentive to cut both output and price and create shortages, because that strategy maximizes bribes. Socialist firms have strong incentives, but these incentives are to maximize the value of bribes rather than the value of official profits.

Our result casts doubt on Kornai's (1979) argument that because socialist firms do not pay for their inputs, they have an incentive to expand output ad infinitum. Perhaps they have an incentive to acquire all the inputs they can lay their hands on, since they do not pay for them and may be able to sell them. But output expansion is not costless to socialist firms, because it limits their ability to collect bribes. As these firms expand, marginal revenue falls, and at some point it falls below the true marginal cost to these firms, which is the official price. Since socialist firms have a well-defined objective of maximizing the value of bribes, they have the incentive to restrict output to the level where the marginal revenue equals the marginal cost they face; this output certainly is not infinite.

The message of this section, then, is that a socialist industry has a very strong incentive to create a shortage. As long as it has some discretion over its price and output, it will do so. Of course we do not really believe that the socialist industry will obtain its maximum bribes and charge a zero official price. The central authorities would then run an enormous deficit and face enormous pressure from consumers to somehow interfere. In the next section, we discuss one plausible form of such interference.

6.3 Response to Shortages

It is implausible to assume, as we have so far, that an industry can generate severe shortages and large official losses without provoking at least some response from the central government. It is more likely that public complaints about shortages and budget deficits will prompt a response. That response, of course, will be muted by the fact that bureaucrats in the ministries and higher up usually share in the bribes and so have a strong incentive not to eliminate them. In particular, they have strong incentives not to stiffen plans and enforce production quotas. Nonetheless, sometimes the center responds to pressure and changes the constraints on an industry. One obvious strategy to combat shortages—used in the Soviet Union in April 1991 and again in January 1992—is to raise prices.

What happens when the center sets the price for the industry is clear from equation (6.2) and is illustrated in Figure 6.3. The industry

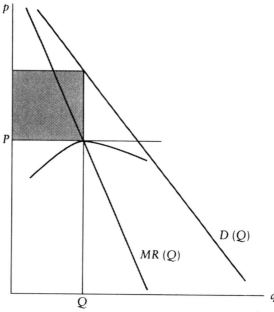

Figure 6.3   The center sets the price *p* for the industry   p↑ q↓

sets output at the point where the marginal revenue is equal to the official price. Because output at this point is below demand, there is a shortage, and the industry collects positive bribes. Suppose that now the central authorities raise prices to reduce shortages. In this model, raising prices reduces rather than raises output, since a higher marginal revenue corresponds to a lower output. The reason for this is that the official price of output is the marginal cost to the socialist industry. Raising official prices is just like raising the marginal cost, and so leads to a reduction in output. Because higher official prices lead to losses of bribes on the marginal units, it pays the industry to cut its output. An official price increase thus has the perverse effect of reducing supply, as the industry struggles to keep up the value of bribes.

This result sheds light on experiences with price increases in the former Soviet Union. In April 1991 the Soviet government raised official prices by an average of 100 percent to 200 percent. Prices remained controlled. A "surprising" consequence of the price increases, discussed in all the Soviet newspapers, was the conspicuous absence of increases in supplies of goods on the store shelves. Even if post-increase prices remained below market-clearing levels, one would still expect a nontrivial increase in the availability of some goods and a reduction in queues. This, however, did not happen. In a second episode, on January 2, 1992, the Yeltsin government freed most prices and sharply raised even the prices of goods that remained controlled. Retail prices rose three- to fourfold on average. In contrast to the earlier reform, there was an instant and tremendous increase of goods on the store shelves. Many items that the Russian consumers had not seen for years, such as coffee, sausages, and chocolates, suddenly appeared in stores.

Our model might explain why goods appeared on store shelves in January 1992 but not in April 1991. In April 1991, although the government raised the prices, the stores' profits were still largely taxed away. Since the store managers did not benefit much from earning higher official profits but could benefit from bribes, it did not pay them to offer any more output at the official prices. In fact, our model predicts that they should have restricted supplies further at official prices. In contrast, in January 1992, property rights to official profits changed dramatically. A much larger chunk of the profits could be kept by the employees and managers of the stores (as well as by suppliers). Moreover, stores could retain some profits to use for a subsequent buyout in privatization. As a result, it became more attractive to sell goods at high prices and keep the share of the legal profits than to keep down official supplies and use bribes. The goods shifted from sale through the back door to sale through the front door. In this way, the change in property rights to official profits may explain why the second price reform worked but the first one did not.

6.4 Conclusion

We have presented a model of shortages in socialist economies intentionally created by an industry—meaning bureaucrats in the ministry and managers of firms—trying to collect rents in the form of bribes when it cannot keep the official profits. This theory suggests that because public ownership of firms and the resulting expropriation of official profits is endemic to socialist economies, so will be shortages. In contrast, because under capitalism firms and their profits are owned privately, capitalist producers will always wish to collect "official" profits by charging higher "official" prices. At a given price, capitalist producers want to sell more, leading to what Weitzman (1984) calls an "excess supply" of goods. Our model thus accords well with the central distinction between capitalism and socialism stressed by both Kornai and Weitzman: "excess supply" of goods under capitalism and excess demand under socialism.

The issue of who keeps the profits arises in market economies as well. For example, public monopolies often underprice output and thus create shortages. In many countries with public phone companies, such as Brazil and France, it takes a long time to obtain a phone line, and a bribe helps to obtain it faster. Since public monopolies and their managers cannot keep a large share of the profits they generate, it is not surprising that they create a situation conducive to the collection of bribes and, more generally, favors. Similarly, inside large firms and other bureaucratic organizations, managers with negligible equity stakes often choose to allocate resources not through market prices but through quantity controls and other transfer-pricing mechanisms that leave them more discretion. This strategy might help them maximize the value of bribes and other favors rather than the firm's profits.

The major theme of our analysis is that socialist planners are self-interested. This assumption contrasts sharply with the one usually made in the debate on market socialism. Since Barone ([1898] 1967), both opponents and advocates of market socialism have assumed a benevolent central planner. As a result, the market socialism literature has focused on the complexity of the computational task facing this benevolent planner (e.g., Lange [1936–37] 1964). But if, contrary to the assumption of this literature, central planners are self-interested, then the possibility of efficient resource allocation under market socialism is in much greater doubt. For as we have shown, it is in the interest of such planners to cut output and to create price distortions. In direct contrast to Lange's claim that monopolistic output restrictions are the likely product of market economies, we have shown that such restrictions are likely to take place under socialism. Even without computational complexities, socialism with self-interested planners will not result in efficient resource allocation.

Last but not least, our analysis has an important implication for reforms in centrally planned economies. A key implication of our analysis is that the question of price reform cannot be separated from the question of property rights. Producers respond to incentives afforded by free prices only if they get the property rights to enough of the profits that can be earned with free prices. Without such property rights to profits, higher prices do not solve the shortage problem endemic to socialist economies, as the Soviet experience in April 1991 has shown. In contrast, giving producers a right to their profits gives them an incentive to respond correctly to free prices as well as to many other signals that will come from free markets. Successful price reform, like most other reforms, boils down to allocating property rights to producers and therefore ultimately depends on privatization of profits.

The Politics of Market Socialism   7

One of the most enduring proposals in modern economics is market socialism: an economy in which firms are owned and controlled by the government but then sell their products to consumers in competitive markets. A reasonable person might expect that recent events in Eastern Europe would put this proposal to permanent and well-deserved rest. Instead, these events seem to have given hope to the market socialists. After all, Eastern European countries are starting out with virtually all firms controlled by the state. In contrast to capitalist economies, where in order to get to market socialism the state must first nationalize the economy, in Eastern Europe and Russia this step was completed decades ago. If only privatization can be stopped, Eastern Europe presents mouth-watering possibilities for experimentation with market socialism. Peculiar as it may seem, the escape from socialism has only encouraged many socialists.[1]

This chapter takes another stab at the problem of market socialism. We focus on an issue that is often mentioned but rarely seriously discussed in the debates over market socialism. Under all forms of market socialism, from Lange ([1936–37] 1964) to the present, the state ultimately controls the firms, and hence politicians' objectives must determine resource allocation. Market socialists have traditionally assumed that politicians will pursue an efficient resource allocation, and have only paid lip service to the idea that the state becomes "bureaucratized."

Originally published in *Journal of Economic Perspectives*, 8, no. 2 (Spring 1994): 165–176.

123

They dismiss the tragic socialist experience as irrelevant because totalitarian systems are not what they have in mind. Rather, market socialists count on a democratic socialist government that pursues efficiency. The question of what such a government will maximize is therefore absolutely central to discussions of market socialism.

We begin by reviewing the debate over market socialism, pointing out the essential role played by assumptions about the objectives of the government. We then discuss a series of economies: totalitarian socialism, democratic socialism, and democratic capitalism. Our argument against democratic market socialism is basically twofold. First, we argue that no democratic government is likely to place sufficient weight on economic efficiency, regardless of whether the economy is capitalist or socialist. Second, we claim that the damage from the government's pursuit of its "political" objectives will be much greater under socialism than under capitalism because, under socialism, the government has a greater ability to determine outcomes at the firm level.

7.1 The Market Socialism Debate

Analytical debate over market socialism started with Barone ([1908] 1935), who has pointed out that the Central Planner, like the Walrasian Auctioneer, can solve n equations with n unknowns and so determine prices that simultaneously clear all markets. The state can then control firms and make lump sum redistributions to promote equality, and still obtain efficient outcomes for any distribution of income.

Barone's argument invited objections from von Mises ([1920] 1935) and Hayek (1935), who argued that the state does not have the necessary information to determine equilibrium prices. These objections, however, were effectively rebutted by Lange ([1936–37] 1964), whose paper remains the most coherent and articulate case for market socialism. Lange argued that while it is true that the state has only limited information, so does the Walrasian Auctioneer. The process of price adjustment in a market economy, according to Lange, takes the form of price increases on goods that are in excess demand, and price declines on goods that are in excess supply. The Central Planner can follow exactly the same procedure: raising prices in response to shortages and cutting prices in response to surpluses. Lange thus established quite convincingly that a benevolent Central Planner can, in principle, clear markets.

Not satisfied with establishing the equivalence between market and socialist resource allocation, Lange went on to present several reasons why socialism is superior. First, the state can distribute income more equitably. Second, since the state controls all firms, it can solve the problem of externalities. Third, since the state sets prices and determines entry, it can avoid monopolies. Aside from excessive prices, monopolies in Lange's model have two disadvantages. They are responsible for rigid prices and therefore contribute to business cycles; and they are only interested in preserving economic rents and hence are incapable of innovation. By crushing monopolies, the socialist state can both solve the business cycle problem and increase the rate of innovation.

Lange's arguments rely heavily on the government's pursuit of efficiency. His basic argument that the government raises prices of goods in short supply presumes that it actually wants to do so—rather than to maintain shortages. The pursuit of income redistribution, of internalizing externalities, and of competition rather than monopoly all presume efficiency-maximizing politicians. Indeed, Lange makes this assumption quite explicitly. For example, he writes: "The decisions of the managers of production are no longer guided by the aim of maximizing profit. Instead, certain rules are imposed on them by the Central Planning Board which aim at satisfying consumers' preferences in the best way possible" (Lange [1936–37] 1964, p. 75).

The actual experience of socialist countries has, of course, been rather different. Instead of raising prices to clear markets, socialist governments typically maintain shortages of many goods for years. Some socialist dictators have pursued economic equality, though murder and repression by others have produced more equality of incomes than of welfare. The notion that the government solves the externality problem is belied by the experience with pollution, which seems to be worse in socialist than in comparably rich market economies (Grossman and Krueger 1995). Also, monopolies, at least as measured by concentration, are much more common in socialist than in market economies (International Monetary Fund 1991). Finally, practically no one believes that technological progress has been faster under socialism.

Market socialists familiar with this experience blame it on totalitarian government, and then get on with the business of praising market socialism in a democratic state. Lange ([1936–37] 1964, pp. 109-110) briefly mentions the dangers of the state becoming bureaucratized, but does not spend much time on this problem: "It seems to us, indeed, that *the real danger of socialism is bureaucratization of economic life,* and not the impossibility of coping with the problem of allocation of resources. Unfortunately, we do not see how the same, or even greater, danger can be averted under monopolistic capitalism. Officials subject to democratic control seem preferable to private corporation executives who practically are responsible to nobody" (emphasis in original).

One obvious problem with this statement is Lange's denial of the importance of incentive and control mechanisms in market economies, including boards of directors, management ownership, large blockholders, takeovers, banks, and bankruptcy (Stiglitz 1991). Subsequent market socialists have indeed focused on this issue, and have added to Lange's model of market socialism incentives for enterprise managers comparable to those in market economies; for example, a group of socially owned large banks might have a controlling interest in large companies (Bardhan and Roemer 1992). In practice, such market-oriented incentive schemes for managers of state enterprises are very uncommon, and are often terminated by politicians when managers begin to actually maximize profits (Nellis 1988). But even more important than the question of incentives for the agent—that is, the manager—is the question of the objectives of the principal—that is, the government. Lange's most controversial assertion is that democratic control of corporate managers will lead to good outcomes, which is effectively a claim that politicians pursue economic efficiency.

In the fifty years since, the discussion of market socialism (except in the public choice literature)[2] has largely swallowed the assumption that the government would maximize efficiency, and focused on the more technical issues, such as the ability of the state to complete the markets, or the relative efficiency of various price adjustment schemes. Hayek's warning (1944) that even democratic socialists turn into Hitlers and Mussolinis made a relatively bigger impression on public opinion than on the economics profession. An analytical discussion of the objectives of a socialist government is still missing. We try to fill this gap by first discussing the likely objectives of a socialist dictator and then turning to the unlikely ideal of democratic socialism.

7.2 Totalitarian Socialism

We begin by considering an ideal dictator, who is completely secure from political or military challenges. This dictator does not need to worry about keeping down unemployment, building up defense, paying off or killing off political competitors, feeding the population, or any other problems. A strictly rational dictator in such a position would maximize personal wealth, which he can either put in his Swiss bank account or use to build himself monuments, such as armies, cathedrals, or industrial plants. The question is: does the pursuit of this objective lead to efficient outcomes?

At first glance, one might think that the unthreatened dictator is just a shareholder in the whole economy, and therefore should be interested in maximizing the value of his shares—that is, the profits of all the firms. Moreover, the dictator would internalize the externalities resulting from the operations of these firms and hence produce an even more efficient outcome than the market. But this is only true if the dictator takes prices as given. In fact, of course, he would control prices as well as production decisions. In this case profit maximization would call for the creation of monopolies in all industries (assuming that the dictator cannot perfectly price discriminate). Far from designing a competitive market equilibrium, the unthreatened dictator would strive for a highly monopolistic and inefficient economy—in stark contrast to Lange's insistence that socialism *prevents* monopolistic tendencies. This result, incidentally, finds empirical support in the tendency of European monarchs to create monopolies precisely to maximize personal revenues (Ekelund and Tollison 1981).

This model seems to better describe the conduct of capitalist dictators, such as Ferdinand Marcos in the Philippines and monarchs in the age of mercantilism, than that of socialist dictators. In socialist countries, rather than observing market-clearing monopoly prices, we see a shortage of most goods. Chapter 6 addresses this issue in a model in which a socialist dictator maximizes his income, but is prevented by the constraint of secrecy from openly putting monopoly profits in his pocket. In that chapter we show that the dictator would behave very similarly to a monopolist, but with one important exception. Instead of charging monopoly prices, the dictator would choose to charge low prices, to create a shortage, and then collect bribes from the rationed consumers. In such a model, the socialist dictator constrained by secrecy would allocate resources very similarly to a capitalist dictator, except for the way in which income is collected.

This simple model has several empirical implications consistent with the experience of socialist countries. First, it explains why shortages in socialist economies are so pervasive, since bribe collection afforded by a shortage is the main mechanism for the dictator and his ruling elite to receive income. Second, the model explains why despite shortages prices in socialist economies are often not raised for years, even on consumer luxuries for which income distribution arguments cannot justify artificially low prices. For example, Russian Communists kept the prices of cars and apartments fixed for decades despite years-long waiting lists. Raising prices would eliminate bribe income, contrary to the interest of the ruling elite. Third, the model explains the tendency of socialist economies to produce many goods monopolistically, since monopoly prevents competition in bribes that would bring prices down to competitive levels. In sum, the socialist dictator model goes some way toward explaining why the inefficiency of socialist economies is so much larger than Lange predicted.

While modeling a socialist dictator as maximizing his wealth oversimplifies reality, more realistic models would probably imply an even smaller interest in efficiency on his part. Most dictators, for example, are politically insecure, and hence pursue personal security for themselves and their supporters. To this end, they spend enormous resources on armies and police, refocus production on military rather than consumer goods, organize firms to make them easy to control and managed by supporters rather than experts, alter prices to transfer resources to their followers, and often kill millions of their opponents. These are more serious costs to economic efficiency than those caused by secure, wealth-maximizing dictators.

7.3 Democracy and Economic Efficiency

Market socialists will deem the above discussion historically relevant, at best, but surely immaterial to their visions of democratic socialism, in which the government is extremely responsive to the will of the people. So let us consider the case of a democratically elected socialist government in control of a nation's firms. Most market socialists presume that such a government will strive for efficient resource allocation. How likely is this objective to materialize?

Before proceeding with this question, we must mention three issues that we do not address. First, Hayek (1944) has followed the inspiration of Smith ([1776] 1976) and argued that democracy is impossible in a country where a single leader has all the power that comes with controlling capital. We are sympathetic to Hayek's argument. But here we will grant market socialists the possibility of democratic socialism, and only examine its consequences. Second, Stigler (1965) has complained that even economists skeptical about the state, such as Adam Smith, usually focus on the state's intentions rather than on its ability to implement its announced goals. While Stigler is right that even a benevolent state might have serious implementation problems, that is not our focus here.

Third, and most important, market socialists often obfuscate the importance of politicians' intentions by imagining complex corporate governance structures. Thus Bardhan and Roemer (1992) imagine a system in which the government controls banks, which also have other shareholders, and which in turn control enterprises. Our view on this issue is simple, but realistic: no matter what smoke and mirrors are used, as long as the government remains in ultimate control of enterprises, which it does by definition in all market socialist schemes, its objectives are going to be the ones that are maximized. Any manager who dares to stand up to the government, or to the bank controlled by the government, will be acting against his personal interest. Similarly, no manager of a bank controlled by the government will refuse to lend money to a large state enterprise when the government that hired him "advises" in favor of the loan. The right focus is therefore on the objectives of the government, regardless of the governance structure through which these objectives are implemented.

The futility of trying to insulate public firms from political pressures is best illustrated by the experience of public enterprises in Western Europe, where democratic institutions are strong and hence the conditions for such insulation are ideal. Despite extensive mechanisms for independent governance, most public firms in Western Europe are subject to heavy-handed government interference. Recall the experience of British coal, where Parliament refused to accept layoffs from enormously inefficient coal mines. Or consider the failure of Air France to cut labor, as the government opted for strikers' support and fired the manager. In countries with weaker democratic institutions, such as Italy as well as many countries in Africa, Asia, and Eastern Europe, public enterprises are simply used by politicians to gain political support and the concept of government noninterference is totally foreign. The experience with public enterprises suggests grave skepticism about the possibility of insulating public firms from the objectives of the government.

So what objectives will the government inherit from the democratic process? Two leading models of democratic decision making are majority voting and pressure groups. Neither model predicts that the democratic government will maximize economic efficiency, although they differ in the nature of deviations from efficiency that they predict.

The majority voting model predicts that the majority will redistribute resources from the minority to itself even at the cost of reduced efficiency. The reason for inefficiency is that majority voting schemes do not weigh the intensity of preferences. As a result, if a majority can obtain a gain as a result of a redistribution from a minority, it will do so even if the costs to the minority exceed the benefits to the majority. In other words, majority voting does not lead to efficient outcomes (Tullock 1959).

This prediction of majority voting seems to hold true in a variety of cases. Most democratic countries (whether capitalist or socialist) practice sharply progressive taxation. Industrial workers sometimes gang up on farmers and expropriate their crops and land even when this strategy leads to devastating losses to farmers and meager benefits to workers. A majority of tenants in a city routinely impose inefficient rent control on the minority of landlords. Ethnic majorities throughout the world force minority businesses to charge prices below cost, hire members of the majority, and pay exorbitant taxes (Sowell 1990). In light of the multiple examples of the tyranny of the majority, the claim that a majority will elect a government committed to economic efficiency is simply false.

An alternative model for democratic politics is the interest group model (Olson 1965; Becker 1983). In this model, interest groups form and pressure the government to pursue policies that benefit these groups at the expense of the rest of the population. Interest group politics leads to efficient resource allocation only under very restrictive conditions.

First, forming an interest group and collecting contributions must be completely costless, so that free rider and other problems are circumvented. In this case, all groups that have a common interest will form. Second, there should be no resource cost of lobbying the government; that is, interest groups should simply bid in cash, which they raise in a nondistortionary fashion, for the policies they want. If both of these conditions hold, then the interest group model predicts efficient outcomes simply because the interest groups that put a higher value on a policy will bid more for it. Thus if an industry wants protection that reduces efficiency, the consumer lobby will value free trade more than the industry, pay more for it, and thus ensure free trade. The public interest model, with costless group formation and lobbying, reduces to an efficient auction of policy choices.

Of course, organizing interest groups is actually quite expensive, because the free rider problem discourages joining (Olson 1965). Many interest groups in which benefits are small and diffuse, such as "consumers for free trade," simply do not form. The interest groups that do form and lobby the government are generally small groups with concentrated benefits, such as "automobile industry for protection." As a result, the organized minorities tend to gang up on the disorganized majority, creating inefficient resource allocation. The assumption of costless lobbying is also false, as rent seeking can absorb substantial resources.

Examples of inefficiencies resulting from interest group politics are numerous; they form the substance of a vast public choice literature. The well-organized managers of the military-industrial complex can form a lobby that makes sure that the state allocates to them, and not to other firms, the majority of state credits. Farmers, doctors, and other groups form effective lobbies that raise prices and redistribute public resources to themselves. Many industries demand and receive protection. We are unaware of any evidence that interest group politics leads to anything like the efficient outcome.

In a provocative but ultimately unpersuasive article, Wittman (1989) argues that the two biases—from majority voting and from interest group pressures—should cancel each other out. Specifically, the majority will vote against candidates who are too favorable to the interests of well-organized minority groups. An example might be that consumers will always vote against protectionist presidential candidates.

However, it is hard to see why these two deviations from efficiency in democratic politics should cancel out in any exact sense. In fact, sometimes the majority is better organized. For example, the majority of the population may be employed in import-competing industries, and hence the majority would favor protection. The disorganized minority that is not employed in such industries will then bear the double cost of neither getting higher wages nor having access to cheap imports. Or consider the case of "democracy" in Russia immediately after the collapse of Communism, where something close to the majority of the population benefited from state subsidies to inefficient industrial enterprises, and was also vastly better organized through industrial lobbies than the remainder of the population. This majority could extract tremendous resources from the rest of the population at a huge cost to efficiency.

In sum, there is no presumption that democratic politics will lead to anything like an efficiency-pursuing government (see also Kornai 1993). Vast amounts of evidence from the U.S. and West European democracies confirm this point. Even Sweden, long the darling of all socialists, has been suffering from a "crisis" brought about by heavy government intervention in the economy, and has been trying to restore "a highly competitive market system" (Lindbeck et al. 1993).

7.4 Democratic Socialism versus Democratic Capitalism

A market socialist would intercede at this point (if not earlier) and note, quite correctly, that the inefficiencies of democratic politics plague capitalist as well as socialist economies. After all, protection, subsidies, and state loans to declining firms are common in capitalist economies as well. Why, then, is democratic politics a special problem for democratic socialism?

The public choice literature establishes that democratic politics do not lead to governmental interest in efficiency, regardless of the economic system. To establish our main point—that democratic socialism must be a less efficient economic system than democratic capitalism—we must show that a democratic government does more damage under socialism than under capitalism.

Our argument boils down to a single assertion: when the government controls firms, it has considerably more ability to convince them to pursue its political objectives than when the government must persuade private shareholders. Becker (1983, p. 385) is characteristically perceptive: "Even though Schumpeter and others have identified selfish pressure groups with democratic capitalism, I believe that pressure groups of workers, managers, intellectuals, etc. have an incentive to be more rather than less active under democratic and other forms of socialism because a larger fraction of resources is controlled by the State under socialism than under capitalism."

We may examine this argument for the superiority of democratic capitalism in greater detail. Suppose the government wants a firm owned by private shareholders to do something that they might not want to do if they maximized profits, such as employ extra people, pay extra wages, undertake a "socially desirable" investment project, produce output for the war effort, and so on. If the government does not control this firm through regulation, it must pay the shareholders the opportunity cost of meeting the government's wishes, since these shareholders, rather than the government, have the control rights over the decisions of the firm. For example, governments often pay firms to maintain employment through tax breaks, procurement contracts and so on. And however the government raises money to make those payments—whether through taxes, borrowing, or the printing press—it is likely to encounter opposition from the broader public. As a result, such political interference in privately owned firms is rather limited.

Of course, governments often find a cheaper way to get firms to pursue political objectives, through regulation. Regulation gives governments some control rights over firms whose profits are privately owned, so that it can compel them to follow the political will without compensating shareholders. By effectively expropriating the wealth of a few shareholders rather than taxing a broader segment of the population, the government faces a lower political price of enforcing inefficient allocations through regulation. Nonetheless, as any form of taxation, regulation is not free to politicians.

Under true market socialism, the government both owns the cash flows from firms and controls their decisions. In this case, when the government makes a firm produce inefficiently, the treasury pays the opportunity cost of such production. From this viewpoint, market capitalism and market socialism appear quite similar: under capitalism, the government must pay shareholders to pursue politically motivated policies and must raise taxes to do it; under socialism, the treasury gives up profits because of the same politically motivated policies, and hence must pay for the forgone profits by raising taxes. Since a democratically elected government bears the political cost of having to raise taxes in either case, its willingness to enforce economic inefficiency might be similar under socialism and capitalism.

But there is a crucial difference between capitalism and socialism. Under socialism, the government is much richer relative to the wealth of the economy than under capitalism: it owns the cash flow of most or all of the firms in the economy. As a result, the government can afford many more politically motivated inefficient projects that lose money than it could in a capitalist economy. For example, the Soviet government could use the wealth from the country's natural resources to build an extremely inefficient, militaristic economy. Many African countries have wasted their mineral and agricultural wealth on failed industrialization. When, in contrast, resources are privately owned, the government cannot as easily spend them to pursue its objectives. It can tax and regulate to extract some wealth, but that gives it much less wealth than owning all the assets to begin with. The reason that democratic socialist economies must be much less efficient than market economies is not that the democratic process leads to worse government objectives under socialism than under capitalism, but that the government can afford to pay for much more inefficiency under socialism than under capitalism.

7.5 Conclusion

Under both capitalism and socialism, the democratic process does not generate governmental objectives consistent with the pursuit of efficiency. But under socialism, the government turns these inefficient objectives into much more damage to the economy than does a capitalist government. The theoretical case for economic efficiency under democratic socialism simply does not hang together.

For the purposes of our argument, we have granted market socialists the assumptions that democratic socialism will not degenerate into totalitarianism and that it has the power to implement its plans. Removing either of these assumptions, or adding the actual economic record of socialism in the Soviet Union and Eastern Europe, would only strengthen the case for democratic capitalism.

In this context, it is instructive to keep in mind who the supporters of "market socialism" in Eastern Europe have been. The supporters, who inevitably talk about Sweden, have tended to be former Communist officials and managers of doomed state enterprises—the people who stood to personally benefit the most from continued government ownership. It is unfortunate that, like the Soviet Communists in the 1930s, these advocates of market socialism have received support from idealists in the West.

A Theory of Privatization

8

In the last decade, privatization of state enterprises has swept the world. Thousands of state firms in Africa, Asia, Latin America, and Western and Eastern Europe have gone private (Kikeri, Nellis, and Shirley 1992). A critical factor behind this move to privatization is the well-documented poor performance of public enterprises. Donahue (1989) surveys multiple studies showing the significantly higher cost of public relative to private provision of municipal services in the United States. Lopez-de-Silanes (1997) documents the inferior profitability of state relative to private firms in Mexico in the 1980s. Mueller (1989) and Vining and Boardman (1992) survey dozens of studies of public and private firms around the world, most of which show that private firms are more efficient. More recent studies have shown that efficiency improves after privatization (World Bank 1995; Megginson, Nash, and van Randenborgh 1994). Here we develop a model of privatization that explains the relative inefficiency of public firms and the improvements of efficiency after privatization as well as several other empirical findings concerning privatization.

The starting point of our analysis is the commonplace observation that public enterprises are inefficient because they address the objectives of politicians rather than maximize efficiency. One key objective of politicians is employment: they care about the votes of the people whose jobs are in danger, and in many cases unions have significant influence

By Maxim Boyko, Andrei Shleifer, and Robert W. Vishny; originally published in *Economic Journal,* 106, no. 435 (March 1996): 309–319.

on political parties. For example, Donahue (1989) describes evidence showing higher employment per unit of output in publicly provided municipal services. The British government for a long time refused to close grossly inefficient coal mines to preserve mining jobs. Although excess employment is not the only politically demanded inefficiency of state firms, it is surely the most commonly noted one. Below we focus on the implications of the political demand for excess employment by public enterprises.

In section 8.2, we present a simple model in which a spending politician, such as an industrial minister, who controls the decisions of a public enterprise, forces it, for political reasons, to spend too much on labor. This politician does not fully internalize the cost of the profits forgone by the treasury and by private shareholders that the firm might have. The manager can bribe this politician to agree to lower employment, and in some cases corruption improves efficiency. Corruption contracts are usually neither legal nor enforceable, however, so inefficiency is not necessarily cured by corruption.

This analysis raises a question: can a reformer make it more difficult for spending politicians to benefit from excess employment in public enterprises? A reformer in this model is a newly elected leader, such as Margaret Thatcher in Britain, Carlos Salinas in Mexico, or Vaclav Klaus in the Czech Republic, who derives political benefits not from excess employment in public enterprises, but from low public spending and taxes. It is not that reformers are benevolent, but rather that their political constituents are the taxpayers rather than the beneficiaries of public largesse. These reformers want to constrain the actions of their own spending ministries or, alternatively, to tie the hands of future governments (such as future Labour governments in Britain) that might be more inclined to spend money on public enterprise employment. In effect, these reformers represent the interests of the treasury against those of the spending ministries.

This chapter discusses privatization as a strategy available to reformers to reduce the inefficiency of public enterprises. By privatization we mean a combination of the reallocation of control rights over employment from politicians to managers and the increase in cash flow ownership of managers and private investors.[1] At first glance, it seems that privatization should reduce employment if managers maximize profits and have no interest in excess employment. However, spending politicians still want to influence firms and can use government subsidies to convince their managers to keep up employment. In principle, there is nothing magic about privatization: just as the spending politician was willing to give up profits of a public firm on excess labor spending, he is willing to subsidize a privatized firm to "buy" excess labor spending. How, then, does privatization serve the reformer's interests and separate the firm from the spending politician?

This question has been addressed by several authors. Schmidt (1996) argues that privatization reduces the amount of information that politicians have, which may lead to the reduction of subsidies and restructuring. Shapiro and Willig (1990) make a clear case that privatization must draw a line between politicians and firms, and like Schmidt use an information argument to show how it works. We agree with the general approach of these papers, although we are not sure why privatization necessarily changes the information of politicians.

We argue that it may be politically less costly for the politician to spend the profits of the firm on labor without remitting them to the treasury than to generate new subsidies for the privatized firm. The public and the reformers may not be aware of the potential profits that a state firm is wasting, but they are keenly aware of the alternative uses of tax revenues, and would not wish to spend public money to subsidize private firms not to restructure. This difference between the political costs of forgone profits of state firms and of subsidies to private firms is the channel through which privatization works here. One important conclusion of this analysis is that a tough monetary policy makes privatization much more effective.

8.1 Political Control of Firms

8.1.1 A SIMPLE MODEL

We consider a firm that only chooses its level of spending on labor E. It can spend an efficient amount L or a higher amount $H > L$. The higher spending comes from excess wages and employment. The restriction of only two levels of spending is introduced for simplicity.

There are two players in this model who have preferences over E: the politician and the manager. The manager here is assumed to represent private shareholders. We begin by assuming that the manager and share-holders own a fraction α of the firm's profits, while the treasury owns a fraction $(1 - \alpha)$. The politician himself owns no equity. In a public firm, α is close to zero, whereas in a private firm, α is close to 1.

To begin, we assume that the objective function of the politician (in dollars) is given by:

$$(8.1) \qquad U_p = qE - m(1 - \alpha)E.$$

The politician prefers higher labor spending since it is a source of political benefits, such as voting support from the employees and labor unions. The marginal benefit to him of an extra dollar of such spending is $q < 1$. But spending more on labor reduces the value of the treasury's share of profits of the firm. The politician cares about these profits because the treasury can impose sanctions on him if the firm loses (or fails to make) money. Importantly, the politician does not care directly about the share of profits forgone by the manager and private shareholders, which matter only to the extent that angering shareholders reduces the net potential political benefit of excess employment, q. The cost to the politician of a dollar of profits forgone by the treasury as a result of spending on labor is m. We assume $m < 1$ because the politician cares less about the treasury's income than he does about his own money. This too creates a bias for too much employment. The politician's objective function thus trades off the political benefits of higher employment against the political costs of the profits forgone by the treasury.

The objective function of the manager (shareholders) is simply given by his share of profits:

$$(8.2) \qquad U_m = -\alpha E.$$

We can extend the model to allow the manager to care about employment directly; the results are very similar as long as the manager cares relatively more about profits than the politician does.

The critical parameter in this model is who controls labor spending. Initially, we assume that the firm is publicly controlled, meaning that E is chosen by the politician. This assumption accurately represents the situation of most public enterprises, where the government exerts substantial influence over their key decisions, particularly when political issues such as employment are involved. For example, the French government refused to back the management of Air France in its attempt to reduce labor costs, with the result that the management left and the employees stayed.

When the politician controls E, we assume he chooses $E = H$. Denote by $\Delta E = H - L$ the incremental gain in labor spending from switching from L to H. Then the assumption that the politician uses his control rights to choose $E = H$ can be rewritten as

$$m(1 - \alpha) < q.$$

3)

This condition says that political benefits per dollar of extra spending on labor exceed political costs per dollar of profits forgone by the treasury from such spending. In this way, we illustrate the idea that political control leads to inefficiencies that benefit politicians at the expense of the treasury and other shareholders.

8.1.2 CORRUPTION

Even if the politician controls labor spending and (8.3) holds, it might be in the interest of the manager (and shareholders) to bribe the politician to cut the firm's labor spending. There are two ways of thinking about this bribe. First, it could be a payoff to change E (or some other decision that the politician imposes on the firm) from H to L. Second, it could be a payment to transfer the control rights over E from the politician to the manager. Since in this model the manager chooses $E = L$ once he gains control rights, the bribe necessary to buy control from the politician is the same as the bribe needed to persuade the politician to change his decision. We show below that corruption reduces the set of parameter values for which labor spending is excessive.

Denote the necessary bribe by b. With bribes, the politician's utility is given by

$$U_p = -m(1 - \alpha)E + qE + b,$$

.4)

and the manager's utility is given by

(8.5) $U_m = -\alpha E - b.$

Since utility is transferable, the manager succeeds in bribing the politician to choose $E = L$ if their combined utility is higher at L than at H, that is, if

(8.6) $m(1 - \alpha) + \alpha > q.$

Both (8.3) and (8.6) can be satisfied simultaneously: the politician chooses H without corruption but is willing to be bribed and choose efficient labor spending. The bribe divides the surplus between the manager and the politician according to the Nash or some other bargaining solution.

This result illustrates the Coase theorem for our model. When side payments in the form of bribes are allowed, the manager and the politician choose the outcome that, from their joint viewpoint, is the most efficient. If (8.6) holds, the "jointly efficient" outcome coincides with the socially efficient one $E = L$, but if (8.6) fails, the two may differ. Condition (8.6) is different from social efficiency in two ways. First, when $m < 1$, the politician does not fully internalize the forgone profits from excessive labor spending. The treasury is too soft to make him act as a full shareholder. Second, excess labor spending benefits the politician since it enables him to take votes away from other politicians, but it should not enter the social welfare function. Thus corruption generally raises efficiency, in that it allows private investors to buy their way out of some of the inefficiencies demanded by politicians, but it does not always lead to first best.[2]

There are, however, problems with using corruption to renegotiate to a more efficient resource allocation, even if (8.6) holds. First, corruption in most societies is illegal, so both the giver and the receiver of a bribe risk going to jail. The illegality of corruption is a particular problem when the bribe-supported outcome leads to substantial losses by the workers, who have an incentive to expose the politician. For the same reason of illegality, the corruption contract is unenforceable in court. After collecting a bribe, the politician can renew his demand that labor spending be kept at a high level, or ask for another bribe. Since the manager has no recourse to enforce the initial agreement, he might never offer a bribe in the first place. Of course, there are other mechanisms of contract enforcement, such as reputation, but in transition economies the horizons of politicians are often too short to develop a reputation for efficient bribe taking.[3] We are back to the case of the politician choosing the inefficient outcome as long as condition (8.3) holds.

8.2 Privatization

By privatization we mean a combination of two changes undertaken by a reformer. The first is turnover of control from spending politicians to managers, often referred to as corporatization. Such a turnover can be implemented by a strong reform government that effectively suppresses the ministries and the bureaucracy, as happened in the Czech Republic. Alternatively, such a turnover can happen more spontaneously, as the power of bureaucracy to protect its control rights diminishes. Such a slow turnover of control from politicians to managers occurred in Russia in the early 1990s.

The second change that is usually part of most privatizations is the reduction of the cash flow ownership by the treasury and the increase of cash flow ownership by managers and outside shareholders. The treasury can sell its shares for cash, or it can give them away through vouchers or some other allocation scheme. Our model shows how both the reallocation of control rights and the increase in private cash-flow rights contribute to restructuring.[4]

When the managers and shareholders interested in maximizing profits gain control over labor spending, they obviously choose $E = L$. This, however, is not the end of the story. For just as before a manager paid a politician with control rights to agree to $E = L$, the politician can now try to pay shareholders not to restructure. The mechanism that politicians use is typically not bribes, but subsidies from the treasury to the firms, also known as soft budget constraints.[5] Indeed, this is the main question about privatization: why would a politician fail to buy his way to high labor spending through subsidies? To show how privatization leads to restructuring, we must establish conditions under which managers with control rights choose to restructure even when they must forgo subsidies from the treasury.

Denote the subsidy from the treasury to the firm by t. Since the treasury owns $(1 - \alpha)$ of the cash flow, it gets the fraction $(1 - \alpha)$ of this subsidy back, so the effective subsidy is αt. If the politician could ask the treasury to subsidize the firm at no cost to himself, he would pay the firm infinite subsidies not to restructure and no restructuring would ever take place. But the treasury has to raise the money for the subsidies through either taxes or inflation, both of which are unpopular. We denote the cost to the politician of making a (net) subsidy αt by $k\alpha t$. In the plausible case, $k < 1$, since subsidies are less expensive to the politician than bribes out of his own pocket, which correspond to $k = 1$.

This model has two parameters that reflect the cost to the politician of forgone treasury revenue: m and k. The first measures the cost to the politician of profits forgone by the treasury, the second measures his political cost of subsidies. If the treasury suffers no illusions from the corporate veil, then $m = k$. However, it is more reasonable to suppose that it is easier for the politician to squander a firm's profits on inefficiencies than to obtain additional subsidies for it, in which case $m < k$. When a firm squanders its profits, most members of the government do not know that it is potentially profitable and hence do not claim a piece of its profits for the treasury and indirectly for their own pet projects. As a result, the minister who oversees this firm can spend the profits on political benefits, such as employment, at a relatively low political cost. In contrast, when a firm receives a subsidy, the minister must compete for the resources of the treasury with all the other politicians who argue for their favorite projects. As a result, buying political benefits with the money that is already in the treasury is more expensive than spending the profits of the firm. We keep the two parameters k and m separate to be able to evaluate the effect of each on the likelihood of restructuring.

We assume that corruption is infeasible (bribes are equivalent to the case of $k = 1$) since we have already noted some problems with bribes, and we want to focus on new issues. The objective function of the politician is given by

$$(8.7) \qquad U_p = -m(1 - \alpha)E + qE - k\alpha t,$$

and the objective function of the manager is given by

$$(8.8) \qquad U_m = -\alpha E + \alpha t.$$

We can compute the Nash bargaining solution to this problem. Without subsidies, the manager chooses efficient labor spending L. He and the politician then bargain, and he chooses labor spending H if he is better off with H and a transfer than he is with L. The politician's incremental utility from switching to H is given by

$$-m(1 - \alpha)\Delta E + q\Delta E - k\alpha t$$

and the manager's incremental utility from switching to H is given by

$$-\alpha \Delta E + \alpha t.$$

The Nash bargaining solution is given by maximizing the product of (8.9) and (8.10) over t, which yields the equilibrium transfer

$$t = \Delta E[-m(1 - \alpha) + q + k\alpha]/(2k\alpha).$$

This bargain fails to be struck if the manager (or the politician) is worse off with $E = H$ and transfer t than he is with $E = L$ and no transfer. The condition for neither of them benefiting from the switch (that is, both (8.9) or (8.10) are negative with t given by (8.11)) is

$$k\alpha + m(1 - \alpha) > q.$$

When (8.12) holds, privatization leads to restructuring in that the politician cannot successfully use subsidies to convince the manager to choose $E = H$.

The left-hand side of (8.12) measures the cost to the politician of getting the firm not to restructure, in terms of both the forgone profits and the needed subsidies. The right-hand side is the benefit to the politician of high labor spending. When the cost exceeds the benefit, the politician cannot convince the manager not to restructure. To understand why privatization works in this model, we can compare (8.12) to (8.3) and (8.6).

The difference between (8.12) and (8.3) is the presence of the term αk in (8.12): the cost of getting the firm not to restructure is higher for the politician after privatization. Privatization works because, to convince the manager who has control rights to have high labor costs, the politician must compensate him (and shareholders) for forgone profits, which are proportional to the privatized cash-flow stake α. In contrast, when the politician controls the firm, he does not need to pay for the profits forgone by the private investors. The politician pays for the profits forgone by the private shareholders with subsidies, and the cost to him of a dollar of subsidies is k. The term αk thus measures the cost to the politician of convincing the manager with control rights not to restructure.

The difference between (8.12) and (8.6) is that (8.12) has αk where (8.6) has α. When the manager bribes the politician to allow low labor spending, his forgone profits from high labor spending are also fully internalized, except now the cost of a dollar of forgone profits is exactly a dollar. With privatization rather than bribes, the cost of a dollar of forgone profits is k rather than a dollar, so privatization is not quite as effective as corruption ((8.12) is harder to satisfy than (8.6)). However, corruption and privatization work in similar ways: they get the politician to internalize the cost of profits forgone by the manager and outside shareholders. Since corruption has its own problems, privatization may be the best available way to stimulate restructuring.

When does (8.12) hold and (8.3) fail? First, even for a fixed α and $k = m$, the left-hand side of (8.12) is higher than that of (8.3) because, once control rights are turned over from the politician to the manager, the politician has to compensate the manager for the forgone profits if he wants high employment. By making the politician internalize the cost of the inefficiency borne by the manager and shareholders, this transfer of control encourages restructuring.

Second, when $k > m$, the left-hand side of (8.12) rises with α, and hence higher private ownership is conducive to restructuring. As cash-flow ownership is transferred from the treasury to the manager (and outside shareholders), the politician must pay for excess labor spending not in terms of relatively cheap to him profits forgone by the treasury, but in terms of relatively expensive to him subsidies. As a result, as more cash flows are privatized, condition (8.12) is more likely to become satisfied even when (8.3) fails. When subsidies are costlier to the politician than forgone profits, privatization of cash flows and not just the transfer of control rights raises the overall cost to the politician of preventing restructuring. In this case, which we regard as the most plausible, a high α is essential for the restructuring to take place.

A high k is naturally interpreted as a tough monetary policy stance. Because a tough monetary stance makes subsidies costly to the politician, it facilitates restructuring. Indeed, condition (8.12) shows that there is an interaction between k and α: the harder the monetary policy stance, the lower the management ownership necessary to bring about restructuring. This result may describe the restructuring in Poland of public but managerially controlled firms during the regime of a restrictive monetary policy, which occurred even before privatization (see Pinto, Belka, and Krajewski 1993). At the same time, when monetary policy is extremely loose, as it was in Russia in 1993, even high management ownership does not induce managers to give up huge government subsidies and restructure. Indeed, if k is low, no α may be high enough to satisfy (8.12). More generally, both a high k, meaning a restrictive monetary policy, and a high α might be needed to ensure restructuring. We have made this argument informally in our earlier paper on the Russian privatization (Boycko, Shleifer, and Vishny 1993).

We began this chapter by asking: how does privatization work? In this section we have proposed a channel through which privatization widens the separation between the manager and the politician, and in this way stimulates restructuring. By transferring control from politicians to managers privatization makes politicians accountable for the profits used on excess labor spending, since they need to subsidize the firm to convince managers to incur this spending. By transferring cashflow rights from the treasury to the managers (and outside shareholders), privatization forces politicians to pay for these forgone profits not through the relatively cheap mechanism of failing to remit profits to the treasury, but through a more expensive mechanism of extracting subsidies from the treasury. Privatization thus works because, first, it makes politicians pay for the private share of profits, and, second, it raises the cost of such payments.

8.3 Desirable Ownership Structures

In the previous sections, we examined two types of control over firms: by politicians and by managers. Managers were not distinguished from outside shareholders. The reality is more complicated. In many countries, enterprise employees get significant control rights even before privatization. In addition, managers do not always have the same preferences as outside shareholders. In thinking about desirable control structures, we can rank potential shareholders in terms of their concerns for labor spending versus profits. Thus employees are even more concerned about labor spending relative to forgone profits than the politicians. After all, the politicians' interest in labor spending derives from the pressure from the unions and the (potentially) unemployed. Managers in reality are in between politicians and outside shareholders, since managers have some concern for empire building/employment whereas outsiders have none.

The fundamental implication of our analysis is that the closer are shareholders' tastes to those of politicians, the less likely is restructuring to occur. When these shareholders gain control rights, it is relatively cheaper for politicians to convince them not to restructure through the use of subsidies.

This simple logic has several implications. First, it suggests that worker control is bad for restructuring. Workers are unlikely to want layoffs necessary for restructuring to begin with, especially if they can get subsidies. Formally, if we replace the manager's objective function (8.2) by one that puts some weight on labor spending, it is easy to check that restructuring is less likely. This result confirms well-established skepticism about worker control (as opposed to control free cash-flow ownership common in the United States and other countries—see Hansmann 1990). It is also consistent with skepticism about significant worker ownership in privatization (Lipton and Sachs 1990; Boycko, Shleifer, and Vishny 1993).

Second, very similar logic suggests that, from the point of view of restructuring, control by large outside investors, who are unlikely to care about employment, is superior to control by managers, who care about it more. The reason, as before, is that large investors are harder to convince through subsidies not to restructure since their tastes are farther away from those of the politicians. In addition, large outside investors, unlike managers, need not be cash constrained, and hence could afford a larger ownership stake α, which also makes effective subsidization harder. This result suggests that the presence of large outside investors is conducive to efficiency (see Shleifer and Vishny 1986). It accords well with recommendations for core investors for East European privatization programs (see Frydman and Rapaczynski 1991; Lipton and Sachs 1990; and Phelps et al. 1993) and also happens to be a common practice in other countries, such as Mexico and France.

The result on the desirability of large shareholders should be interpreted carefully. The reason that outside shareholders promote restructuring is their interest in profits. If large shareholders are politicized, in the sense that they are pressured or bribed to bring their objectives in line with those of the politicians, they can become detrimental to restructuring. In Russia, for example, some politicians want to create industrial holding companies that become core investors in privatized firms. This strategy is designed to increase political influence on firms, not to reduce it. Indeed, throughout the world, government holding companies come to represent the tastes of the politicians, and as a result slow down rather than encourage restructuring.

A more subtle example of the same potential danger would be privatization in Poland, in which several government-sponsored mutual funds are to become controlling shareholders of privatizing companies through a free allocation of shares to these funds, which in turn are to be owned by Polish citizens. This program is intended to be a quick way to bring core investors to privatized firms, provided that those investors maximize profits. If, in contrast, the government-regulated mutual funds come to represent the preferences of politicians, they may work to prevent restructuring rather than facilitate it. To be effective, large blockholders must be private parties whose objective is to maximize profits.

8.4 Conclusion

We began with an empirically plausible assumption that the inefficiency of state firms results from their pursuing well-specified objectives of politicians, such as excess labor spending. We have presented a model in which privatization effectively drives a wedge between politicians and managers, that is, depoliticizes firms and leads to their restructuring, even when politicians can use subsidies to convince privatized firms not to restructure. In this model, privatization and an effective stabilization policy can work together to make restructuring more likely by making it too costly for politicians to subsidize firms.

At a more general level, we have tried to show that the critical agency problem that explains the inefficiency of public firms is the agency problem with politicians rather than that with managers. We believe that managerial discretion problems are usually minor relative to political discretion problems. Privatization works because it controls political discretion.

Politicians and Firms

9

9.1 Introduction

Economists traditionally view public enterprises as curing market failures (Atkinson and Stiglitz 1980). Public enterprises are controlled by governments maximizing social welfare, and improve on the decisions of private enterprises when monopoly power or externalities introduce divergence between private and social objectives. Public enterprises are productively efficient, and charge prices that more accurately reflect social marginal costs.

This view of public enterprises is contradicted rather remarkably by a large body of empirical accounts of such firms in market, socialist, and mixed economies (e.g., Vernon and Aharoni 1981; Donahue 1989). Observers of such enterprises stress two features contradicting the conventional view: public enterprises are highly inefficient and their inefficiency is the result of political pressures from the politicians who control them. Examples abound. Most public enterprises are encouraged by politicians seeking votes to employ too many people. Thus "operating costs at Europe's [state] airlines are 48% higher than at America's [private ones]," primarily because of excess employment (*The Economist* 1994b). Some plants built by state companies, such as the Italian state-owned steel giant ILVA near Naples, never produce goods and only put people on the payroll (*The Economist* 1994a). Government agencies providing munic-

Originally published in *Quarterly Journal of Economics,* 109, no. 4 (November 1994): 995–1025. © 1994 by the President and Fellows of Harvard College and the Massachusetts Institute of Technology.

ipal services in the United States typically employ 20 to 30 percent more people for a given output level than do private contractors (Donahue 1989).

The beneficiaries of the excess employment are often political supporters of the government, who value these jobs because they pay more than market wages. In Greece, all employees and not just top managers of public enterprises turn over when an opposition party wins an election. In many American cities, such as Chicago, most city jobs used to be patronage jobs (Royko 1971). Donahue (1989) presents evidence that government employees in local municipal services in the United States are both less productive than their private counterparts and better paid.

Excess employment and wages in public enterprises are not the only source of political benefits. Public enterprises in many cases produce goods desired by politicians rather than by consumers. For example, the decision to produce the Concorde rather than a jetliner with a broader market appeal was made by French politicians despite their knowledge that the demand for the Concorde would be low (Anastassopoulos 1981). Crédit Lyonnais, the giant state bank, lost billions of dollars making dubious loans to the friends of the socialist party (*The Economist* 1994c). Public enterprises are also frequently asked to locate their production in politically desirable rather than economically attractive regions. Thus Italian state firms were told to build production facilities in the South, the bedrock of support of the ruling Christian Democrats (Martinelli 1981). Renault, Airbus Industries, and Aéroports de Paris all chose locations that pleased politicians rather than locations that minimized costs (Anastassopoulos 1981). More generally, a substantial body of empirical evidence documents both the superior efficiency of private firms relative to comparable public firms (Mueller 1989; Vining and Boardman 1992; Lopez-de-Silanes 1997), and the improvement of efficiency after privatization (Kikeri, Nellis, and Shirley 1992; Megginson, Nash, and van Randenborgh 1994). The examples presented above suggest an explanation of this evidence, namely that public enterprises pursue political goals.

Nor is it typically the case that public enterprises cure market failures. Far from dealing with externalities from pollution, public enterprises are often the worst polluters, as the sad experiences of Russia, Romania, East Germany, and other countries of Eastern Europe illustrate (Grossman and Krueger 1995). Some public enterprises charge prices significantly below marginal cost to win political support, as the underpricing of railroad services in many European and Latin American countries and cheap food policies in Africa show (Bates 1981). In the case of food pricing in Africa, the beneficiaries are the relatively rich and politically active city dwellers and the losers are the poor and politically inactive farmers (Bates 1981). Such pricing policies are strictly regressive, contrary to the view that public pricing redistributes income to the poor.

Here we continue the research started in Boycko, Shleifer, and Vishny (1993, Chapter 8) and focus on political considerations to study both public enterprises and private enterprises subject to political influence. We describe a game between the public, the politicians, and the enterprise managers. We assume that, because the public is disorganized, politicians cater to interest groups, such as labor unions, rather than the median voter (see Olson 1965; Stigler 1971). We also assume that the relationship between politicians and managers is governed by incomplete contracts, so that residual rights of control rather than incentive contracts become the critical determinant of resource allocation (see Grossman and Hart 1986). Under these assumptions we derive implications of bargaining between politicians and enterprise managers over what enterprises do. In particular, we focus on the role of transfers between the public and private sector, including subsidies to enterprises and bribes to politicians.

An alternative approach to these issues is to focus on asymmetric information and incentive contracts. This approach has been pursued by Dewatripont and Maskin (1990), Schmidt (1996), and Laffont and Tirole (1993). We believe that several new and empirically valid insights can be derived by focusing on the distribution of control rights. Section 9.2 presents a simple model of a firm that can deliver political benefits to politicians. We distinguish such firms based on who owns their cash flows (the treasury or the private shareholders) and who has control rights over employment (the politician or the shareholders). Subsidies to firms from the treasury and bribes between managers and politicians emerge naturally in our model when politicians and managers bargain over the allocation of resources.

Section 9.3 solves the basic model. It begins with an irrelevance proposition: with full corruption, the allocation of control rights and cash-flow rights between managers and politicians does not affect either the efficiency of the firm or the transfers it receives. This result implies, in particular, that with full corruption, neither commercialization nor privatization matters. The irrelevance proposition raises the basic puzzle: how does private ownership make a difference? After all, politicians are interested in influencing both private and public firms to deliver political benefits and can use subsidies to convince private firms to deliver these benefits. In principle, there is no magic line that separates firms from politicians once they are privatized.

Section 9.3 begins to address this puzzle by also discussing the case with no corruption. In this case, we establish several empirically plausible results. First, managerial control leads to more efficient resource allocation than does politician control. Second, corruption under plausible circumstances improves efficiency. Third, as long as politicians maintain control over firms through direct public control or regulation, privatizing cash flows reduces efficiency and increases corruption. Fourth, economic stabilization can promote restructuring through hardening budget constraints of all firms.

The assumption of limited corruption does not fully eliminate the counterintuitive irrelevance results. Even without bribes, the allocation of cash-flow rights remains irrelevant once control is turned over to the manager. Thus, while corporatization matters without corruption, the puzzle of how privatization makes a difference remains. To address this puzzle, in section 9.4, we introduce a "decency" constraint that limits subsidies to profitable firms. We show that, for profitable manager-controlled firms, increasing the managers' cash-flow rights reduces excess employment. That is, privatization and not just corporatization stimulates restructuring. The model implies that potentially profitable firms are the best candidates for privatization, because they restructure after privatization, whereas unprofitable firms continue providing political benefits in exchange for subsidies.

In section 9.5, we ask what determines the government decision to relinquish control over enterprises or to privatize their cash flows. In our model, politicians never want to relinquish control over firms. They also do not like high management ownership of firms with significant managerial autonomy. However, politicians in control prefer private to public ownership of cash flows, since higher private ownership enables them to extract more from private shareholders through excess employment and bribes. To explain why politicians sometimes give up control, we need to make taxpayers' interests more active, since politicians responsive to taxpayers are interested in privatization. The model sheds light on patterns of public and private ownership and control across countries.

9.2 A Model

We begin with a very simple model that enables us to analyze political influence on firms. There are three players in this model: the treasury, the politician, and the manager of the firm. We make the first player passive, while the second two bargain over the decisions of the firm. In this model we do not distinguish between the manager and the shareholders of the firm, and assume that the manager serves the interests of shareholders.

Denote by L the unneeded employment of the firm, or employees in excess of what are needed to efficiently produce its output. Assume that these extra employees produce nothing. Let w be the wage of each of these employees. Presumably, w exceeds the (effort adjusted) market wage since otherwise being a redundant worker is of no value to that worker and hence to the politician.

Suppose that the politician derives political benefits from excess employment L with a dollar value of $B(L)$. The excess employees may be union members, and the politician may want the support of the union. The employees may refrain from rioting if hired by the firm, or even offer their services in suppressing other rioters. We could more generally assume that the politician benefits both from excess employment and from higher wages, and so write $B(L, w)$. In that model, the wage is endogenously determined. We could not obtain substantial additional insights from the more general model.[1]

We assume that the firm earns profits π before it hires any extra employees. Fraction α of this firm's cash flow is owned by the manager and outside shareholders (who are viewed here as the same), and fraction $(1 - \alpha)$ is owned by the treasury. In a publicly owned firm, α is close to zero, whereas in a private firm, α is close to one. We will treat α as a continuous variable rather than distinguish sharply between private and public firms.

In the game between the politician and the manager, the politician generally wants the firm to employ extra people L, because he derives political benefits $B(L)$ from excess employment. To persuade the manager to do that, the politician might subsidize the firm, that is, make a transfer t from the treasury to the firm. Such subsidies are extremely common, and often go under the name of "soft budget constraints" (Kornai 1979). Since the treasury owns some of the cash flows, it cares not about the gross transfer t to the firm, but about the transfer net of the amount it gets back as a shareholder and the net of its share of the spending on extra employment:

$$(9.1) \qquad T = t - (1 - \alpha)(t - wL) = \alpha t + (1 - \alpha)wL.$$

Since the treasury owns $(1 - \alpha)$ shares, it gets back fraction $(1 - \alpha)$ of the transfer t as a shareholder, but must pay fraction $(1 - \alpha)$ of the excess wage bill in terms of forgone profits. For concreteness, note that in a purely public firm, with $\alpha = 0$, $T = wL$: the treasury gets back its transfer but effectively pays for wL. In contrast, in a purely private firm, with $\alpha = 1$, the net transfer is equal to the gross transfer, since shareholders fully pay for wL. Note also that π does not enter the calculation of the net transfer T since the treasury gets $(1 - \alpha)\pi$ with or without the subsidy T and extra employment L.

In general, the subsidy T is not costless to the politician, who has to overcome the objections of the ministry of finance, the treasury, the central bank, or any other taxpayer voice in the government. Rather than model the treasury or the finance minister explicitly, we simply assume in this model that the political cost to the politician of making the transfer T is $C(T)$. We could alternatively forget the treasury and simply interpret $C(T)$ as the political cost to the politician of raising tax revenue to provide subsidy T. In section 9.5 we briefly discuss what happens if the treasury is an active player. Importantly, $C(T)$ is generally smaller than T since the politician is spending the public's rather than his own money.[2]

With the treasury passive, the politician and the manager bargain over L and T. In general, we allow the manager to bribe the politician and vice versa. The bribe from the manager to the politician (positive or negative) is denoted by b. Corruption is an absolutely pervasive feature of the relationship between politicians and economic agents whose fortunes they affect, yet it remains at best a side issue in most economic models.[3] Since managers (and shareholders) pay the bribes out of their own pocket, the cost of bribe b is exactly b.

Under these assumptions, the utility function of the politician is given by

$$U_p = B(L) - C(T) + b;$$

that is, the political benefits of excess employment net of the political cost of subsidies, plus the bribe. The utility function of the manager is given by

$$U_m = \alpha(\pi + t - wL) - b = \alpha\pi + T - wL - b.$$

The manager's utility is given by his share of the net profits minus the bribe.[4] As the last expression in (9.3) shows, the manager can be thought of as owning α of the profits, getting the full net transfer, and then paying the full cost of excess employment and the bribe. When bribes cannot be paid, b is set identical to zero. We examine a Nash bargaining game between the politician and the manager with these utility functions.

While α describes the ownership of cash flows of the firm, we have not specified who has control rights over L and T. We assume throughout that the politician controls T, but that L can be controlled by either the politician or the manager. These control rights over L determine the threat points in the negotiation between the manager and the politician. The allocation of cash-flow rights and of control rights in our model also has an economic interpretation. In a conventional state firm, the politician controls L, and the cash flow is mostly owned by the treasury (α is low). In a regulated firm, the politician still controls L (through regulation of L or of other decisions of the firm), but the manager and private shareholders have cash flow rights (α is close to 1). In a "corporatized" or "commercialized" firm, the control rights over L are turned over from the politician to the manager, yet the treasury retains ownership of the cash flows. Finally, in a truly private firm, the manager both controls L and owns the cash flow. This four-way classification is useful in the analysis that follows.

As we specified the model, cash-flow and control rights are completely separable. That is, the government can turn over control of the firm without getting rid of its cash-flow rights and, conversely, can get rid of its cash-flow rights without surrendering control. In market economies, equity usually combines both cash-flow and control rights, often in the form of one share one vote. As a result, privatization simultaneously transfers cash-flow and control rights from politicians to private agents. However, in principle, the two attributes of equity are separable: in Eastern Europe, corporatization often takes place without privatization. In fact, some market socialists have advocated corporatization without privatization (Bardhan and Roemer 1992). Finally, regulation after privatization can mean a transfer of cash-flow rights without a transfer of control. For these reasons, we assume that cash-flow and control rights can be allocated separately.

In our model, the fact that a firm is private does not mean that it is free of political influence and therefore sets $L = 0$. Indeed, the politician would try to convince the manager of even a private firm to hire extra workers in exchange for a positive transfer T. Many private firms in Europe and the United States receive subsidies and tax breaks in exchange for hiring more people or locating in particular areas. Similarly, the fact that a firm is public does not mean that the politicians try to make it as inefficient as possible, since managers can always bribe politicians in exchange for agreeing to somewhat lower excess employment. Because politicians in this model try to influence all firms through subsidies and bribes, and all firms try to influence politicians through bribes, corporatization or privatization does not self-evidently change resource allocation. Thus the question that we are interested in is how reallocations of cash-flow and control rights change outcomes.

Before solving the model, we briefly discuss our notion of social efficiency. We assume that political benefits to politicians represent effective transfers from their political competitors, that is, that the political benefits are not social benefits. If one politician is able to hire his political supporters, social welfare does not rise, but rather the politician receives the votes that another politician would have gotten instead. Thus excess labor enters the social welfare function as $-\mu L$, where μ is the social opportunity cost of labor. Similarly, we assume that the political cost to the politician of a subsidy from the treasury is not its social cost, but that this transfer does have some positive net social cost, since the resources must be raised through distortionary taxes. We simply assume, therefore, that the social cost of the transfer T is σ. The social welfare function is thus $-\mu L - \sigma T$.

With this social welfare function, first-best efficiency dictates that $L = T = 0$: there is no excess employment or subsidies. However, our model follows Olson (1965) and others in assuming that the public is not organized and hence cannot get together to convince or bribe the politicians and managers to be efficient. As a result, politicians and managers can use public money to arrive at an outcome that is efficient between them, but is not the first best. We are not particularly interested in the deviations of the outcome in this model from first best. Rather, we are interested in how L and T depend on the allocation of cash-flow and control rights.

9.3 Analysis

9.3.1 THREAT POINTS AND JOINT EFFICIENCY

To begin, we compute the before-bribes allocations where the manager and the politician, respectively, control L. These allocations determine the threat points for the two control structures from which the manager and the politician can bargain to a different allocation either with or without using bribes.

When the *politician* has control rights over both T and L, he chooses L and T to maximize

$$B(L) - C(T),$$

subject to the constraint that the manager be kept to his reservation utility of zero:

$$\alpha\pi + T - wL \geq 0.$$

When the politician has control rights, he can force the manager to hire enough labor L to wipe out the firm's profits π and not just the transfers.

The first-order conditions to this problem are given by

$$T = wL - \alpha\pi,$$

$$B'(L) = wC'(T).$$

When the politician has control rights, he keeps the firm down to zero net profits, and uses the firm's cash flow to hire extra labor until the marginal political benefit of doing so exactly offsets the marginal political cost of getting extra transfers from the treasury to pay for it.

When the *manager* has control rights over L, the threat point is determined by the Nash equilibrium in which the manager and the politician noncooperatively choose L and T respectively. Obviously, at this Nash equilibrium, $L = T = 0$.

Finally, we need to compute the "jointly efficient" outcome from the viewpoint of the manager and the politician with fully transferable utility, which is given by maximizing the combined utility of the manager and the politician:

$$(9.8) \qquad\qquad B(L) - C(T) + \alpha\pi + T - wL.$$

Solving this problem yields the following first-order conditions:

$$(9.9) \qquad\qquad B'(L) = w,$$

$$(9.10) \qquad\qquad C'(T) = 1.$$

At the jointly efficient point, the excess employment and transfer decisions are completely separable. First, the manager and the politician together raise the extra employment to the point where the marginal political benefit of an extra person is exactly equal to the marginal cost, which is his wage. They then suck the cash out of the treasury until the marginal cost of getting an extra dollar is exactly equal to a dollar. At this efficient solution, the marginal political benefit of an extra employee is exactly offset by the marginal political cost of getting subsidies to pay his wage.

Figure 9.1 illustrates this basic model together with the threat points and the joint efficiency point. It depicts the set of points (L, T) at which $B'(L) = wC'(T)$ and the manager's individual rationality constraint. At the threat point with the politician's control of L, the manager's individual rationality constraint binds. The threat point with the manager's control of L has $L = T = 0$. Using this basic model, we next ask what happens when bargaining is allowed.

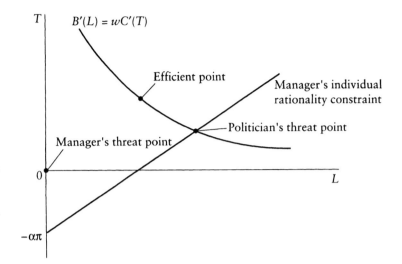

Figure 9.1 Transfers and excess employment in the basic model

9.3.2 EQUILIBRIUM WITH BRIBES

To compute the equilibrium when the manager and the politician are allowed to bribe each other, we examine the cases of politician and manager control separately. With politician control, the manager and the politician bargain from the politician control threat point given by equations (9.6) and (9.7). Denote by L_d and T_d the labor and transfer at the disagreement point. Then the politician's incremental utility from bargaining is given by

$$11) \qquad B(L) - C(T) + b - [B(L_d) - C(T_d)],$$

and the manager's incremental utility from bargaining is given by

$$12) \qquad \alpha\pi + T - wL - b,$$

since the manager's disagreement utility is zero. The Nash bargaining solution maximizes the product of (9.11) and (9.12) over L, T, and b. The solution is given by $B'(L) = w$ and $C'(T) = 1$, that is, the efficient outcome. The equilibrium bribe is given by

$$13) \qquad b = 0.5\{[\alpha\pi + T - wL] - [B(L) - C(T) - B(L_d) + C(T_d)]\},$$

that is, the manager and the politician split the gains from trade.

With manager control, the threat point utility of the manager is $\alpha\pi$, whereas the threat point utility of the politician is zero. Again, the outcome of Nash bargaining is the efficient point, while the bribe is given by

(9.14)
$$b = 0.5\{[T - wL] - [B(L) - C(T)]\}.$$

These calculations can be summarized in our first result:

Proposition 9.1   With bribes, the allocation of resources is independent of either the allocation of cash-flow rights α or the allocation of control rights over L.

When bribes are allowed, the decisions on L and T are governed by the joint desire of the manager and the politician to maximize resources under their combined control and use them efficiently. Thus they extract cash from the treasury until the marginal political cost of the last dollar is equal to a dollar, and employ extra labor until the marginal political benefit is just equal to the wage. Having allocated resources efficiently, they use bribes to divide the surplus.

This result is a variant of the (restricted) Coase theorem in our model. Regardless of who has control and cash-flow rights over L, the politician and the manager internalize the full costs of making inefficient decisions, and hence act as full owners. For example, when the politician controls L, he effectively pays for higher L in terms of lower bribes, and hence does not want to raise L above the jointly efficient level (even when the firm's cash flows are privately owned). Conversely, when the manager controls L, he effectively pays for reducing L below the jointly efficient point in terms of lower bribes, and so does not want to cut L below the jointly efficient level (even when the firm's cash flows are publicly owned). As always in the Coase theorem, with bargaining and side payments, each party acts as a full owner whether or not it is. Since the public does not participate in the bargaining, the first-best outcome with $L = T = 0$ does not obtain. Rather, bargaining with transfers only leads to efficiency vis-à-vis the manager and the politician. The allocation of control rights and cash flows can influence bribes, but not the allocation of resources.

This result has a rather dramatic implication. It says that, with full corruption, neither privatization nor commercialization matters. Even with public ownership, if corruption is unrestricted, on the margin, politicians are paying for inefficient decisions in the form of lower bribes. With full corruption, public ownership is not a problem. Proposition 9.1 thus formally raises the question we are interested in: how do privatization and corporatization affect the allocation of resources?

A second result concerning this equilibrium is given by

Proposition 9.2 Under politician control, the equilibrium bribe is increasing in α; under manager control, the equilibrium bribe is independent of α.

The proof follows from equations (9.13) and (9.14). Intuitively, under politician control, a higher α raises the value of profits $\alpha\pi$ that the politician can extract from the manager, and therefore raises the politician's utility at the disagreement point. Since the final allocation is unchanged, the politician benefits from his higher disagreement utility through higher bribes. Under manager control, the manager receives $\alpha\pi$ regardless of whether he agrees with the politician, and hence the bribe is independent of α. The result with politician control might shed light on the large amount of corruption in countries like Italy or the Philippines, where firms are privately owned (α is high) and then pay enormous bribes to politicians who control them through regulation.

9.3.3 EQUILIBRIUM WITH NO BRIBES: POLITICIAN CONTROL

The assumption of unrestricted corruption is not completely plausible. Part of the problem is that, in most countries, corruption is illegal, so taking bribes is costly to the politician. More important, corruption contracts are not enforceable in courts, and so the Coasian bargain between the manager and the politician may not be sustainable. Specifically, after receiving a bribe in return for agreeing to lower employment (or the relaxation of some other regulation), the politician can come back and demand again that employment be raised. The manager cannot appeal to a court to enforce relief from political demands on the grounds that a bribe has been paid. Because corruption contracts are not enforceable in courts, the usefulness of corruption in moving to the jointly efficient outcome is limited.[5] For this reason, the case of limited corruption is of greater empirical relevance. In fact, we go further and assume that bribes cannot be paid at all. Again we treat the cases of politician control and manager control separately.

In the case of politician control of both L and T, the manager and the politician cannot bargain to an allocation that is better for both of them without bribes. Hence the politician's threat point remains the no-bribes allocation even when bargaining is allowed.

The first question to ask is whether this threat point has a higher L and a lower T than the jointly efficient point. In the case shown in Figure 9.1, when the politician controls L but cannot take bribes, he inefficiently extracts surplus by forcing too much excess employment on the firm and giving it too few transfers even when he does not value the employment too much. At this equilibrium, $C'(T) < 1$, and $B'(L) < w$. When bribes are allowed, the politician extracts surplus more efficiently through bribes rather than through excess employment. As a result, L is lower and T is higher with bribes. To get this lower L and higher T, the manager bribes the politician in the equilibrium with corruption.

However, it is also possible that the jointly efficient point has a higher L and a lower T than the no-bribes politician control equilibrium. This happens if the politician cares a lot about L, but the cost of transfers is also very high. To satisfy the manager's individual rationality constraint, the politician keeps both T and L low when bribes are forbidden. At this equilibrium, $B'(L) > w$, and $C'(T) > 1$: the politician is buying the L that he wants with very expensive T. Once bribes are allowed, the politician can use the cheaper bribes rather than the more expensive transfers to buy L. As a result, in the equilibrium with bribes, the politician bribes the manager to have a higher L and a lower T than in the no-bribes equilibrium, even though the politician has control rights over L. This result obtains when it is cheaper for the politician to pay for L with cash than with increased subsidies. This analysis can be summarized in our next result:

Proposition 9.3   With politician control, the no-bribes equilibrium can have either a higher or a lower L than the equilibrium with bribes. When the no-bribes equilibrium has a higher L, the manager bribes the politician in the equilibrium with bribes. When the no-bribes equilibrium has a lower L, the politician bribes the manager in the equilibrium with bribes.

The second question we ask is what happens to the politician control no-bribes equilibrium when cash flows are transferred from the treasury to the manager. This yields

Proposition 9.4   With politician control, an increase in α leads to an increase in L and a cut in T.

The proof of this proposition can be inferred from Figure 9.1, since an increase in α represents a downward shift of the manager's individual rationality constraint, and hence a rise in L and a reduction in T at the politician's threat point. Intuitively, an increase in α enables the politician to extract more from the manager, since at his threat point the politician can extract $\alpha\pi$. Because (with no bribes) the politician extracts surplus by raising L and reducing T, the proposition follows. This result is similar to Proposition 9.2, where a higher α increased bribes rather than excess employment.

Proposition 9.4 has an important implication. It says that, in this model, a regulated private firm might have higher excess employment than a public firm. While in a public firm the politician needs to pay for excess employment through politically costly subsidies, in a regulated firm he can force the private sector to pay for the inefficiency. This result suggests that, without bribes, regulation might be an even greater problem than public ownership.

Together, Propositions 9.2 and 9.4 suggest the dangers of privatizing without deregulating. When the government maintains control over firms, privatizing cash flows simply enables politicians to extract more from the managers, in the form of either bribes or excess employment. This also implies that if the government wants to continue tight regulation over firms, it will not get much revenue from privatization. For privatization of cash flows to lead to restructuring, surrender of control by politicians to the managers and private shareholders is the first essential step.

9.3.4   EQUILIBRIUM WITH NO BRIBES: MANAGER CONTROL

Next we compute the no-bribes equilibrium under manager control of L. Since now the manager controls L and the politician controls T, they can bargain to a superior allocation by raising

L and T simultaneously. Because the manager's disagreement utility is $\alpha\pi$, his incremental utility from bargaining is given by $(T - wL)$. Since the politician's disagreement utility is zero, his incremental utility from bargaining is given by $B(L) - C(T)$. The no-bribes Nash bargaining solution is given by

(9.15)
$$C'(T) = [B(L) - C(T)]/[T - wL],$$

(9.16)
$$B'(L) = w * [B(L) - C(T)]/[T - wL].$$

Note that at this solution, we again have $B'(L) = wC'(T)$. Without bribes, the manager and the politician can agree to raise both L and T to make each of them better off.

We ask the same two questions here as we did for the case of politician control. First, where does the no-bribes manager control equilibrium lie relative to the jointly efficient point? As before, in one case, L is lower and T is higher in the no-bribes equilibrium than they are with bribes. When the manager cannot obtain bribes from the politician, he earns a return from his control of L through too little excess employment and too many transfers. At this equilibrium, $B'(L) > w$ and $C'(T) > 1$. If the manager could collect bribes, he and the politician would bargain to a higher L and a lower T, and the politician would bribe the manager to get to this point. In this mirror image of the first case of politician control, the politician would buy more L through the more efficient corruption rather than the less efficient transfers.

However, with manager control, we also have the second case in which L is higher and T is lower at the no-bribes equilibrium than at the jointly efficient point. This occurs when $B(L)$ and $C(T)$ are both relatively low. The manager wants transfers T. When bribes are not allowed, he "buys" these transfers through a channel that is expensive to him, and not that highly valued by the politician, that is, excess employment. As a result, at the no-bribes equilibrium, $C'(T) < 1$ and $B'(L) < w$. With bribes, the manager can buy transfers more efficiently, and so can get more T with a lower L. In this equilibrium with bribes, the manager is bribing the politician to get the T that the politician controls, even though the manager controls L.

This analysis can be summarized in

Proposition 9.5 With manager control, the no-bribes equilibrium can have either a higher or a lower L than the equilibrium with bribes. When the no-bribes equilibrium has a lower L, the politician bribes the manager in the equilibrium with bribes. When the no-bribes equilibrium has a higher L, the manager bribes the politician in the equilibrium with bribes.

The second question is what happens to the manager control no-bribes equilibrium when cash flows are transferred from the treasury to the manager? Conditions (9.15) and (9.16) imply

Proposition 9.6 With manager control, the allocation in the no-bribes equilibrium is independent of management ownership α.

Intuitively, the reason for this result is that the manager obtains $\alpha\pi$ regardless of whether he agrees with the politician, and hence the bargaining solution is independent of α. Proposition 9.6 is a surprising result. Recall that we have pursued the no-bribes assumption to get away from the implausibility of the irrelevance result in Proposition 9.1. Indeed, without bribes, we have shown that L and T depend on whether the manager or the politician controls L. That is, corporatization matters (below we show how it matters). However, Proposition 9.6 says that, without bribes, once control rights are turned over to the manager, giving him additional cash-flow rights does not influence the allocation. While corporatization matters, privatizing cash flows afterward has no incremental effect. Thus the question of why *privatization* matters remains open, and motivates our analysis in Section 9.4. First, however, we present some comparative statics results of this model.

9.3.5 COMPARATIVE STATICS

This section establishes four results that deal with the effects of (1) changing control rights (with no bribes), (2) corruption, (3) political competition, and (4) macroeconomic policy. These results are established in Propositions 9.7–9.10.

Proposition 9.7 Holding α constant, with no bribes, L is lower and T is higher under management control of L than under politician control of L.

The proof is straightforward. At both allocations, we have $B'(L) = wC'(T)$. The manager's indifference curves in Figure 9.1 are straight lines with the slope of w. Under politician control, the manager's utility is zero (hence the equilibrium lies on his individual rationality constraint, which has the intercept of $-\alpha\pi$). Under manager control, the manager's utility is at least $\alpha\pi$ and hence the equilibrium lies on an indifference curve above that with the intercept of zero. That is, under manager control, we must have a lower L and a higher T than under politician control. This result, incidentally, does not depend on which of the cases described in Propositions 9.3 and 9.5 obtains.

Proposition 9.7 is an important and intuitive result. It says that, when managers gain control (without bribes), they partially restructure. At the same time, the budget constraint softens endogenously. When managers obtain control over L, they can extract higher transfers from the treasury. Interestingly, this result may capture the experience of Russia, where the spontaneous turnover of control to enterprise managers during the late 1980s has led to an increase in subsidies. Of course, the assumption of no bribes is questionable for Russia.

More important, Proposition 9.7 shows the critical role of corporatization, that is, the transfer of control from politicians to managers, in stimulating restructuring. Corporatization has frequently been advocated by Western economists interested in Eastern Europe (Lipton and Sachs 1990; Sachs 1992; Boycko, Shleifer, and Vishny 1993), and has been an integral part of all major privatization programs, including those in Poland, Czechoslovakia, and Russia. This model suggests formally why corporatization is so important for restructuring, but also shows why corporatization might make stabilization even more difficult.

The effects of corruption are also easy to establish:

Proposition 9.8   Bribes from politicians to managers raise L and reduce T. Bribes from managers to politicians raise T and reduce L.

The proof of Proposition 9.8 follows from Propositions 9.3 and 9.5. The politician bribes the manager in two cases: one of manager control, and the other of politician control. In both of these cases, the effect of bribes is to raise L and to reduce T. Similarly, the manager bribes the politician in two cases: one of politician control, and the other of manager control. In both of these cases, the effect of bribes is to reduce

L and to increase T. In all cases, the party paying the bribe shifts the equilibrium toward more of what it wants, which is L in the case of the politician and T in the case of the manager. In particular, the effect of the more common bribes from managers to politicians is to promote restructuring and to raise the subsidies to the firm.

Although it is common to observe direct payments to individual voters in return for political support, cash bribes from politicians to managers are less common. There are several reasons for this. First, politicians always have some control rights over firms, such as the power to offer them government contracts and other favors, and hence always have some ability to make transfers to the firm and receive kickbacks. Second, politicians and political parties might be cash constrained and hence unable to afford bribes. Third, obtaining political benefits from public enterprises that politicians control might be much cheaper than obtaining them from privately controlled enterprises. For all these reasons, politicians do not typically give cash bribes to managers. In fact, the common language meaning of corruption involves private parties bribing government officials, not vice versa. In this sense, the effect of corruption in this model is to reduce L and raise T. That is, in our model, corruption as it is commonly understood promotes restructuring.

Under some plausible circumstances described below, reducing L and raising T is socially efficient. In this model, then, corruption increases efficiency. This result seems inconsistent with the findings of Mauro (1993) that corruption in a cross-section of countries is associated with both lower income and lower economic growth. The reason that corruption is beneficial in this model is that it enables private agents to buy their way out of politically imposed inefficiencies. Corruption is only good because it undoes the detrimental effect of political control. Thus it is true that private business is slower in Russia in part because corruption is so rampant, but this statement is misleading. What raises the costs of private business in Russia is political control of space, distribution, and other essential inputs. Conditional on this control, corruption reduces costs. Proposition 9.8 is thus very similar to Leff's (1964) argument that corruption is good because it reduces regulatory damage. One way to reconcile this argument with the evidence is to note that corruption goes hand in hand with the extent of political control, and hence the empirical observation that corruption is bad for growth simply reflects the fact that government regulation (omitted from the regression) is bad for growth.

Two additional results come from looking at changes in $B(L)$ and $C(T)$, which have very intuitive interpretations. $B(L)$ represents the degree of competition among politicians who compete in patronage. In a perfectly secure dictatorship, $B(L)$ is arbitrarily close to zero. But if politicians compete for votes by promising jobs and pork barrel projects, then competition for votes raises $B(L)$.

With respect to this kind of political competition, we can establish

Proposition 9.9   With bribes, an increase in $B(L)$ raises L and keeps T constant. Without bribes, an increase in $B(L)$ raises both L and T regardless of who has control rights.

One interesting implication of this result with bribes is that, as $B(L)$ converges to zero, L converges to zero as well, and the model turns into a pure kickback model. The manager collects T from the treasury and turns some of it over to the politician. Arguably, this case accurately describes dictators who perceive themselves to be safe, such as Marcos in the Philippines. When corruption is not allowed, an increase in $B(L)$ makes the politician willing to pay more for L. When he has control rights, he raises T to get more L while keeping the manager down to zero utility. When the manager has control rights, he extracts more T from the politician for the L he is willing to hire. With and without bribes, then, increased political competition in this model strictly reduces efficiency since it raises demand for politically motivated resource allocation.

This result on political competition should be interpreted carefully. Politicians can also compete with one another by promising a smaller government, or lower taxes. If this kind of competition is incorporated in the model, it will probably increase efficiency. We cannot claim in general, therefore, that political competition is bad for efficiency. At the same time, politicians do compete in some cases by making escalating promises of patronage employment and pork barrel projects. Proposition 9.9 shows that such competition reduces efficiency. These results have their counterparts in economic markets as well, where price competition raises efficiency but competition in other dimensions, such as advertising, might reduce efficiency.

In this model, $C(T)$ can be interpreted as the monetary policy stance. The higher is $C(T)$, the stronger is the finance ministry (or the central bank, or the taxpayers' voice in the government) relative to branch ministries and other politicians, and the more restricted is monetary policy. As $C(T)$ rises to infinity for a given T, subsidies are completely eliminated.

Proposition 9.10   With bribes, when $C(T)$ rises, subsidies and bribes fall while L stays constant. Without bribes, as $C(T)$ rises, L and T fall regardless of who has control rights.

Interestingly, with bribes, as $C(T)$ rises to infinity, subsidies fall to zero, L stays constant, but bribes do not disappear. The politician and the manager simply exchange L for bribes. Conversely, when the monetary policy stance loosens, we again see no change in equilibrium L, but bribes rise. Perhaps one reason for increased corruption in Russia in the early 1990s was the loose monetary policy.

Without bribes, when credit policy becomes tighter, in equilibrium both T and L fall. That is, a harder monetary stance now both reduces subsidies and increases efficiency, consistent with the general intuition and perhaps the experience of Poland (Pinto, Belka, and Krajewski 1993). In fact, as $C(T)$ rises to infinity, both L and T converge to zero. This result comes from the fact that tighter budget constraints lead to restructuring only if the bribe channel is closed and inefficiency rather than bribes must be cut.

9.3.6   SUMMARY

This section has produced five principal results. First, the allocation of control and cash-flow rights does not influence resource allocation with full corruption. This result raises our main question: why do corporatization and privatization matter?

Second, privatization without commercialization, that is, with continued heavy regulation of firms, may actually make things worse. Politicians continue to use their control of regulated firms to pursue political objectives, but it is now less costly for them to do so.

Third, without corruption, commercialization promotes restructuring even though it softens budget constraints. This result makes the case for mandatory corporatization in Eastern Europe.

Fourth, corruption stimulates restructuring by enabling managers to pay for reduced political control of their firms. This result is less of an endorsement of corruption than a further indictment of political control.

Fifth, stabilization has significant allocative benefits. It cuts subsidies and bribes with corruption, but also stimulates restructuring without it. Consistent with Boycko, Shleifer, and Vishny's (1993) analysis of the Russian privatization, stabilization and restructuring are intimately linked.

Throughout this section, we have discussed the effect of different environments on the excess employment and subsidies to firms rather than on "social efficiency." The social efficiency consequences of changes in L and T depend on the social welfare function. If the social cost of transfers σ is high relative to the social cost of excess labor μ, then changes that reduce L and raise T are a bad idea. Thus giving managers control over L or allowing them to bribe politicians are efficiency-reducing policies. Conversely, if the social cost of transfers is low relative to the social cost of excess labor, then giving managers control or allowing them to bribe politicians is a sound policy.

In Russia and Eastern Europe, we believe that the inefficiency of the former state enterprises is the more important social cost, so that policies reducing L are beneficial even if they raise T. If that assumption is granted, the principal results summarized above can be restated in terms of improved efficiency and not just restructuring. In particular, the turnover of control from politicians to the managers—commercialization—is not just conducive to restructuring but is also socially good. To be sure, this welfare interpretation is not general.

Although the analysis has delivered several plausible results, it implies that, even without bribes, once managers have control over L, giving them extra cash-flow ownership does not change the resource allocation. That is, privatization does not add much to corporatization. Of course, if we assumed that the only way to give managers control rights is by giving them cash-flow rights as well, we would have established the benefits of privatization and corporatization simultaneously, but we have kept the two separate. Alternatively, if we expanded the model to include a reason to give managers performance incentives, management ownership would make a difference, but such a model would have trouble explaining why most cash flows need to be allocated to private investors, rather than just a small stake to the managers. In the next section, we suggest one plausible change in the model that generates the result that privatization promotes restructuring.

9.4 A Model with Restricted Subsidies

So far we have assumed that subsidies to firms are unrestricted. This may be a valid assumption for money-losing firms, since the government can make the political claim that it is saving jobs by subsidizing them. But the assumption of unrestricted transfers does not seem plausible for profitable firms, where subsidies would enrich already wealthy shareholders. This may lead to a politically unacceptable scandal as voters see politicians enriching their friends. In this section, we introduce a "decency" constraint (DC) that disallows positive gross subsidies to highly profitable firms, and examine its consequences.

The simplest form of the decency constraint is

(9.17) $t > 0$ if and only if $\alpha\pi + T - wL < K$ for some constant K.

That is, the government cannot openly subsidize a firm if this provides its manager with a utility level above K. Since bribes are secret, the politician can certainly bribe the manager to give him a higher level of utility, but he cannot do so with transfers from the treasury. Constraint (9.17) is shown in Figure 9.2 for the case of a profitable firm that has $\alpha\pi > K$; that is, the manager, if left alone, has utility above the maximum he is allowed with transfers. When $L < (\alpha\pi - K)/(\alpha w)$, the maximum net transfer is $T = (1 - \alpha)wL$. The politician can only pay for the excess employment through the reduction of profits accruing to the treasury. When $L > (\alpha\pi - K)/(\alpha w)$, the maximum net transfer is $T = wL + K - \alpha\pi$. For a sufficiently high L, the firm spends enough on excess employment that, on margin, the politician can fully compensate the manager for extra workers. Note that as α converges to 0, the decency constraint converges to the manager's indifference curve through $L = T = 0$, whereas as α converges to 1, the first segment of the decency constraint converges to the L-axis.

The case of politician control of L is simple. The threat point remains as before at the intersection of the $B'(L) = wC'(T)$ curve with the

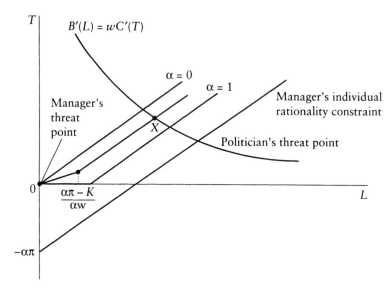

Figure 9.2   Transfers and excess employment with the decency constraint

manager's individual rationality constraint. Without bribes, this threat point remains as before the final allocation. The decency constraint is irrelevant with politician control and no bribes. With bribes, if the *DC* is not binding at the jointly efficient point, the politician and the manager just bargain to that point, as before. If the constraint is binding, the manager and the politician bargain to the intersection of $B'(L) = wC'(T)$ curve and *DC* (point *X*), which will yield a higher *L*, a lower *T*, and a lower bribe than without the constraint. Note that for high enough $\alpha\pi$, the decency constraint is always binding.

Under manager control of *L*, the threat point as before is $L = T = 0$. When bribes are not allowed, and $\alpha\pi > K$, this threat point is the equilibrium allocation: the manager and the politician will not bargain to a higher *L* and *T*. The reason for this is that *DC* lies strictly below the manager's indifference curve through zero, and hence no combination of *L* and *T* satisfying *DC* will make the manager better off than he is at $L = T = 0$ (see Figure 9.2). In sum,

Proposition 9.11   With manager control, the decency constraint, $\alpha\pi > K$, and no bribes, the manager chooses zero excess employment.

Suppose now that bribes are allowed, and assume that the DC is binding at the jointly efficient point. For this case, we can establish

Proposition 9.12 Suppose that bribes are allowed, the manager controls L, and the decency constraint with a particular K applies. Then for $\alpha \pi$ sufficiently high, the manager chooses a lower L than he does with $\alpha = 0$ and the firm collects no subsidies.

Proposition 9.12 establishes that under the decency constraint, profitable commercialized firms with high management ownership stop receiving subsidies and reduce L. These firms may still receive bribes from politicians in exchange for a positive L, so constraint (9.17) is not violated. In the general case where bribes are more expensive than transfers, this leads to a lower L than in the case without the decency constraint. Moreover, as we argued before, direct cash bribes from politicians to managers are uncommon. Proposition 9.12 then implies that a firm with either high profits, or high management ownership, or both is likely to restructure under the decency constraint. Moreover, as we also argued before, direct cash bribes from politicians to managers are uncommon. Proposition 9.12 then implies that a firm with either high profits, or high management ownership, or both is likely to restructure under the decency constraint. Intuitively, managers of profitable firms who own many shares would rather take the profits than use them on inefficient overemployment and take the small transfers they can get. The decency constraint is thus one mechanism through which privatization can lead to restructuring of profitable firms.

In contrast, for unprofitable firms the decency constraint does not bind, and hence private ownership does not encourage restructuring. It is politically easier to subsidize such firms, and hence they keep getting subsidies rather than restructure even when management ownership is high. These results accord well with the Russian experience. Consistent with the model, privatization of very unprofitable firms results in continued subsidies and very little restructuring. In contrast, potentially profitable firms appear to begin laying off people, changing product lines, and otherwise restructuring. From the point of view of restructuring, privatization of "good" firms is the best strategy, in contrast to the conventional wisdom that the worst firms are the best candidates for early privatization (Kikeri, Nellis, and Shirley 1992).

Propositions 9.11 and 9.12 also show the role of significant outsider ownership in ensuring that privatization leads to restructuring of profitable firms. With trivial ownership, the decency constraint is too weak and so does not preclude subsidies, making it possible for politicians to convince managers to stay inefficient. Propositions 9.11 and 9.12 thus deliver the key result that high management ownership stimulates restructuring, even when managers are already in control.[6]

9.5 Privatization and Nationalization

In this section we discuss the determinants of privatization and nationalization. We begin with politicians' interest in control, and then turn to their preferences regarding the ownership of cash-flow rights by the treasury or private investors. Finally, we abstract from the model and ask what would happen if the treasury were a more active player.

Perhaps the most obvious result in our model is

Proposition 9.13 Politicians always prefer their own control over L to that of the managers.

Politicians are better off when they have control rights—whether through regulation of private firms or through nationalization—because control gives them better bargaining opportunities. As a result, control brings them both political benefits and bribes. One conspicuous example of this interest in control is the nationalization of money-losing firms, which might otherwise go bankrupt and leave potential political supporters of the government without employment. A money-losing firm, which has a negative value to shareholders, can still have a positive value to a politician who is able to secure the votes of its employees.

Of course, the greater the likelihood that politicians will actually obtain the votes of people whose jobs are saved (the higher is $B(L)$), the more likely they are to try to keep the firms afloat. Thus the Labour government in Britain, which almost automatically got the votes and political contributions of union members, nationalized many bankrupt industries in the 1960s. And it was a Democratic president in the United States, encouraged by midwestern Democratic congressmen, who insisted on subsidizing Chrysler. Interestingly, both politicians and the treasury prefer nationalization (that is, obtaining both cash-flow and control rights) to subsidizing privately controlled money-losing firms. Control brings bribes, and even without bribes, politicians get both a higher L and a lower T when they have control rights. The lower T is also attractive to the treasury, which therefore also supports nationalization.

While nationalization of money-losing firms is most common, politicians insist on controlling profitable firms as well. Indeed, railroads, telephone, banking, and oil are typically either publicly owned or at least publicly regulated, even though few of them are natural monopolies. Unlike in a traditional model, where political control of monopolies is justified on social welfare grounds, here political control of monopolies results from politicians pursuing their selfish objectives. Monopolies tend to be large, and hence enable politicians to hire many political allies ($B(L)$ is larger). State railroad and alcohol monopolies present opportunities for hiring thousands of political allies. Monopolies also enable politicians to control prices to pursue political ends. Finally, according to Section 9.4, politicians pursue control or treasury ownership of profitable firms precisely because such firms have a strong incentive to restructure when outsiders have control and a large cash-flow stake (Propositions 9.11 and 9.12). To ensure that these firms pursue political objectives, politicians must control them.

Although the model delivers the unambiguous prediction that politicians want to control firms if they can, the question of whether they want the cash flows to belong to the treasury or to private investors is more interesting. The answer depends on who controls L.

Proposition 9.14   Under the decency constraint, politicians prefer managers who control L to have a low ownership stake.

Recall that without the decency constraint, management ownership of cash flows does not matter. With the decency constraint, however, a higher α means a tougher decency constraint, and hence a greater likelihood that the manager does not want subsidies and restructures instead. Higher management ownership makes managers more difficult to seduce into staying inefficient, and hence is unattractive to politicians. This result may explain why politicians do not like to put managers of corporatized enterprises on incentive plans. Once managers get incentive contracts, convincing them to follow political objectives requires giving them a very high, even indecent, standard of living through exorbitant subsidies. Low management ownership, in contrast, makes it much easier for politicians to bargain with managers without making them too rich. Proposition 9.14 might thus explain the prevalence of low-powered incentives in commercialized firms that was stressed by Nellis (1988). It might also explain why public procurement contracts often take a cost-plus form. Since these contracts often deliver political benefits such as new high-wage jobs, giving suppliers incentives for cost minimization only gets them to reduce these political benefits.

When politicians control firms, however, the result is just the reverse:

Proposition 9.15   With or without bribes, politicians who have control of firms prefer higher private and lower treasury ownership.

Politicians prefer a higher α because it implies a higher $\alpha\pi$ and hence a greater amount that politicians can extract from private shareholders when they have control. When corruption is feasible, politicians extract resources from managers by getting higher bribes. This may well explain why politicians in Italy are happy with regulated private firms, from which they can extract large kickbacks. When corruption is not feasible, politicians can still extract more surplus with a higher α—except now they do it through a higher L rather than higher bribes. Thus politicians in Sweden have been happy with private ownership and heavy regulation of firms, since this arrangement has enabled them to force firms to deliver social services to employees. The ruling party benefited without much corruption. From the viewpoint of politicians, treasury ownership of cash flows is a waste (except if it benefits them through an income effect), while private ownership of cash flows presents opportunities for resource extraction from the private sector through bribes or politically desired inefficiencies.

Our analysis raises a question: why have politicians in many countries failed to control all firms through regulation, even when they allow cash flows to be privately owned? Indeed, many countries in the last ten years have reduced government control of firms, even privatizing many of them (Kikeri, Nellis, and Shirley 1992). Why would rational politicians ever agree to privatization?

To persuade politicians to be interested in privatization, we must move away from the model and make the treasury and the interests of taxpayers more active. The decision to privatize then becomes the outcome of competition between politicians who benefit from government spending (and bribes) and politicians who benefit from low taxes. We expect the treasury to win out and privatize when the political benefits of public control are low, and the desire of the treasury to limit the subsidies is high. This would happen when, presumably, $C(T)$ is high and $B(L)$ is low.

Indeed, privatization usually occurs when conservative governments, favored by taxpayers, replace leftist governments, favored by public employees (or democratic governments replace Communist governments). For these new governments, $B(L)$ is relatively low, since employees of public companies rarely vote for them, and $C(T)$ is relatively high, because taxpayers do. Privatization was pursued by relatively conservative governments in, for example, Britain, France, and almost everywhere in Eastern Europe. In the United States, municipal services are usually privatized under pressure from taxpayers (Donahue 1989). When a government has a high $C(T)$ and a low $B(L)$, "spending" politicians do not resist privatization strenuously, and the treasury favors it strongly, at least for potentially profitable firms which, according to our model with limited transfers, restructure as a result of privatization.

More generally, we expect a new government to privatize a state firm if it cannot significantly change this firm's decisions to address its own political goals, and to keep the firm public if the decisions of the firm can be radically changed. For example, the conservative governments in Britain and France did not expect the votes of the employees of state firms, and could not really change whom these firms employed. As a result, they privatized them. Conversely, the conservative government of Greece could change almost all employees of state firms (including air traffic controllers at the airports), reaping a much larger political benefit from keeping firms in state hands than the conservative governments in Britain and France ever could. Not surprisingly, there was not much talk of privatization in Greece even under the conservatives, let alone the socialists.

This discussion brings out an important determinant of whether politicians want firms to be private or public, namely their ability to get tangible political benefits from public ownership. The greater the independence of public firms from politicians, the less attractive is public ownership to politicians, and hence the less sustainable is public ownership in the long run. Recent movements of firms between public and private ownership in France illustrate this observation very clearly. Because France has an extremely independent civil service, the ability of changing governments to radically alter the policies of state firms is limited. Because of their constituency, French socialists care relatively more about the employment benefits of public ownership and relatively less about the budget consequences, and hence they prefer public ownership of firms. Gaullists, on the other hand, unable to reap substantial political benefits from public ownership because of the entrenched socialist civil service, are inclined to privatize. Protection of state firms from aggressive political control, according to our model, makes them much likelier candidates for privatization. In particular, privatization is more likely to occur in countries with an independent civil service.

9.6 Conclusion

We have examined the behavior of private and public enterprises in situations where politicians try to influence firms to pursue political objectives. When managers control firms, politicians use subsidies and bribes to convince them to pursue political objectives. When politicians control firms, managers use bribes to convince them not to push firms to pursue political objectives. In this context, we established that the allocation of control rights and cash-flow rights does not influence resource allocation when corruption is costless and treasury subsidies are equally costly across all firms. This conclusion raised a puzzle: do corporatization and privatization matter and if so how do they work?

We approached these questions by showing how restrictions on corruption and subsidization lead to real effects of corporatization and privatization. Corporatization raises the likelihood of restructuring when corruption is limited. Privatization of cash-flow rights further encourages restructuring when the government is limited in subsidizing profitable firms with rich private shareholders. This result implies that the potentially profitable firms are the best candidates for privatization, since they refuse to dissipate their profits on excess employment, whereas the hopeless firms continue to be subsidized. Finally, privatization is more likely to be implemented when reformers want to restrict government spending and cannot obtain large political benefits from public firms.

The main limitation of the models is that they simply posit objective functions for politicians rather than derive them from explicit models of the political process. Although the benefit of this approach is a realistic set of implications about the effects of political influence on firms, the results are not completely derived from "first principles." The next step in this research, then, is to model the political process explicitly and to examine the new insights that emerge as a result.

Privatization in the United States   **10**

10.1 Introduction

In the United States, "privatization" mainly refers to the contracting out by the government of local public services to private providers. A city or county government may contract with a private company to pick up garbage, to keep city parks clean, to manage its hospitals, to provide ambulance services, to run schools and airports, or even to provide police and fire protection. In the last twenty-five years this method of providing public services has become more popular, although it is still less common than in-house provision of public services by city or county employees. Nonetheless, the growth of the private provision of public services has stimulated a lively discussion on the wisdom of contracting by the government.

The main argument for contracting is the accumulating evidence that it usually saves local governments money, sometimes a great deal of money, relative to public provision (Savas 1982, 1987; National Commission for Employment Policy 1988; International City Management Association 1989; Donahue 1989; and Kemp 1991). Savings are made possible because private contractors use fewer people than governments do to provide the same service (Savas 1987), pay 10 to 20 percent lower wages, and offer much lower employee benefits than the government does (Stevens 1984). In Los Angeles County, one of the leaders in

By Florencio Lopez-de-Silanes, Andrei Shleifer, and Robert W. Vishny; originally published in *RAND Journal of Economics*, 28, no. 3 (Autumn 1997): 447–471.

contracting out, the average service cost reduction achieved from contracting has been around 36 percent, giving the county in 1988 an estimated savings of $133 million (National Commission for Employment Policy 1988).

This evidence raises the obvious question: why does private contracting remain much less popular than in-house provision? Why aren't more local government services privatized? In this chapter we try to examine the determinants of the decision to contract out or provide services in house.

To this end, we explore three types of potential determinants of the provision mode: efficiency (social goals), political patronage, and ideology. The efficiency view suggests that the government can sometimes deliver services that better address social goals if the provision is carried out by its own employees, because politicians and civil servants place more weight on these goals than do the private contractors (Hart, Shleifer, and Vishny 1997). Such attention to social goals may in some cases be efficient despite the higher cost of in-house provision. The political patronage view argues that politicians get political support from public employees when services are provided in house, and so favor this mode unless pressured by taxpayers into lower-cost private contracting. The ideology view states that some voters simply hate big government and so support privatization.

We empirically examine the merits of these three views of the determinants of privatization using a sample of public services for the 3,042 U.S. counties. We have little direct evidence on the efficiency view, but try instead to find evidence bearing on the political patronage view and, to a lesser extent, on the ideology view. Specifically, we explore the trade-off between the political benefits of in-house provision and the pressure to curb government spending.[1]

We examine a range of services that counties commonly provide, including hospitals, landfills, libraries, nursing homes, public transit, sewerage, stadiums, fire protection, airports, water supply, electric utility, and gas utility, and look at two modes of provision of these services: contracting and in house. We do not look at the less common alternatives to public provision, such as volunteerism, franchising, or vouchers, which are also sometimes described as privatization (Savas 1987). Since different services are provided by different levels of government, in most cases only a small subset of the counties provides a given service at all. We do not focus on the alternative of nonprovision, also known as service shedding.

We look at the determinants of the provision mode in 1987 and at how it changes from 1987 and 1992. To do that, we consider a variety of political and budgetary variables, focusing primarily on state laws that influence the political benefits and costs of in-house provision by the counties. For example, some states require a merit system in county hiring, set local purchasing standards (such as a requirement of competitive bidding), or forbid political activity by public employees. Under the political patronage model, these laws should reduce the county politicians' discretion and hence reduce the political benefits obtainable from hiring government employees to provide services. This, in turn, should raise the likelihood of privatization.

Along similar lines, the main benefits of in-house provision accrue to public employees, who are also the greatest opponents of privatization. We use a variety of labor market and unionization measures to gauge their role in determining the provision mode.

Under the political patronage model, the harder budget constraints of local governments raise the likelihood of privatization. We focus on the role of state laws, such as restrictions on bond issues, balanced budget amendments, and restrictions on taxation by counties. In addition, following Poterba (1994), we look at state fiscal crises as stimuli to privatization. These enable us to examine empirically how political patronage becomes constrained by pressure from taxpayers.

10.2 Theoretical Issues

The three leading theories of the determinants of the privatization decision—efficiency (social goals), political patronage, and ideology—have different implications for the data. Our empirical analysis focuses on the effects of clean government laws, hard budget constraint laws, and labor market conditions on privatization decisions. Accordingly, we evaluate the predictions of the three theories for the effects of these variables.

Some of the reasons for in-house provision of government services are purely normative. Private contractors might fail to pursue social goals that politicians want to attain (Sappington and Stiglitz 1987; Shapiro and Willig 1990). If these politicians cannot write a complete contract that specifies exactly what contractors are supposed to do in all circumstances, they need a public bureaucracy they can control better to make sure these goals are achieved (Hart, Shleifer, and Vishny 1997).[2] For example, private providers of health care might turn down the sickest patients to avoid incurring the high cost of treating them if they can find a reason within their contract to do so. A publicly run hospital, in contrast, would be more likely to accept such patients, especially if a politician asked. Similarly, it may not be efficient for a government to contract out the imprisonment of dangerous criminals. The contractor might abuse the criminals, or reduce security in the prison, to cut costs. The government may be unable to specify in the contract all the actions that must be taken to ensure the safety and the security of the prisoners, but if it asks for changes after the contract is signed, the contractor can refuse unless the terms are improved. More generally, private providers may cut quality if they don't care about repeat business and if quality levels are not fully specified in the contract.

These examples suggest that incomplete contracts can give the contractor room to cut costs and quality, as well as the power to hold up the government that wants to maintain quality. The problem of excessive contractor power, incidentally, becomes much more severe if the politicians writing the contract with the private suppliers make a mistake (forget to include performance measures in the contract) or are simply bribed to write a contract that benefits the private supplier (AFSCME 1984; Hart, Shleifer, and Vishny 1997). This logic suggests some potential efficiency benefits of in-house provision of government services. Of course, there may be efficiency benefits of private contracting as well, such as contractor specialization and investment in specific assets. In equilibrium, both delivery modes will be observed.

Under this simple efficiency model, the privatization decision should be determined only by the tradeoff between achieving social goals and providing services at the lowest possible cost. Clean government laws should have no effect on the privatization decision. The efficiency model does, however, predict that hard budget constraint laws increase the likelihood of privatization. A poorer government is less likely to care about the uncontractible aspects of prison security or the assurance of high-quality health care. It would also be more interested in the cost savings that contractors can obtain.

An alternative view of the privatization decision focuses on politics and patronage. Specifically, local politicians might choose to provide services in house because they derive political benefits from such provision, including the support of local public sector unions, the opportunity to purchase supplies from political allies, the ability to hire relatives and campaign activists, the ability to use local government employees on political projects, and so on. It is more difficult to derive all these benefits from private contractors, since the politician loses a large measure of control once the contract is signed. Following Stigler's (1971) theory of regulatory capture, Chapters 8 and 9 argue that the pursuit of political benefits is the principal reason for the pervasive political control over firms around the world.

The existing literature on contracting recognizes the pivotal role of political factors as well. In the United States, the main political factor favoring in-house provision is the clout of public employee unions, which have emerged as the strongest opponents of privatization (see the readings in Kemp 1991; AFSCME 1984; Kodrzycki 1994).[3] Politicians seek to win the support of these unions, which are the major beneficiaries of in-house provision, or at least avoid their active opposition. If politicians could use the public provision of services to pursue their goals without a budget constraint, they would keep everything public.[4] The pressure for privatization must come from voters' preference for lower taxes, which leads to lower public budgets and hence makes in-house provision less affordable. Indeed, the hardening budget constraints of local governments are often mentioned as the main stimulus for privatization (Savas 1987; Kemp 1991).

The political model has clear empirical implications. Clean government laws reduce the political benefits of in-house provision, since they restrict politicians' freedom of action and hence make privatization more likely. Hard budget constraint laws also make it more difficult for politicians to spend public money to procure political benefits, and hence they too encourage privatization.

A different interpretation of the effect on clean government laws is that they are "nuisance laws" which are difficult to comply with and therefore raise the cost of providing services in house. In this interpretation, even public-spirited politicians might find it attractive to contract out a service to avoid costly compliance with clean government laws. On both political and "nuisance" interpretations, the degree of privatization differs from the efficient level under clean government laws, in the first case, because of the direct benefits of patronage, and in the second case, because of the indirect compliance costs of fighting real or imaginary patronage. On the nuisance-laws interpretation, however, there need be no real patronage, just deadweight costs from antipatronage laws. Unfortunately, we are unable to disentangle these two types of costs or their effects in our data.

The third theory stresses the importance of voter ideology. It is hard to imagine that voters have preferences on something as technical as the mode of delivery of government services, but voters surely have views about government more generally. It is possible, therefore, that privatization, clean government laws, and budgetary limit laws are simultaneously determined by the degree of voters' antigovernment sentiment.

To evaluate this view, we control for voting patterns (Republican versus Democrat) in different counties. We also look at correlations between voting patterns and the presence of various clean government and budgetary limit laws on the states' books, as well as the correlations among the laws themselves. This evidence gives us an indication of whether a single factor called antigovernment sentiment can simultaneously explain voting patterns and restrictive state laws.

10.3 Data

10.3.1 THE MODE OF PROVISION

This analysis is based on the 1987 and 1992 Censuses of Governments, which surveyed all 3,042 counties in the United States. The 1987 Census collected information about the following twelve services: airports, water supply, electric utility, gas supply, hospitals, landfills (dumps), libraries, nursing homes, public transit, sewage system, stadiums/convention centers, and fire protection. The key question was whether a county (a) provided and operated a service, (b) provided and contracted out a service, or (c) neither of these. Not every service is provided by every county, since many services are provided by townships, municipalities, or even states. Moreover, there are several additional modes of providing services, including totally private provision (individuals pay private vendors), franchise agreements, grants/subsidies to private suppliers, vouchers to consumers who buy from private suppliers, volunteers, and self-help. In the 1987 Census of Governments, these alternative, but much less frequent, modes of paying for public services are grouped together with nonprovision. Our analysis therefore focuses only on those observations where the county provided a service either in-house or through a private contract.

The 1992 Census of Governments asked about five additional services: refuse collection, ambulances, maintenance of streets and highways, industrial development, and resource recovery/recycling. Some of these services, such as refuse collection, are often provided by counties, and it is peculiar that they were not included in 1987. The 1992 Census also distinguished between contracting out when the county owned the capital and contracting out when the contractor did. The 1992 Census continued to group together nonprovision and provision through a method other than contract or in house supply. As of 1996, the 1992 Census had not been completed. We have the data on the mode of provision in 1992, but not on many of the explanatory variables. For this reason, we focus on a 1987 cross-section, as well as on switchers from 1987 to 1992. Table 10.1 summarizes the data used in the analysis.

Table 10.2 presents some of the basic information on the mode of provision of the twelve services that were asked about in both 1987 and 1992. Some services are provided by many counties, including libraries (42.9%), landfills (52.1%), and airports (27.5%). Others, such as gas and electric utilities, are hardly ever provided at the county level. Altogether, less than 20 percent of the possible county-service combinations are actually provided either in house or by contract, giving us a total of 7,185 county-service observations. In 1987, there are roughly three times as many cases of in-house provision as of contracts. Libraries are hardly ever contracted out, but utilities almost always are, whereas hospitals and airports are contracted out about half as often as they are managed in house. Overall, contracting out appears to be a significant, but still relatively small, mode of provision of public services.

The right panel of Table 10.2 presents the same information for 1992. The incidence of county provision of services increases by almost 15 percent, so there are a total of 8,243 county-service pairs in

Table 10.1 Summary statistics of variables for the population of 3,042 counties in the United States

Variable	Observations	Mean	Median	Standard deviation	Minimum	Maximum
A. Clean Government Variables						
State law requires merit system for county	3,042	0.3418	0	0.4744	0	1
State law sets purchasing standards for counties (type of auction and preferences)	3,042	0.7870	1	0.4095	0	1
State law forbids county employees to engage in political activity	3,042	0.4494	0	0.1859	0	1
B. Labor Market Laws and Conditions						
State law does not allow county employees to strike	3,042	0.9494	1	0.2192	0	1
Fraction of county government employees represented by bargaining units	3,036	0.0948	0	0.2103	0	0.9917
Equivalent full-time county government employees per 1,000 inhabitants	3,042	10.196	6.9405	10.8039	0	288.653
Unemployment rate in county in 1986	3,041	0.0875	0.0790	0.0412	0.018	0.379

Table 10.1 (continued)

Variable	Observations	Mean	Median	Standard deviation	Minimum	Maximum
Wage premium of county employees over private sector employees	3,042	1.1541	1.1072	0.3586	0.2128	4.3708
C. Budget Constraints						
State law does not authorize counties to issue short-term debt	3,042	0.4820	0	0.4859	0	1
State law imposes debt limits on counties	3,042	0.7765	1	0.4166	0	1
State constitution or statutory law mandates a balanced budget for counties	3,042	0.2158	0	0.4114	0	1
State law does not allow state to take over county financial administration	3,042	0.9441	1	0.2297	0	1
State law gives the state the power to assess county property taxes	3,042	0.0746	0	0.2628	0	1
State "rainy day fund" in 1987 as a percentage of state government's total expenditures	3,042	3.3302	3.29	6.3076	−11.72	41.27

Table 10.1 (continued)

Variable	Observations	Mean	Median	Standard deviation	Minimum	Maximum
D. Ideology						
Fraction of county gubernatorial votes for Republican candidate	3,042	0.4704	0.4834	0.1473	0.0323	0.8330
E. Controls						
County belongs to a regional organization	3,040	0.6615	1	0.4733	0	1
Fraction of county population living in municipalities in 1987	3,042	0.4685	0.4792	0.2128	0	1
Percentage of county population above 25 years old with at least high school degree	3,042	0.6961	0.7137	0.1038	0.3156	0.9892
Bank deposits per capita in county in 1987	3,020	7,032.7	6,429.2	3,336.2	0	38,027.9
Resident population in county in 1987	3,042	72,205.1	22,300	247,539.8	100	8,481,500

Table 10.1 *(continued)*

Variable	Observations	Mean	Median	Standard deviation	Minimum	Maximum
Population per square mile of land in county in 1987 (in thousands)	3,042	1.2283	0.3728	4.1282	0.0006	117.1704
Personal per capita income in county in 1987	3,013	12,410.35	12,173	2880.213	4,033	30,469
State unemployment rate in 1986	3,042	0.0739	0.0700	0.0196	0.028	0.131
Percentage of state population above 25 years old with at least high school degree	3,042	0.7469	0.7516	0.0553	0.6428	0.8663
Bank deposits per capita in state in 1987	3,042	7,712.4	7,200.4	2,241.1	3,861.7	28,325.9
Personal per capita income in state in 1987	3,042	14,078.61	14,008	1,884.04	10,318	20,344
Resident population in state in 1987	3,042	6,434,280	4,807,000	5,579,408	490,000	27,700,000

Table 10.2 Service provision by county governments in the United States

Service	Counties with service provision in 1987			Counties with service provision in 1992		
	Provided by the county government (% of counties)	Provided by a private contractor (% of counties)	Total (% of counties)	Provided by the county government (% of counties)	Provided by a private contractor (% of counties)	Total (% of counties)
Hospitals	476 (15.7%)	245 (8.1%)	721 (23.7%)	391 (12.9%)	337 (11.1%)	728 (23.9%)
Landfills	1,261 (41.5%)	323 (10.6%)	1,584 (52.1%)	1,208 (39.7%)	415 (13.6%)	1,623 (53.4%)
Libraries	1,128 (37.1%)	177 (5.8%)	1,305 (42.9%)	1,133 (37.3%)	340 (11.2%)	1,473 (48.4%)
Nursing homes	489 (16.1%)	155 (5.1%)	644 (21.2%)	437 (14.4%)	214 (7.0%)	751 (21.4%)
Public transit	148 (4.9%)	87 (2.9%)	235 (7.7%)	187 (6.2%)	176 (5.8%)	363 (11.9%)
Sewerage	310 (10.2%)	69 (2.3%)	379 (12.5%)	321 (10.6%)	139 (4.6%)	460 (15.1%)
Stadiums	140 (4.6%)	38 (1.3%)	178 (5.9%)	151 (5.0%)	62 (2.0%)	213 (7.0%)

Table 10.2 (continued)

Service	Counties with service provision in 1987			Counties with service provision in 1992		
	Provided by the county government (% of counties)	Provided by a private contractor (% of counties)	Total (% of counties)	Provided by the county government (% of counties)	Provided by a private contractor (% of counties)	Total (% of counties)
Fire protection	607 (20.0%)	173 (5.7%)	780 (25.6%)	640 (21.0%)	368 (12.1%)	1,008 (33.1%)
Airports	585 (19.2%)	250 (8.2%)	835 (27.5%)	574 (18.9%)	328 (10.8%)	902 (29.7%)
Water supply	312 (10.3%)	81 (2.7%)	393 (12.9%)	336 (11.1%)	178 (5.9%)	514 (16.9%)
Electric utility	18 (0.6%)	50 (1.6%)	68 (2.2%)	6 (0.2%)	149 (4.9%)	155 (5.1%)
Gas utility	14 (0.5%)	49 (1.6%)	63 (2.1%)	17 (0.6%)	136 (4.5%)	153 (5.0%)
Total number of services provided (% of services)	5,488 (15.0%)	1,697 (4.7%)	7,185 (19.7%)	5,401 (14.8%)	2,842 (7.8%)	8,243 (22.6%)

Note: For the twelve services recorded by the Census of Governments this table shows the number of counties providing each service and the percentage of the total of 3,042 U.S. counties that these providers represent.

Table 10.3   Provision across time

| | Service provision in 1992 by | | | |
	County government	Private contractor	None of the above	Total
Service Provision in 1987 by				
County government	3,888	533	1,067	5,488
	(10.7%)	(1.5%)	(2.9%)	(15.0%)
Private contractor	363	647	687	1,697
	(1.0%)	(1.8%)	(1.9%)	(4.7%)
None of the above	1,150	1,662	26,507	29,319
	(3.2%)	(4.6%)	(72.6%)	(80.3%)
Total	5,401	2,842	28,261	36,504
	(14.8%)	(7.8%)	(77.4%)	(100%)

1992, or 22.6 percent of the feasible universe. Landfills, libraries, fire protection, and airports remain the most popular. Interestingly, in-house provision is now less than twice (as opposed to three times in 1987) more common than contracting. The reason for this can be gleaned from Table 10.3, which examines the switching of observations from 1987 to 1992. Table 10.3 shows that relative to the available universe, there has been much less privatization than nationalization between 1987 and 1992. Contracted-out services had a higher likelihood of being brought in house (363 out of 1,697) than county-government-provided services had of being contracted out (533 out of 5,488). There is no wave of privatization of county-provided services in this sample.

Table 10.3 also shows, however, that when counties began to provide services they did not provide before, they were 50 percent more likely to provide them through contract. Of these newly provided services, 1,150 were delivered by the county government and 1,662 were delivered by private contractors. This is especially noteworthy since overall contracting remains relatively less common than in-house provision. The much higher incidence of private contracting in the provision of new county services accounts for the greater overall prevalence of contracting in 1992 than in 1987. These results are understandable if public sector unions are effective opponents of privatization, but are not organized enough to stop private provision of services not currently provided by public employees. Later in this chapter we return to the question of changes in provision mode between 1987 and 1992, but first we focus on the 1987 cross-section.

10.3.2 CLEAN GOVERNMENT

The principal hypothesis of this chapter is that the more difficult it is to pursue political ends through in-house provision of public services, the more likely are local politicians to privatize these services. To measure the political benefits of in-house provision, we rely primarily on variation in state "clean government" laws. Our source of data on these variables is a compilation of state laws governing local government structure and administration from the U.S. Advisory Commission on Intergovernmental Relations (USACIR 1993). Since local governments in the United States are legally created by the states, they are established in accordance with state constitutions and statutes. All states therefore decide how much authority can be exercised by each type of government. We use information collected by the USACIR for 1990 for all U.S. states regarding three clean government measures (USACIR 1993). These are all the measures from USACIR that we thought could be reasonably interpreted as conducive to privatization.

First, we use a dummy for whether state law requires its counties to use a merit system in hiring. A merit system presumably makes it more difficult for politicians to hire relatives, friends, and campaign activists for government posts, and therefore makes in-house provision less attractive. Chapter 9 conjectures in the context of West European privatizations that an independent civil service might encourage politicians to divest state firms, since they are less able to control these firms and staff them with political allies.

Second, we use a dummy for whether state law sets local purchasing standards for its counties. A local purchasing standard generally requires counties to use competitive bidding on all purchases over a specified amount, or on all purchases of a designated type. As a result, a local purchasing standard makes it less attractive to use in-house providers of services to favor politically desirable suppliers, and therefore promotes privatization. But such a standard might also sometimes discourage corrupt contracting with suppliers who are allies of politicians, which would favor in-house provision over privatization. The interpretation of this variable is ambiguous.

Third, we use a dummy for whether the state law forbids political activity by government employees. If the state law forbids such activity, then hiring government employees becomes less attractive, which would favor privatization.

10.3.3 LABOR MARKET CONDITIONS

We argued that patronage is a key benefit of in-house provision of public services. But patronage is also an important cost of in-house provision, since hiring potential political supporters at high wages is also expensive, and irritating to the taxpayers. As a result, the predictions of the effects of labor market conditions on privatization are sometimes ambiguous.

First, we use a dummy for whether state law allows county employees to strike. On the one hand, if public employees can strike, then they can presumably bargain for higher wages, which makes them more expensive to employ and hence makes privatization more attractive. On the other hand, holding relative wages of public employees constant, as we do in the regression, the ability to strike enables public employees to resist privatization through strikes, which makes privatization more costly. In fact, one of the consistent findings of the earlier literature on local government contracting is that strong public sector unions often succeed in blocking privatization.[5] Since we are holding wages constant, we expect that the ability to strike is a deterrent to contracting out.

Second, we consider each county's civilian unemployment rate in 1986 (from Bureau of Census, County Statistics file 3). Since public hiring is often viewed as a politically desirable solution to unemployment problems, a higher unemployment rate should make privatization less attractive.

Third, we consider the public employee wage premium, defined as the ratio of the average annual pay for a full-time equivalent county employee to the average annual pay for a full-time equivalent private sector employee in that county (from 1987 Census of Governments, Employment Statistics, and 1987 County Business Patterns, respectively). The mean of this ratio in our sample is 1.15. Many observers believe that the greatest difference in public and private pay is not in wages, however, but in benefits, and the number we compute ignores benefits. Whether high relative pay should encourage or discourage privatization is ambiguous. A higher public wage premium should foster stronger support for politicians who deliver it, and hence discourage privatization, but it also raises the cost of in-house provision relative to contracting out. We control for the wage premium in the regressions without a strong theoretical prior about its effect.

Fourth, we consider the fraction of county government workers in unions (from 1987 Census of Governments, Employment Statistics). This variable is similarly interpretable as the state law allowing strikes. A higher union participation by county employees might encourage privatization because it raises costs. However, holding wages constant, higher union participation probably deters privatization by raising the effectiveness of public employees in resisting contracting out.

Finally, we look at the number of county government employees per 1,000 people (from 1987 Census of Governments, Employment Statistics). In a cross-section, a higher density of public employment is almost by definition negatively associated with privatization, and therefore we do not include this variable in the cross-sectional analysis. This variable is, however, useful for looking at switchers between 1987 and 1992. A higher incidence of public employment may encourage privatization as a way to save costs, but may also make opposition to privatization more powerful. The sign on this variable must therefore be determined empirically.

10.3.4 BUDGET CONSTRAINTS

We have interpreted the state laws and the labor market variables largely in terms of the political benefits of in-house provision. But politicians cannot spend on such benefits, or even on socially desirable activities, without limit because their budgets are limited. The harder the budget constraints politicians face, the more likely they should be to privatize government services. As before, our preferred measures of hard budget constraints are state laws limiting a county's ability to tax and to spend. These measures are preferred to county cash-flow measures, which are endogenous. For example, if we find that large budget deficits are associated with more in-house provision, it could be that counties providing services in house spend more and therefore run larger deficits, or it could be that the ability to run a deficit deters privatization. For a clearer interpretation, we focus mainly on state laws.

We have five such state law variables, all as before derived from US-ACIR (1993). The first is a dummy equal to one if the state does not allow its counties to engage in short-term borrowing. Short-term loans are defined as those loans of limited duration that are taken out in anticipation of specific revenues soon to be collected. We conjecture that a prohibition on short-term borrowing hardens the budget constraint and hence fosters privatization. The second is a dummy equal to one if the state imposes debt limits on counties, which can be expressed as a percentage of assessed property value, or in absolute terms, or in some other way. In most states, these debt limits cover only obligations with maturities greater than one year. Hence these restrictions are complementary to the restrictions on short-term borrowing. Once again, we conjecture that such limits harden budget constraints, and hence promote privatization. The third hard budget constraint variable is a dummy equal to one if state law mandates a balanced budget for counties. Counties typically have two budgets, an operating budget and a capital budget. Balanced budget restrictions apply to the operating budget only, which includes items like educational costs and social programs. The capital budget covers items such as highway construction and other infrastructure costs. Much of the long-term debt incurred by counties is associated with the capital budget. Restrictions on long-term debt would have their greatest impact on the capital budget, although counties have some ability to shift excess funds from one budget to the other.

We include all of these variables separately because it does not appear that one restriction subsumes the others. For example, the requirement of a balanced operating budget does not imply that the county cannot engage in large-scale borrowing in the capital budget. Similarly, even if a county is at its debt limit for long-term debt, this does not preclude it from running a deficit in its operating budget and financing it by rolling over short-term debt. The ability to engage in short-term borrowing also gives a county added financial flexibility even if it is restricted to a balanced budget and its long-term debt issues are limited.

The fourth variable is a dummy equal to one if state takeover of county finances is not allowed by state law. The possibility of a bailout by the state should soften the budget constraint, and hence make privatization less likely. The fifth variable we use is a dummy equal to one if the state assesses county property taxes. Such limits on discretionary taxation by county politicians should harden budget constraints, and thus encourage privatization.

Our last budget constraint variable is a state-level cash flow variable motivated in part by Poterba's (1994) analysis of state fiscal crises. All states have so-called rainy day funds, which are reserves that can be made available for unforeseen circumstances. We use the amount of money in each state's rainy day fund at the end of 1987 relative to each state's total government expenditure in that year. Presumably, the less money there is in such an emergency fund, the less financially secure the counties in the state are, and the more likely is privatization. This variable is of particular interest in addressing the question of whether fiscal emergencies trigger privatization, and hence is most useful in the analysis of switchers between 1987 and 1992.

10.3.5 IDEOLOGY

To capture the ideological attitudes to government, we consider the fraction of votes in the county for a Republican gubernatorial candidate in the election closest to 1987 (Inter-University Consortium for Political and Social Research, General Election Data for the United States 1970–1988). When more people vote Republican, the local government should be more likely to privatize. In order to best measure ideological orientation, we have considered various alternatives. For example, because the result of any one election might be idiosyncratic, we have also looked at average results over the two past elections. In addition, we have looked at county-level voting in congressional, senatorial, and presidential elections as alternative measures of ideological orientation of the electorate. The gubernatorial vote in the last election proved to be the single best measure in terms of predicting the probability of private contracting.

10.3.6 CONTROL VARIABLES

To minimize the likelihood that our results capture some unobserved state or county heterogeneity, we control for several county and state characteristics. These include each county's 1987 population, population per square mile of land, county per capita income, county per capita bank deposits, and fraction of county population above twenty-five years old with at least twelve years of education (all from Bureau of the Census, County Statistics file 4, and Census of Population and Housing). These are standard demographic, income, and wealth measures. We also add a dummy equal to one if a county belongs to a regional organization, which tends to be a collaboration between local governments sometimes used for jointly providing or purchasing public services (1987 Census of Governments, Government Organization file). At the county level, we also control for the fraction of county population living in municipalities in 1987, since municipalities, like counties, often provide public services. In addition, we include several state controls, such as state resident population in 1987, bank deposits per capita in the state in 1987, personal per capita income in the state in 1987, state unemployment in 1986, and fraction of the state's population over twenty-five years old with at least twelve years of education (County Business Patterns and Bureau of the Census, County Statistics file 4, Census of Population and Housing). Since we use state-level variation for many of our explanatory variables, including these state controls in addition to county controls is essential.

10.4 Results

The analysis in this section is divided into four parts. First, we present the basic cross-sectional results on the determinants of the provision mode using conditional means of the dependent variables, a probit and a linear regression. Second, we consider two statistical issues that the basic results do not deal with: sample selection bias and potential correlation among the residuals. Third, we interpret the evidence, and in particular attempt to distinguish the political patronage model from the ideology model. Fourth, we present the results on the switchers in provision mode between 1987 and 1992.

10.4.1 BASIC RESULTS

Table 10.4 presents conditional means of the privatization variables as a function of each of the main determinants of privatization discussed above. The unit of observation is county service, so for some counties we have several observations. We do not include observations

Table 10.4 Probability of service provision

		Service provision by private contractor in 1987		Switched to private contractor provision in 1992 (privatization)		Switched to county government provision in 1992 (nationalization)	
		Mean	Difference in means (t-stat.)	Mean	Difference in means (t-stat.)	Mean	Difference in means (t-stat.)
Unrestricted mean		0.2362		0.1206		0.3594	
A. Clean Government Variables							
State law requires merit system to the county	Yes	0.2655	0.0431[a] (3.93)	0.1240	0.0049 (0.44)	0.2820	−0.1248[a] (−4.12)
	No	0.2224		0.1191		0.4067	
State law sets local purchasing standards	Yes	0.2507	0.0426[a] (4.12)	0.1254	0.0131 (1.31)	0.3413	−0.0607[c] (−1.81)
	No	0.2081		0.1123		0.4020	
State law forbids political activity for government employees	Yes	0.2451	0.0177[c] (1.77)	0.1145	−0.0118 (−1.21)	0.3445	−0.0318 (−1.05)
	No	0.2507		0.1263		0.3763	
B. Labor Market Laws and Conditions							
State law does not allow county employees to strike	Yes	0.2387	0.0348[c] (1.87)	0.1236	0.0388[a] (2.43)	0.3637	0.0649 (1.12)
	No	0.2039		0.0848		0.2985	
Fraction of county employees in unions (%)	≥9.5%	0.2001	−0.0485[a] (−4.34)	0.1065	−0.0189[c] (−1.76)	0.4319	0.0915[a] (2.41)
	<9.5%	0.2486		0.1254		0.3404	

Table 10.4 (continued)

		Service provision by private contractor in 1987		Switched to private contractor provision in 1992 (privatization)		Switched to county government provision in 1992 (nationalization)	
		Mean	Difference in means (t-stat.)	Mean	Difference in means (t-stat.)	Mean	Difference in means (t-stat.)
Number of county employees per 1000 inhabitants	≥10.2			0.1209	0.0007	0.3954	0.0633[b]
	<10.2			0.1202	(0.08)	0.3322	(2.07)
Unemployment rate in 1986 (%)	≥8.7%	0.2456	0.0166[c]	0.1295	0.0154	0.3827	0.0422
	<8.7%	0.2290	(1.63)	0.1141	(1.54)	0.3405	(1.39)
Wage premium (1987 average pay of county over private sector employee)	≥1.154	0.2404	0.0068	0.1176	−0.0048	0.3533	−0.0127
	<1.154	0.2336	(0.68)	0.1224	(−0.49)	0.3660	(−0.42)
C. Budget Constraints							
State law does not authorize counties to issue short-term debt	Yes	0.2770	0.0581[a]	0.1623	0.0569[a]	0.3040	−0.0850[a]
	No	0.2189	(5.15)	0.1054	(4.73)	0.3890	(−2.74)
State imposes debt limits on counties	Yes	0.2418	0.0272[a]	0.1237	0.0148	0.3395	−0.1039[a]
	No	0.2146	(2.24)	0.1088	(1.28)	0.4432	(−2.63)
State law mandates balanced budget for counties	Yes	0.2071	−0.0427[a]	0.1101	−0.0161	0.3660	0.0095
	No	0.2498	(−4.07)	0.1262	(−1.59)	0.3565	(0.29)

Table 10.4 (continued)

		Service provision by private contractor in 1987		Switched to private contractor provision in 1992 (privatization)		Switched to county government provision in 1992 (nationalization)	
		Mean	Difference in means (t-stat.)	Mean	Difference in means (t-stat.)	Mean	Difference in means (t-stat.)
State law does not allow the state to take over county finances	Yes	0.2428	0.0800[a]	0.1248	0.0442[a]	0.3568	−0.0376
	No	0.1628	(5.00)	0.0806	(3.10)	0.3944	(−0.62)
State assesses county property taxes	Yes	0.2212	−0.0168	0.1090	−0.0130	0.3246	−0.0392
	No	0.2380	(−1.06)	0.1220	(−0.86)	0.3638	(−0.84)
State's "rainy day fund" as a % of state's total expenditures in 1987	≥3.33%	0.2351	−0.0022	0.1153	−0.0110	0.3216	−0.0768[a]
	<3.33%	0.2373	(−0.22)	0.1263	(−1.12)	0.3984	(−2.55)
D. Ideology							
Fraction of county gubernatorial votes for Republican candidate (%)	≥46.8%	0.2403	0.0081	0.1350	0.0286[a]	0.3558	−0.0076
	<46.8%	0.2322	(0.81)	0.1064	(2.92)	0.3634	(−0.80)

a. Significant at 1 percent.   b. Significant at 5 percent.   c. Significant at 10 percent.

where the county does not provide a service or provides it via a third way. In this sample, 23.6 percent of county services are provided through contract and 76.4 percent in house.

The results on the 1987 cross-section are suggestive. Merit system laws, purchasing standards laws, and prohibitions against political activity by public employees all encourage privatization. Among the labor market variables, low unionization and a prohibition on public employee strikes encourage privatization. Softening county budget constraints, through allowance of county short-term borrowing, possible state takeover of finances, and the lack of a debt limit law, discourage privatization. However, a balanced budget law discourages privatization as well.

The results on switching from in-house provision to contracting between 1987 and 1992 generally have the same sign as the results on the 1987 cross-section, although the magnitude of the effects is smaller and the statistical significance lower. The fraction of county voters who supported a Republican gubernatorial candidate in the previous election is the one variable that is statistically significant in the switchers equation but not in the 1987 cross-section equation.[6] This variable represents a recent event in each county, and hence it is not surprising that it predicts switchers to privatization rather than the level of privatization. The results on switching from private to in-house provision between 1987 and 1992 are also generally in the same direction as the cross-sectional results, but weaker. Contrary to what we would predict, more money in the rainy day fund reduces the likelihood of nationalization.

There is a good reason why in general we have stronger results for the 1987 cross-section than for the switchers, especially using state law variables. Our evidence indicates that, by 1987, the mode of provision of county services has been more or less established; the system is in a steady state. Newly added services are provided disproportionately privately, but there is about as much shifting from in-house to private provision as backward. Without a trend toward privatization, we can estimate the determinants of the steady state modes of provision more precisely than the determinants of switching, which are the faster-moving variables. For this reason, most of our discussion focuses on the 1987 cross-section.

Table 10.5 presents the slope estimates from a probit and an OLS regression that includes all the relevant variables and controls for state and county characteristics as well as service and region effects. We pool all of our county-service observations, a total of 6,997 for 2,453 counties. The OLS and probit results are extremely similar, so we discuss the OLS results and mention probits when there are material differences.

Table 10.5 confirms the significance of state clean government laws in promoting privatization. Counties that are required by their states to use a merit system have a 2.7 percentage point higher probability of privatizing their services. Counties that are required to have purchasing standards have an 11 percentage point higher likelihood of contracting out. Counties in states that forbid government employees to engage in political activity have a 6.2 percentage point higher probability of privatization. All these effects are statistically significant, except for the merit system law which is marginally significant in the OLS regression and insignificant in the probit. This evidence is consistent with the theory that political benefits of public control are an important obstacle to privatization.

The data in Table 10.5 also confirm our preliminary results on the labor market variables. Counties in states that allow strikes by government employees have an 11 percentage point lower probability of privatization. The 1986 unemployment rate has a statistically significant, but small, effect on privatization. A 1 percentage point rise in the unemployment rate in a county reduces the probability of privatization of a service in that county by 0.05 percentage points. The wage premium comes out with a statistically significant and positive (though small) coefficient. A 10 percentage point increase in the wage premium (say, from 1.1 to 1.2) raises the likelihood of privatization by 0.3 of a percentage point. Finally, the fraction of county employees represented by bargaining units comes out highly significant and negative, indicating that strong unions deter privatization. As this fraction rises by 0.1, the probability of privatization falls by 0.9 percentage points. Together with the effect of the strikes variable above, the negative union effect on privatization is a clear finding of our empirical work.

We now turn to the budget constraint variables. The effect of the state law prohibiting counties from issuing short-term debt is to raise

Table 10.5 Cross-section of service provision in 1987

Dependent variable: Service provision by private contractor in 1987	Probit	Linear	Random effects (county effects)	Random effects (county and state effects)
A. Clean Government Variables				
State law requires merit system for county	0.0231 (0.0158)	0.0273[c] (0.0149)	0.0231 (0.0196)	0.0283 (0.0394)
State law sets purchasing standards for county	0.0987[a] (0.0186)	0.1067[a] (0.0193)	0.0975[a] (0.0240)	0.0702 (0.0514)
State law forbids county employees to engage in political activities	0.0544[a] (0.0162)	0.0622[a] (0.0155)	0.0490[b] (0.0199)	0.0450[c] (0.0261)
B. Labor Market Laws and Conditions				
State law does not allow county employees to strike	0.0905[a] (0.0251)	0.1067[a] (0.0289)	0.0929[a] (0.0360)	0.0951[c] (0.0529)
Fraction of county employees represented by bargaining unions	−0.0944[a] (0.0323)	−0.0858[a] (0.0286)	−0.0978[b] (0.0403)	−0.1207[a] (0.0447)
Unemployment rate in county	−0.0458[a] (0.0173)	−0.0458[a] (0.0178)	−0.0278 (0.0239)	−0.0056 (0.0259)
Wage premium of county employees over private sector employees	0.0277[c] (0.0148)	0.0291[b] (0.0143)	0.0114 (0.0194)	0.0113 (0.0207)
C. Budget Constraints				
State law does not authorize counties to issue short-term debt	0.0425[b] (0.0211)	0.0494[b] (0.0208)	0.0277 (0.0259)	0.0267 (0.0552)
State law imposes debt limits on counties	0.0588[b] (0.0246)	0.0664[b] (0.0267)	0.0557[c] (0.0322)	0.0502[c] (0.0260)
State law mandates balanced budgets for counties	−0.0617[a] (0.0159)	−0.0600[a] (0.0162)	−0.0491[b] (0.0215)	−0.0428 (0.0525)
State law does not allow the state to take over county financial administration	0.0904[a] (0.0275)	0.0891[a] (0.0280)	0.0932[b] (0.0395)	0.0743 (0.0544)

Table 10.5 (continued)

Dependent variable: Service provision by private contractor in 1987	Probit	Linear	Random effects (county effects)	Random effects (county and state effects)
State laws give the state the power to assess county property taxes	0.0097 (0.0250)	−0.0101 (0.0230)	0.0294 (0.0317)	0.0561 (0.0824)
State's "rainy day fund" as a percentage of state's total expenditures in 1987	−0.0072[a] (0.0013)	−0.0075[a] (0.0013)	−0.0051[a] (0.0016)	−0.0056[c] (0.0032)
D. Ideology				
Fraction of county gubernatorial votes for Republican candidate	0.0917[c] (0.0482)	0.0904[b] (0.0456)	0.0665 (0.0601)	0.0762 (0.0771)
E. Controls				
County belongs to a regional organization	0.0139 (0.0120)	0.0134 (0.0117)	−0.0142 (0.0153)	0.0235 (0.0158)
Fraction of county population living in municipalities	0.1050[a] (0.0325)	0.1002[a] (0.0280)	0.1043[a] (0.0404)	0.1000[b] (0.0443)
Fraction of county population above 25 years with at least 12 years of education	0.1050[a] (0.0325)	0.1002[a] (0.0280)	0.2934[a] (0.1181)	0.3576[a] (0.1281)
Additional county and state controls	yes	yes	yes	yes
Service and region dummies	yes	yes	yes	yes
Number of observations	6,997	6,997	6,997	6,997
F statistic on overall significance (Prob > chi^2)			.0000	.1539
Adjusted (or Pseudo) R^2 (Overall R^2 for random effects)	.0816	.0842	.0856	.0808

Note: Probit, OLS, and random effects regressions of the cross-section of the twelve different services of the 3,042 counties in the United States. For the probit, derivatives are calculated based on the average of the scale factor in the case of the continuous regressors, and as the average of the difference in the cumulative normal distributions evaluated with and without the dummy variable in the case of binomial regressors. For the OLS, the table reports coefficients and their White-corrected standard errors. The random effects regressions use the GLS estimator and report standard errors.

a. Significant at 1 percent.   b. Significant at 5 percent.   c. Significant at 10 percent.

the probability of privatization by 4.9 percentage points. The effect of the state law imposing debt limits on counties is to raise that probability by 6.6 percentage points. The effect of the balanced budget mandate is still statistically significant and of the wrong sign, implying that counties facing this restriction have a 6 percentage point lower probability of privatization. The impossibility of state takeover of county finances raises the probability of privatization by a somewhat implausible 9 percentage points. The state's power to assess county property taxes—our sole tax variable—is insignificant. Finally, the estimated coefficient on the rainy day fund variable is statistically significant and negative. This is consistent with the prediction that softer budget constraints, which are perhaps associated with larger fund balances, reduce the likelihood of privatization. By and large the evidence here suggests that harder budget constraints on counties are associated with a higher likelihood of contracting out public services.

The fraction of county votes for a Republican gubernatorial candidate is statistically significant, but the effect is small. As that fraction rises by 10 percentage points (a large swing), the probability that a service in that county is privatized rises by approximately 1 percentage point. The relatively small size of the effect may mean that elections primarily affect switchers. Alternatively, ideology may be an unimportant determinant of privatization.

10.4.2 STATISTICAL ISSUES

One methodological issue concerns our estimated standard errors. If there is a county-specific taste for privatization, driven, for example, by a county-specific antigovernment sentiment, then error terms across county-service observations will be correlated and our estimated standard errors will be too low. The same reasoning applies at the state level as well, where all the observations in a state may be reflecting a common state-specific political sentiment. Below we consider some alternative specifications that try to take account of the possible correlation of error terms across observations.

First, instead of using multiple service observations for each county, we look at individual services and run the regressions across counties. Table 10.6 presents the results of probits for the five most common county-provided services in our sample: airports (820 observations), landfills (1,544 observations), hospitals (710 observations), nursing homes (629 observations), and libraries (1,272 observations). For individual services, the coefficients are generally of the same sign as for the pooled sample, although the statistical significance of some of the results is lower. The results that remain most pronounced after disaggregation are on the clean government laws (state merit system, state purchasing standards, and state prohibition of political activities all encourage privatization). Among the labor-market variables, a prohibition on strikes still raises the odds of private provision. Hard budget constraint results are weaker statistically, although the signs of coefficients are generally the same as in the pooled regression. The possibility of issuing short-term debt generally has a negative effect, whereas debt limits generally have a positive effect. The signs on the balanced budget coefficients vary. The effect of the possibility of state takeover of finances on privatization is negative in three out of five cases, and statistically significant in all of those, and not in the other two. The effect of the state having power to assess county taxes is in general positive. Finally, the effect of higher balances in the rainy day fund is very consistently negative and significant, supporting the results of the pooled regression. The effect of the ideology variable continues to be positive, though not significant for any individual service.

In addition to service-specific regressions, we estimate two random effects models: one using county-specific errors and another allowing for state- and county-specific errors. These specifications take explicit account of the correlated errors among our observations and produce consistent standard errors. Results are presented in the two rightmost columns of Table 10.5. In the penultimate row we also present the results of Breusch-Pagan tests, which test the null hypothesis that the variance of the county (state) error terms is equal to zero. For example, if the Breusch-Pagan test for county errors rejects, we need to focus on a random effects model including a county error term in addition to a county-service error.

Random effects results allowing for county-specific effects are consistent with the OLS results but somewhat weaker. The effects of clean government laws are 10 to 20 percent smaller, with two of the three measures remaining significant at the 5 percent level or higher. The merit system variable goes from being significant at the 10 percent level to

Table 10.6 Cross-section of service provision in 1987 for some individual services

Dependent variable: Service provision by private contractor in 1987	Airports	Landfills	Libraries	Nursing homes	Hospitals
A. Clean Government Variables					
State law requires merit system for county	0.1187[b] (0.0536)	0.0119 (0.0317)	0.0122 (0.0275)	0.0748 (0.0519)	−0.0686 (0.0528)
State law sets purchasing standards for county	0.1369[b] (0.0602)	0.1887[a] (0.0352)	0.0188 (0.0325)	0.0590 (0.0604)	−0.1557[b] (0.0735)
State law forbids county employees to engage in political activities	0.0313 (0.0577)	0.0825[a] (0.0314)	0.0445[c] (0.0260)	0.0543 (0.0524)	0.0743 (0.0607)
B. Labor Market Laws and Conditions					
State law does not allow county employees to strike	0.1635[b] (0.0732)	0.0165 (0.0502)	0.0959[a] (0.0346)	0.0830 (0.0756)	−0.0544 (0.1034)
Fraction of county employees represented by bargaining unions	−0.1251 (0.1009)	−0.1608[a] (0.0671)	−0.0135 (0.0561)	−0.2433[a] (0.0974)	−0.1519 (0.1364)
Unemployment rate in county	−0.0959[c] (0.0580)	−0.0113 (0.0368)	−0.0651[c] (0.0340)	−0.0366 (0.0638)	−0.0698 (0.0646)
Wage premium of county employees over private sector employees	−0.0244 (0.0437)	0.0362 (0.0306)	−0.0167 (0.0268)	0.1032[b] (0.0486)	0.0167 (0.0539)
C. Budget Constraints					
State law does not authorize counties to issue short-term debt	0.0479 (0.0684)	−0.0013 (0.0401)	0.0350 (0.0371)	0.0719 (0.0692)	0.2248[a] (0.0749)

Table 10.6 (continued)

Dependent variable: Service provision by private contractor in 1987	Airports	Landfills	Libraries	Nursing homes	Hospitals
State law imposes debt limits on counties	0.0425 (0.0973)	0.1142[a] (0.0462)	0.0664[c] (0.0390)	0.0529 (0.0737)	−0.0865 (0.0920)
State law mandates balanced budgets for counties	−0.0620 (0.0533)	−0.0481 (0.0321)	−0.0260 (0.0299)	0.0302 (0.0554)	0.2123[a] (0.0643)
State law does not allow state to take over county financial administration	0.1105 (0.0859)	0.1142[a] (0.0462)	−0.0068 (0.0536)	0.1361[c] (0.0781)	−0.2960[b] (0.1389)
State law gives the state the power to assess county property taxes	0.2487[a] (0.0894)	0.0454 (0.0563)	−0.0234 (0.0368)	0.1577 (0.1186)	0.0082 (0.1016)
State's "rainy day fund" as a percentage of state's total expenditures in 1987	−0.0065[c] (0.0039)	−0.0069[a] (0.0026)	−0.0059[a] (0.0019)	−0.0035 (0.0040)	−0.0091[b] (0.0038)
D. Ideology					
Fraction of county gubernatorial votes for Republican candidate	0.1193 (0.1488)	0.1069 (0.0988)	0.0659 (0.0823)	0.2033 (0.1504)	0.0251 (0.1757)

Table 10.6 (continued)

Dependent variable: Service provision by private contractor in 1987	Airports	Landfills	Libraries	Nursing homes	Hospitals
E. Controls					
County belongs to a regional organization	-0.0018	0.0269	0.0125	0.0012	-0.0480
	(0.0742)	(0.0233)	(0.0205)	(0.0342)	(0.0415)
Fraction of county population living in municipalities	-0.0742	0.0404	0.1131ᶜ	-0.1068	0.1822
	(0.1008)	(0.0672)	(0.0609)	(0.1069)	(0.1231)
Additional county and state controls	yes	yes	yes	yes	yes
Region dummies	yes	yes	yes	yes	yes
Number of observations	820	1544	1272	629	710
Log likelihood	-456	-707	-456	-274	-414
Pseudo R^2	.0895	.1035	.0840	.2147	.0912

Note: Probit regressions of the cross-section of the twelve different services of the 3,042 counties in the United States. The table reports derivatives and their standard errors. Derivatives are calculated as in previous tables.

a. Significant at 1 percent.   b. Significant at 5 percent.   c. Significant at 10 percent.

being insignificantly different from zero. The coefficients on both the strikes variable and the unionization variable are of comparable magnitude and remain significant. Of the hard budget constraint variables that are significant in the OLS regressions, all but the short-term debt variable remain significant at the 10 percent level or higher. The coefficient on Republican votes is diminished by 25 percent and is no longer statistically significant. The Breusch-Pagan test rejects the null hypothesis that the county error variance is zero at a very high level of significance, indicating that the random effects specification with county errors is more appropriate than the OLS.

Random effects results allowing for both state- and county-specific effects are weaker than the county results. Among the clean government variables, only the political activities variable is significant at the 10 percent level. The strikes and unionization variables remain significant, as do the debt limits and rainy day fund variables among the hard budget constraint variables. Although these results are statistically weaker than either our initial results or the random effects results with county-specific errors, the signs and magnitudes of most coefficients are comparable. Moreover, the Breusch-Pagan test does not provide strong support for the random effects model with state-level errors. The *p*-value associated with the Breusch-Pagan test is .744, so we cannot reject the null hypothesis that the state-level error variance is zero at any conventional level of significance.

A second methodological concern is a sample selection bias resulting from the nonprovision of many services. After all, approximately 20 percent of the counties in our sample did not provide any of the twelve services at all, and more generally close to 80 percent of the possible county services that can be provided are not. Nonprovision can result either because the population in a given area does not get the service from any level of government, or because it gets the service from another level of government, such as the township, the municipality, or the state. We cannot easily ascertain from our data what the situation is; nor do we have a good theoretical prediction of what the selection bias is. Nonetheless, we use two strategies to deal with it.

The simplest strategy is to include in the Table 10.5 regressions a measure of intensity of service provision in each state. We define this measure as the ratio of all county services actually provided in a given state to the total possible number of county services that can be provided by that state (that is, twelve times the number of counties in the state). This variable is not significant in the regressions, and does not materially affect any key coefficients.

Another strategy is to include nonprovision as a third possible outcome and estimate a multinomial logit model. With this approach, we can ascertain whether the estimated effect of our independent variables on the relative odds of private versus public provision is spuriously driven by their correlation with the provision versus nonprovision choice. The results of this estimation are presented in Table 10.7. Not surprisingly, some of the best predictors of nonprovision are low personal per capita income and low resident population, but these variables are not significant in predicting the choice between private and public provision. The ideology variable is also significant in predicting nonprovision, but not in predicting the choice between public and private provision. More noticeable than these differences are the many similarities between the two columns. While we have not pursued this very far, perhaps one can think of nonprovision as a more extreme outcome than private provision in response to some of the same clean government and budget constraint variables.[7] The key observation from Table 10.7, however, is that explicitly taking account of the provision/nonprovision choice does not alter our conclusions about the determinants of privatization.

10.4.3 INTERPRETATION

Most of the evidence we have presented suggests that clean government laws and hard budget constraint laws are associated with more privatization of government services and tough unions are associated with less. This evidence is clear in our basic regressions using county services as units of observation, and it survives the corrections for sample selection bias and the estimation of a random effects model. What does this evidence imply for the three theories of privatization outlined in section 10.2?

The evidence is consistent with the political patronage theory of privatization. State clean government laws that lower the benefits of political control are actually associated with a higher probability of privatization, and the labor market variables, such as strike laws, public

Table 10.7 Multinomial logit of cross-section of service provision in 1987

Dependent variable: Service provision in 1987	Private contracting	No provision by local government or by private contractor
A. Clean Government Variables		
State law requires merit system for county	0.1143 (0.0828)	0.0618 (0.0497)
State law sets purchasing standards for county	0.5817[a] (0.1085)	0.5978[a] (0.0613)
State law forbids county employees to engage in political activities	0.3426[a] (0.0896)	0.2247[a] (0.0517)
B. Labor Market Laws and Conditions		
State law does not allow county employees to strike	0.4879[a] (0.1632)	1.1265[a] (0.0971)
Fraction of county employees represented by bargaining unions	−0.6039[a] (0.1854)	−0.4232[a] (0.1038)
Unemployment rate in county	−0.2451[b] (0.1054)	−0.1430[b] (0.0612)
Wage premium of county employees over private sector employees	0.1913[b] (0.0814)	0.0197 (0.0505)
C. Budget Constraints		
State law does not authorize counties to issue short-term debt	0.2518[b] (0.1129)	0.0027 (0.0661)
State law imposes debt limits on counties	0.3498[a] (0.1329)	0.5083[a] (0.0805)
State law mandates balanced budgets for counties	−0.4354[a] (0.0963)	−0.3949[a] (0.0571)
State law does not allow the state to take over county financial administration	0.7251[a] (0.1800)	0.7799[a] (0.1022)
State law gives the state the power to assess county property taxes	−0.0482 (0.1407)	−0.1586[b] (0.0818)

Table 10.7 (continued)

Dependent variable: Service provision in 1987	Private contracting	No provision by local government or by private contractor
State's "rainy day fund" as a percentage of state's total expenditures in 1987	−0.0419[a] (0.0080)	−0.0276[a] (0.0046)
D. Ideology		
Fraction of county gubernatorial votes for Republican candidate	0.3671 (0.2609)	0.6381[a] (0.1543)
E. Controls		
County belongs to a regional organization	0.0921 (0.0682)	−0.0651[c] (0.0395)
Fraction of county population living in municipalities	0.6517[a] (0.1857)	0.5096[a] (0.1050)
Fraction of county population above 25 years old with at least 12 years of education	1.1340[b] (0.5260)	0.0931 (0.3045)
Personal per capita income in county in 1987	−0.000102 (0.000071)	−0.000189[a] (0.000037)
Resident population in county in 1987	−0.000081 (0.000074)	−0.000124[a] (0.000041)
Additional county and state controls	yes	
Service and region dummies	yes	
Number of observations	36,504	
Log likelihood	−17407	
Prob > chi^2	.0000	
Pseudo R^2	.1907	

Note: Multinomial logit regression of the cross-section of the twelve different services of the 3,042 counties in the United States. The table reports coefficients and their standard errors.
a. Significant at 1 percent.   b. Significant at 5 percent.   c. Significant at 10 percent.

unionization, and the unemployment rate, generally support this theory as well. An alternative interpretation is that clean government laws increase the likelihood of privatization through raising the "nuisance" costs of public production, rather than through decreasing its political benefits. This evidence does not imply that efficiency and social goals do not matter, but only that they are not the whole story.

Some of the evidence may also be compatible with the ideology theory, according to which voters in some regions have a strong antigovernment sentiment, which causes them to pass antigovernment laws (such as hard budget constraint laws and clean government laws) as well as to privatize. According to this theory, all we are capturing is unobserved heterogeneity among regions of the country. Although we have tried to control for the political sentiment of the population by looking at the Republican votes in each county, as well as for a variety of other variables that might be correlated with local antigovernment sentiment, such as education, income, and wealth, distinguishing between the two interpretations of the evidence is difficult.

One further piece of evidence that we found informative is presented in Table 10.8. This table shows the correlations across states between Republican votes and the existence of the various laws in these states. Two points about this table are noteworthy. First, many of the clean government laws—including those involving a merit system and the prohibition of employee participation in politics—are negatively correlated with Republican votes. Similarly, some hard budget constraint laws—including those placing state debt limits on counties and those authorizing the state to assess county property taxes—are negatively correlated with Republican votes. This evidence is inconsistent with the view that all the laws are driven by voter antigovernment sentiment, which is probably at least somewhat related to Republican votes. Second, the correlations between different clean government and budgetary limit laws are typically small and often "of the wrong sign." This evidence too makes us skeptical about the ideology interpretation of the results.

10.4.4 SWITCHERS

As we showed earlier, there is no significant trend toward either privatization or nationalization between 1987 and 1992. However, we do have some "fast-moving" variables that may be as important

Table 10.8 Correlations of variables at the state level

Variable	Merit system	Purchasing standards	No worker politics	No strikes allowed	No short-term debt	Debt limits	Balanced budget	No state takeover	Assess taxes	% votes Republican
State law requires merit system for county (merit system)	1.000									
State law sets purchasing standards for counties (purch. stands.)	0.039	1.000								
State law forbids county employees to engage in political activity (no worker politics)	0.155	0.090	1.000							
State law does not allow county employees to strike (no strikes allowed)	-0.051	-0.183	-0.176	1.000						
State law does not authorize counties to have short-term borrowing (no short-term debt)	0.151	0.160	0.098	0.183	1.000					

Table 10.8 (continued)

Variable	Merit system	Purchasing standards	No worker politics	No strikes allowed	No short-term debt	Debt limits	Balanced budget	No state takeover	Assess taxes	% votes Republican
State law imposes debt limits on counties (*debt limits*)	0.151	-0.146	-0.037	-0.134	0.021	1.000				
State constitution or statutory law mandates a balanced budget for counties (*balanced budget*)	0.027	-0.067	0.094	-0.048	0.067	0.072	1.000			
State law does not allow state to take over county financial administration (*no state takeover*)	-0.131	-0.157	-0.108	-0.078	0.157	0.115	-0.096	1.000		
State law gives the state the power to assess county property taxes (*assess taxes*)	0.203	-0.155	0.176	0.091	-0.014	0.135	0.048	-0.421	1.000	
Fraction of gubernatorial votes for Republican candidate (*votes Republican*)	-0.183	0.247	-0.189	0.138	0.297	-0.013	-0.026	0.051	-0.240	1.000

for determining the transitions in the provision mode as they are for the long-run equilibrium. For example, the rainy day fund variable, which captures the 1987 available emergency resources of the state government, should theoretically determine the transition in provision modes between 1987 and 1992. Similarly, the percentage of votes for the Republican gubernatorial candidate is likely to reflect recent ideological shifts and not just the long-run political sentiment of the electorate.

Table 10.9 deals with the switchers. First, we look at the subsample of county services that were provided in house in 1987, and examine which ones of these switched to provision by private contract in 1992 and which ones stayed in house. We control for 1987 county government employment per 1,000 inhabitants, on the theory that a higher concentration of public employees might deter privatization. Consistent with the view that the system has achieved an equilibrium by 1987, the results are considerably weaker than for the cross-section. The competitive bidding variable remains an important predictor of switching to private supply, although it is possible that states where privatization is favored also try to make sure that contracting is clean, and hence introduce purchasing standards. Allowing public employees to strike remains a key factor in preventing the switch to privatization. Two budget constraint variables are statistically significant. State laws that prohibit counties from issuing short-term debt make contracting out more likely. High balances in state rainy day funds make contracting less likely. The Republican votes variable also has the predicted effect.

Although these results are weaker than the cross-sectional results, the two fast-moving variables that are likely to be the short-run stimuli to privatization, Republican votes and rainy day balances, both enter significantly. Moreover, the signs of other coefficients are generally consistent with the cross-sectional evidence.

The only statistically significant variables in the nationalization regression are state purchasing standards, county unemployment rate, union representation, concentration of public employees, and state power to assess county taxes. With the exception of the last variable, all have the signs predicted by the political theory. This regression suggests that union and labor market pressures are most important for counties bringing contracted-out services in house. The other effects are not statistically significant, but usually have the right sign for the political

Table 10.9 Privatization and nationalization switchers from 1987 to 1992

Dependent variables	Privatization switchers between 1987 and 1992	Nationalization switchers between 1987 and 1992
A. Clean Government Variables		
State law requires merit system for county	0.0028 (0.0154)	−0.0515 (0.0510)
State law sets purchasing standards for county	0.0385[c] (0.0186)	−0.2135[a] (0.0689)
State law forbids county employees to engage in political activities	−0.0042 (0.0155)	0.0432 (0.0565)
B. Labor Market Laws and Conditions		
State law does not allow county employees to strike	0.0547[b] (0.0235)	0.0781 (0.0891)
Fraction of county employees represented by bargaining unions	−0.0067 (0.0296)	0.1979[c] (0.1152)
Equivalent full-time county government employees per 1,000 inhabitants	−0.0007 (0.0004)	0.0096[a] (0.0030)
Unemployment rate in county	−0.0088 (0.0178)	0.1078[c] (0.0616)
Wage premium of county employees over private sector employees	0.0101 (0.0146)	−0.0373 (0.0534)
C. Budget Constraints		
State law does not authorize counties to issue short-term debt	0.0437[b] (0.0216)	−0.0459 (0.0669)
State law imposes debt limits on counties	−0.0063 (0.0273)	−0.0192 (0.0954)
State law mandates balanced budgets for counties	−0.0129 (0.0157)	−0.0454 (0.0519)

Table 10.9 (continued)

Dependent variables	Privatization switchers between 1987 and 1992	Nationalization switchers between 1987 and 1992
C. Budget Constraints (continued)		
State law does not allow the state to take over county financial administration	0.0165 (0.0285)	−0.1363 (0.1115)
State law gives the state the power to assess county property taxes	0.0317 (0.0274)	−0.2613[a] (0.0854)
State's "rainy day fund" as a percentage of state's total expenditures in 1987	−0.0026[b] (0.0012)	0.0047 (0.0035)
D. Ideology		
Fraction of county gubernatorial votes for Republican candidate	0.0775[c] (0.0457)	−0.0981 (0.1592)
E. Controls		
County belongs to a regional organization	0.0218[c] (0.0114)	−0.0586 (0.0394)
Fraction of county population living in municipalities	0.0499[c] (0.0294)	−0.0037 (0.1163)
Additional county and state controls	yes	yes
Service and region dummies	yes	yes
Number of observations	4,290	991
Log likelihood	−1518	−594
Pseudo R^2	.0473	.0850

Note: Probit regressions of the cross-section of the twelve different services of the 3,042 counties in the United States. The table reports derivatives and their standard errors. Derivatives are calculated as in previous tables.

a. Significant at 1 percent.   b. Significant at 5 percent.   c. Significant at 10 percent.

theory. These results, therefore, continue to provide evidence favoring the importance of the political determinants of the contracting decision.

10.5 Conclusion

We have presented systematic evidence on the political determinants of the privatization decision. This evidence suggests that political factors are important. Politicians derive significant benefits from the in-house provision of public services—such as political patronage, support from public employee unions, control of unemployment through public payrolls—and may lose these benefits as a result of privatization. We find that, consistent with this theory, factors that reduce the political benefits from in-house provision, especially state clean government and antiunion laws, make privatization more likely. Politicians give up their patronage benefits when they are not too large. On the other hand, we cannot with these data reject the possibility that clean government laws are just nuisance laws that raise the cost of public production for public-spirited politicians.

The other side of the coin, of course, is that voters do not like taxes, and the only way politicians can pay for the patronage is through higher government spending. Taxpayer opposition to such spending is the political cost of in-house provision, and the political benefit of privatization. Consistent with this theory, the factors we examined that increase the cost of government spending, such as state laws restricting government financing and measures of a state's financial trouble, make privatization more likely. Politicians give up their patronage benefits when they become too expensive.

These results are consistent with the theory that the privatization decision is determined in part by the tradeoff that politicians face between in-house provision of public services, which brings them political benefits, and higher government spending, which brings them political costs. This political tradeoff, and not just the efficiency and ideological factors, is likely to determine the decision to privatize.

Government in Transition

11.1 Introduction

In one of his most celebrated, though not most clairvoyant, books, *Capitalism, Socialism, and Democracy* (1942), Joseph Schumpeter reluctantly predicted the inevitable collapse of capitalism around the world and a transition to socialism. Schumpeter's pessimism about the world he saw is understandable: in the late 1930s, as he was writing his book, Europe and America had not quite emerged from a major depression and Hitler's armies were marching across Europe. Still, the inaccuracy of Schumpeter's forecasts is remarkable. Half a century later, the transition the world is experiencing is the reverse of the one he expected: from socialism to capitalism. Market economies around the world are limiting the scope of their governments by privatizing everything from industry to social security. Even more remarkably, the Soviet bloc countries, including all the East European economies and countries of the former Soviet Union (FSU), have initiated a transition to capitalism. As an admirer of capitalism and of entrepreneurial spirit, Schumpeter would have surely rejoiced over his error.

The transition to capitalism has sparked an intense controversy among economists concerning its optimal speed. Jeffrey Sachs (1993,

By Andrei Shleifer; originally delivered as the Schumpeter Lecture to the European Economic Association's annual meeting in Istanbul, August 1996, and published in *European Economic Review*, 41, nos. 3–5 (May 1997): 385–410. Reprinted with kind permission from Elsevier Science-NL, Sara Burgerhartstraat 25, 1055KV Amsterdam, The Netherlands.

1995) and other advocates of so-called shock therapy have argued that a transition economy must undertake the three essential steps of rapid liberalization—price liberalization, stabilization, and privatization—as quickly as possible to restart economic growth under normal market conditions. Opponents of this view have focused on the potential costs of shock therapy, such as the rapid decline of state firms, job loss, and dislocation of labor (Murrell 1991; Goldman 1994). They preferred the transition economies to progress slowly and to continue inflation, subsidies, and government ownership for a longer period of time.

By the mid-1990s the advocates of shock therapy had won, at least in the context of East European transition.[1] Depression had occurred almost everywhere in Eastern Europe and the FSU, caused to a large extent by the demilitarization of national economies, the collapse of state firms, and the breakdown of trade ties both between and within countries.[2] This depression, however, has been if anything milder in the countries pursuing radical liberalization (World Bank 1996; Aslund, Boone, and Johnson 1996). Moreover, the countries in Eastern Europe—such as Poland and the Czech Republic—that have been the prototypical radical liberalizers were growing rapidly by the mid-1990s. The countries that deferred reforms or proceeded slowly—such as Romania and Bulgaria—were growing less rapidly. Inside the FSU, the relatively more radical liberalizers, such as the Baltic States, Russia, and Kyrghizstan, maintained higher living standards and experienced a milder depression than the go-slow countries, such as Belarus and Ukraine. This particular debate about transition, then, has been resolved by experience.

Some nagging questions nonetheless remain, many of them raised by Russia. Between 1992 and 1995, Russia went through all the major treatments of shock therapy. Prices were liberalized on January 2, 1992. Most of the economy was privatized between 1992 and 1994 so that the private sector produced over half of Russia's output by 1995. Finally, inflation was dramatically reduced in 1995. Yet despite the fact that Russia undertook all these measures, its official GDP continued to shrink in 1995 and 1996, and even if the unofficial sector is counted, the economy grew at best lethargically. Some advocates of shock therapy (e.g., Aslund, Boone, and Johnson 1996; World Bank 1996) confronted this uncomfortable evidence by reclassifying Russia as a go-slow reformer whose experience confirms rather than contradicts the virtues of shock therapy.[3] In contrast, the opponents of shock therapy, including several American Nobel laureates in economics in collaboration with several Soviet economists (Abalkin et al. 1996), have argued that the Russian experience proves what an error shock therapy has been. The definitional squabbles aside, Russia's experience—especially as compared with Poland's—raises several genuine puzzles.

Why was Russia not growing in the mid-1990s, whereas Poland was expanding by over 5 percent a year? Why, at least in the short run, have the effects of liberalization on private sector growth been stronger in Poland? More generally, what are the mechanisms through which radical liberalization—in the form of price liberalization, stabilization, and privatization—leads to economic growth? Are these mechanisms less effective in Russia, or are there other factors that determine growth? If there are other factors, what are they and what can be done to make them work in Russia?

The comparison of Russia and Poland is germane for several reasons in addition to their common economic policies. To begin, unlike China, both were industrial economies at the time reforms began. Both economies faced substantial disruption from the collapse of COMECON and other trade following the demise of the Soviet Union. Indeed, both economies were in shambles at the beginning of reforms, overwhelmed by inflation, goods shortages, and declining production. The two countries have political similarities as well. Both experienced a near-collapse of the state prior to transition. In Poland, martial law led to the total demise of the Communist Party and its military regime. In Russia, the Gorbachev government faced a similar crisis, which led to the dissolution of the Soviet Union and the creation of an independent Russia. After Communism collapsed, both countries moved to fragmented, rapidly changing party systems and "semi-presidential" regimes, in which a conflict between president and legislature was built in from the start. Both were led in their transition by charismatic, populist presidents committed first and foremost to the destruction of Communism. Yet, despite these similarities as of 1990, the two countries' reforms had had very different results as of 1996.[4]

This chapter argues that an essential part of transition to capitalism is the transition of government. To understand the Russian experience by comparison to the experiences of other fast reformers such as Poland, one needs to examine the nature of political control of economic life that remains after the reforms as well as the support that government offers private business. Despite similar economic reforms, government in Russia continues to retain substantial political control over economic life and, moreover, often uses this control to pursue predatory policies toward business. The political transition in Russia has not gone nearly as far as it has in Poland, and this slowness of political transition retards economic growth.

The next section develops the argument that the speed of economic reform is not the whole story, and that transition of government is a distinct and crucial determinant of economic performance. Three questions are then asked. First, does the performance of governments in Russia and Poland actually differ? The answer is yes. Second, why does the performance of governments in different countries, particularly Poland and Russia, differ so much? Six theories of determinants of government performance are evaluated, leading to the conclusion that the retention of old politicians in Russia and the creation of inappropriate incentives for them accounts for their predatory conduct. Finally, the chapter examines potential policies of reforming the government in Russia.

11.2 Government in Transition

The economics of transition typically focuses on the economic factors that shape the process.[5] How strong is the entrepreneurial response to liberalization? How rapidly do state and privatized firms restructure? How quickly is labor reallocated between activities? Yet this approach does not pay nearly enough attention to the basic element of transition: the transition of the government from a Communist police state to an institution supporting a market economy. This transition of government is as essential for economic transformation as it is for the democratization of societies escaping Communism.

A discussion of the transition of government calls for an assessment of the costs of political control of economic life, of which socialism is only the extreme example.[6] The politicians controlling economic life are almost always interested in using business to achieve personal political and economic objectives.[7] The principal political objectives are to maintain voting support and prevent dissent. To this end, politicians provide jobs for political supporters through state firms, deliver services to their allies at subsidized prices, often at the expense of political opponents, and more generally direct national resources not to economically efficient use but to the use of friends and allies. Because the cost of such a use of resources is borne by society at large and not by the politicians personally, political control of economic life is generally grotesquely inefficient, as the vast empirical literature on the inefficiency of state firms illustrates. The personal economic goals of politicians do not generally further efficiency either, since they use their regulatory powers to create rents for their allies, who presumably share with them, as well as to collect bribes. Corruption is directly related to the government's role in the economy.

Under socialism, the effects of political control are especially pernicious. The politicians are the Communist Party, which uses its control of economic life to maintain power. Through planning, the party controls all aspects of economic life, from prices and wages to major investment decisions to minute aspects of resource allocation. Such control aimed at preserving Communism leads to the commitment of massive human and physical resources to the military, the heavy industry that supports it, the infrastructure for the heavy industry, and the internal police— all at the expense of consumer goods and services. Throughout Eastern Europe, politicization of the economy has created militarized economies with pitifully low standards of living.

When the Communists' power collapsed, so did the Communist government machines that supported it and controlled economic life. Yet the remnants of a large government often remained, ready to continue political control. A principal goal of the political transition, and of the few reformers who undertook it, was to replace these remnants with institutions supportive of capitalism. Such transition of government entailed two separate steps. First, the economies needed to be depoliticized: control by market forces had to replace control by the government. That meant ridding the government of the levers and resources it could still rely on to control firms. But second, the transition also required the government to take on new functions, such as the provision of laws and regulations that support a market economy. The state had to be weakened overall, yet strengthened in a few areas. Some muscles needed to atrophy, others to develop.

All the treatments of shock therapy contribute to depoliticization. Price liberalization eliminates price controls, which are the principal weapons of the central planners, used to stimulate and discourage the production of particular goods or to create shortages that allow planners to maintain their power over resource allocation. Stabilization imposes a harder budget constraint on the government, and hence prevents politicians from using subsidies to encourage firms—and often whole regions—to pursue political ends. Finally, privatization deprives the government of direct control over firms, which enables it to force firms to pursue political goals. Privatization and stabilization actually reinforce each other: privatization deprives the state of its direct power to influence firms, while stabilization deprives it of the means of buying such influence (Chapter 9).

The available evidence on stabilization and privatization supports the essential role of depoliticization. Pinto, Belka, and Krajewski (1993) show how even state firms in Poland began to restructure after stabilization in response to hardening of their budget constraints. A large body of evidence from around the world points to efficiency improvements after privatization (e.g., Megginson, Nash, and van Randenborgh 1994; La Porta and Lopez-de-Silanes 1997). For Russia in particular, survey evidence by Earle and Estrin (1995) and Earle and Rose (1996) reveals dramatically faster restructuring by privatized firms than by state firms, measured not just by layoffs but also by new product introductions and capital investment. Earle and Rose (1996) also find much less political influence on privatized firms than on state firms, as well as a clear influence of large investors on the privatized firms. Such replacement of government control with shareholder control is an essential element of depoliticization (Boycko et al. 1995; Chapter 8).

But the three radical reforms are only part of depoliticization, and of public sector reform more generally. Even with the three measures taken, the government retains much regulatory power that it can use either to support a market economy or to prey on it. The government still grants export and import licenses, regulates the entry of new firms, enforces or fails to enforce law and order, and so on. Shock therapy does not guarantee depoliticization, since politicians can still exercise control in many ways. Nor does shock therapy guarantee a transformation of government institutions, which is a separate endeavor altogether.

This endeavor, however, is an equally essential element of the transition of government. It includes first and foremost the creation of laws and legal institutions that protect private property and enforce contracts between private parties, but also limit the ability of officials to prey on private property.[8] It also includes the creation of regulatory institutions that deal with competition, securities markets, banking, trade, patents, and so on. These institutions need to support a market economy, rather than use their powers to enrich the regulators and their political allies. Such a transformation of government may be as radical as shock therapy itself.

As shown in the next section, the experiences of Russia and Poland are best understood by comparing the performance of their governments. Shock therapy has greatly contributed to depoliticization in both countries by weakening the control of the central government over the economy. Yet shock therapy is far from the whole story. Despite shock therapy, politicians in Russia, particularly at the local level, retain enormous control over economic life, which they use to pursue political ends and to enrich themselves. This makes them rather different from politicians in Poland. Russia is also behind in creating the institutions of a new market economy. In short, the performance of the two countries is best understood in terms of the different stages of transition of their governments.

11.3 Local Government Performance in Moscow and Warsaw

The previous section argued that the failure of depoliticization and the continued predatory role of the state may explain slow growth even after shock therapy. One way to evaluate this argument is by comparing Russia and Poland.[9] Although Poland began reforms two years earlier than Russia and stabilized five years earlier, by the end of 1995 both countries had completed radical reforms. Nonetheless, in 1995 Poland grew by 7 percent, and Russia probably not at all. Small business—the engine of growth of all transition economies—is growing faster in Poland than in Russia. According to the European Bank for Reconstruction and Development (1996), in 1995 Poland had two million small businesses, compared with only one million officially registered small businesses in Russia, despite its four times larger population. Even if one triples this number for Russia to account for the gray economy, small business development in Poland remains more impressive.[10] Can this difference in private sector growth in the two countries be explained by the conduct of their governments?

The anecdotal evidence, at least, appears to be consistent with the view that government performance differs significantly between the two countries. Many Russian entrepreneurs, particularly founders of small businesses, complain about the difficulties of starting and operating a business in Russia. They always point to multiple permits, inspections, and registrations, all requiring interactions with multiple officials many of whom need to be bribed before the necessary documents are issued. Then of course there are complaints about the rackets and their take. To compare this with the situation in Poland, consider the February 1996 comments of a wealthy Polish businessman on the difficulty of opening a shop in Poland: "Oh, it is very, very difficult. There are now so many shops and so much competition that it is impossible to make money." When asked about permits, registrations, inspections, bribes, and other obstacles from the government, he answered, "These are not a problem, but the competition is awful; I would never recommend opening a shop in Poland."

Since, as George Stigler has reminded us, the plural of anecdote is data, it made sense to ask shop owners in the two countries more systematically about their interactions with the state. Accordingly, in March and April of 1996, Timothy Frye and Shleifer (1997) surveyed 55 shop managers in Moscow and 50 in Warsaw about their relationship with the local government—the level of government that affected their lives most directly. The survey focused on relatively small shops, mostly in the food business and employing between 5 and 50 people. Moscow shops were a bit larger (23 versus 15 employees on average), a bit newer (3 versus 4.5 years in operation), and their managers were a bit older (45 versus 42 years old, on average), but in general the shops were chosen to be similar. Each shop manager answered a brief questionnaire about his legal and regulatory environment.

Table 11.1 reports answers to questions about law and order, or courts and protection. In both countries, courts are rarely used. Only 19 percent of shop managers in Moscow and 14 percent in Warsaw report

Table 11.1 Legal environment in Moscow and Warsaw: The fraction of affirmative responses and *t*-tests of differences in responses

	Warsaw (*n*)	Moscow (*n*)	T-statistic
Used courts in the last two years	.14 (50)	.19 (53)	.66
Needed to use courts, but did not	.10 (50)	.45 (53)	4.32
Can use courts against government	.41 (46)	.50 (52)	.86
Can use courts against business partner	.45 (38)	.65 (52)	1.97
Contacted by rackets in the last six months	.08 (50)	.39 (54)	3.91
Does one need roof/umbrella to operate	.06 (50)	.76 (54)	10.10

having used them in the last 2 years ($t = .66$). This may simply reflect the high cost of using courts in both countries. However, when asked whether they needed to use courts but did not, 45 percent of Moscow managers answer yes, whereas in Warsaw, only 10 percent do ($t = 4.32$). Either the Moscow shop managers have less faith in their courts, or they face more frequent disputes that require court intervention than their counterparts in Warsaw.

When asked whether they "could use courts to defend their rights if the government grossly violated their property rights," 50 percent of Moscow respondents, and 41 percent of Warsaw respondents, answered affirmatively ($t = .86$). Evidently business people in both countries retain significant skepticism about the independence and effectiveness of courts in disputes with the government. On the other hand, when "the government" is replaced by "a business partner" in this question, 65 percent of Moscow respondents, and only 38 percent of Warsaw respondents, answered yes ($t = 1.97$). In this circumstance Moscow shop managers appear to be more prepared to resort to courts. Finally, Frye and Shleifer find that 57 percent of Moscow shops have hired legal counsel, compared with only 36 percent of Warsaw shops ($t = 2.2$). This may reflect a greater interest in litigation, but more likely lawyers are needed in Russia to deal with bureaucrats.

Opinions on private rather than public protection were also solicited. In Russia, it is common for shop owners to pay private security agencies to protect them from crime and help resolve disputes. This institution is known as a "roof" in Russia, and is apparently is referred to as an "umbrella" in Poland—perhaps to reflect the greater fragility of the requisite private protection in Poland. Respondents were asked whether it was true that one could not operate a store in their city without a roof (an umbrella). In Moscow, 76 percent answered yes, whereas in Poland only 6 percent did ($t = 10.10$). A related question is whether a shop manager has been contacted by the rackets in the last six months. In Moscow, 39 percent of the respondents answered yes, whereas in Warsaw only 8 percent did. In short, these data make clear that the private enforcement of rules (as opposed to law) and order plays a greater role in Russia than in Poland. Since the respondents in both cities are equally skeptical about courts, the likely reason for the higher incidence of protection rackets in Russia is the greater failure of simple police protection there.

The next set of questions deals with the regulatory environment and the closely related problem of corruption. Table 11.2 presents the results. When asked how long it took to register their business, Moscow respondents reported an average of 2.7 months, compared with .7 months in Warsaw ($t = 5.02$). When asked how many inspections they had last year, Moscow residents said that they averaged 18.56, and Warsaw managers 9.00 ($t = 3.46$). Moscow shop managers are also more likely to be fined by inspectors than are their counterparts in Warsaw: 83 percent of them report having paid fines compared with 46 percent in Warsaw ($t = 2.72$). Fines may be a good measure of regulatory burden as well as a proxy for corruption.

One measure of the severity of the regulatory burden is the concern of the shop managers about being in violation of certain regulations. To get at this issue, shop managers were asked how "legally vulnerable" they felt, on a scale of 1 to 10. The mean answer in Warsaw was 3.6, compared with 5.1 in Moscow ($t = 3.9$), which is consistent with the greater regulatory and tax burden in Russia. Another measure of regulatory burden is corruption, since a standard way to get around

Table 11.2 Regulatory environment in Moscow and Warsaw: Responses to questions about government regulation and corruption and *t*-tests of differences between Warsaw and Moscow

	Warsaw (*n*)	Moscow (*n*)	*T*-statistic
Time to register business (months)	.72 (47)	2.71 (51)	5.02
Inspections last year	9.0 (49)	18.56 (55)	3.46
Percentage of shops fined by inspectors last year	46 (49)	83 (52)	2.72
Number of different agencies conducting inspections	2.65 (49)	3.58 (55)	1.84
How legally vulnerable do you feel on a scale of 1 to 10	3.6 (50)	5.1 (55)	3.91
How often does one need to bribe officials on a scale of 1 to 5	2.21 (47)	2.9 (53)	2.52

difficult regulations, requirements, delays, and fines is to pay a bribe. Respondents were asked somewhat discreetly: how often does one need to bribe officials to do business in your city, on a scale of 1 to 5 (1 is almost never, 2 is rarely, 3 is sometimes, 4 is often, and 5 is almost always). The mean response in Warsaw is 2.2, compared with 2.9 in Moscow (*t* = 2.52). The structure of corruption was also explored by asking how many different agencies visited the shop. On average, 3.58 different agencies conducted inspections of Moscow shops, compared with 2.65 in Warsaw (*t* = 1.84). If the amount of bribes rises with the number of independent bribe takers, this evidence points further to the greater burden of regulation in Moscow than in Warsaw.

In sum, the Frye-Shleifer evidence indicates that shop owners in neither country are particularly keen on using the courts, although the Russian respondents have a greater need for them. On the other hand, private protection is used much more extensively in Russia than in Poland. Regulations in Russia appear to be a good deal more oppressive to business than they do in Poland. This is reflected in the frequency of inspections and in the greater legal vulnerability that Russian respondents feel, as well as in the greater burden of corruption in Moscow. The survey has not obtained much information about taxes, although the respondents in both countries view taxes as their most important problem, and respondents in Russia report heavy reliance on bribes to avoid taxes. It appears that the tax burden, like the regulatory burden, is more severe in Russia, at least if we take the enormous underground economy there (which does not exist in Poland) as evidence. Indeed, if taxes and regulations drive businesses in Russia underground, it is not surprising that they need to rely on criminals rather than the police for protection.

One final question corroborates the anecdote that began this section. When asked to rate the problem of product market competition on the scale from 1 to 10, Moscow shop managers' average answer is 4.8, compared with 6.2 in Warsaw ($t = 2.3$). Evidently, the Polish shopkeepers have their rents extracted by competitors, while the Russian ones are extracted by the bureaucrats.

These results suggest that the transition of government into one that supports markets from one that preys on them has gone further in Poland than in Russia. Regulators of small business exert more power over business in Moscow than in Warsaw, and use this power to enrich themselves. Nor has the Russian government yet successfully taken on the basic market-supporting functions, including police protection. Russia is much more of a laggard in the transition of its government than it is in shock therapy.

11.4 Possible Causes

The previous section has presented evidence indicating that the Russian government remains a good deal less supportive of private business than the government in Poland. It has focused on local government, but similar observations can be made about the central government as well. This section examines some of the possible causes of this difference in government performance. A large number of possible causes can account for this difference in public sector performance. Six are examined here.

11.4.1 SHOCK THERAPY AS A CAUSE OF
GOVERNMENT FAILURE IN RUSSIA

It has been argued that the radical reform itself—in the form of privatization and stabilization—is responsible for the ineffectiveness of the Russian state. For example, the limitations on public spending in Russia may have caused its government to abandon its basic functions, such as police protection. Privatization has allegedly turned state assets over to the mafia, and thus has caused crime.

The evidence does not support these arguments. First, as already mentioned, Poland and the Czech Republic were the champions of shock therapy, yet neither experienced the same collapse of the state as Russia did. Ukraine has been a prototypical go-slow (if at all) reformer, yet the data indicate that its government is at least as predatory as Russia's (Kaufmann and Kaliberda 1997). The disorganized, predatory state was fully operational in Russia in 1991 and 1992, even though privatization did not occur until 1993–1994 and stabilization until 1995. Sachs's (1995) claim that radical reform by itself revives the bankrupt state may go too far, but certainly radical economic liberalization and government reform are two necessary and distinct elements of transition.

11.4.2 TRUST, SOCIAL CAPITAL, AND THE CIVIL SOCIETY

An alternative set of explanations of government failure in Russia deals with trust, social capital, and civil society. In recent years, various authors—including Gambetta et al. (1988), Coleman (1990), Putnam (1993), Gellner (1994), and Fukuyama (1995)—have used these concepts to explain why some societies function better than others. Putnam (1993) invokes the concept of social capital to explain why governments in northern Italian regions function better than governments in southern Italy. Putnam shows that, empirically, some measures of trust among people in a region—such as participation in nongovernmental associations—are strongly correlated with the quality of government performance in that region.

It is important to distinguish two views of how social capital contributes to better government. On the first view, taken by Coleman, Fukuyama, and Putnam, trust promotes cooperation between people, and cooperation leads to better performance of all institutions in the society, including the government. On the second view, which is similar to Gellner's theory of civil society but has also been stressed by János Kornai and Jeffrey Sachs, the essential manifestation of social capital is the presence in a country of nonstate institutions that watch, criticize, and restrain the government. Active participation by citizens in such institutions enables them to limit the predatory tendencies of public officials. On this view, countervailing power rather than cooperation among people per se improves the performance of the government.

La Porta, Lopez-de-Silanes, Shleifer, and Vishny (1997) test both of these views of trust using data from the World Values Survey, a sociological survey of 1,000 people in each of forty countries conducted last in the early 1990s. One question that the survey asked might bear on the "cooperation" view of trust: "Generally speaking, would you say that most people can be trusted, or that you cannot be too careful in dealing with people?" The percentage of people answering yes to this question is one measure of trust in a country. La Porta and colleagues (1997) examine the relationship between this measure of trust and several proxies for government performance across countries, such as infant mortality and public education expenditure, but also perceived corruption, bureaucratic quality, and judicial efficiency. They find a positive correlation between trust and government performance across the world, even controlling for per capita income.

The World Values Survey also asked whether respondents participate in a variety of civic activities, including (a) social welfare services for the elderly and deprived, (b) education, art, and cultural activities, (c) local community affairs, (d) activities related to conservation, the environment, and ecology, and (e) work with youth. The percentage of these activities in which an average respondent in a country is involved may measure the intensity of civic participation. La Porta and colleagues (1997) examine how this participation variable affects their proxies for government performance. Although this variable does not work as well as the measure of trust, it is generally also positively correlated with government performance, controlling for per capita income.

This evidence suggests that, in principle at least, low social capital might be a valid explanation of the poor performance of Russia's government. To examine this possibility, Table 11.3 presents data on the answers to the trust and participation questions in the World Values Survey. The data seem quite plausible. On trust, the Scandinavian countries are at the top, and Turkey and Brazil are at the bottom. On participation, Scandinavia is again very high whereas the East European countries appear to be at the bottom. On trust, Russia and Poland are in the middle, with 37 percent of the Russians and 34 percent of the Poles believing that people can be trusted. This puts the two countries very close together: a bit below Germany and Japan, but higher than the Czech Republic and France. The participation variable is unfortunately not available for Poland, although Russia is in the middle of the East European pack, lower than the Slovak Republic but higher than Hungary and Romania.

These data do not support the view that poor social capital is responsible for government failure in Russia. If cooperation is the essential benefit of social capital, then Russia should not expect to have a government as good as that in Sweden and Denmark, but can surely count on one as good as that in France. If participation in civic organizations is the key benefit, Russia's future is not as attractive, but still typical of Eastern Europe, where some countries with lower rankings, such as Hungary and Romania, are succeeding in the transition of their governments.

It is possible, of course, that our measures—particularly that of participation—do not adequately capture the efficacy of the civic countervailing power to the government. Poland, in particular, had two institutions at the beginning of reforms that played a critical role in the transition of its government: the Catholic Church and the Solidarity labor union. The Catholic Church, while not in general a friend of economic reforms, nonetheless used its influence to demand a clean government. Solidarity essentially destroyed Communism and became the basis of Poland's first non-Communist and reformist political party. The Orthodox Church in Russia has not played a significant role in politics, and there was no anti-Communist political movement comparable to Solidarity. In fact, as of this writing, Russia still does not have a reform-minded political party. Still, putting too much emphasis on the role of these two institutions neglects the fact that many countries in Eastern Europe, including Hungary, the Czech Republic, Slovakia, and Romania, managed a government transition without counterparts to either Solidarity or the Polish Catholic Church. This makes one

Table 11.3 Social capital around the world: World Values Survey, 1981–1984 and 1990–1993, Inter-University Consortium for Political and Social Research

Country	*Trust:* The percentage of people that answered "yes" when asked "Generally speaking, would you say that most people can be trusted or that you can't be too careful in dealing with people?"	*Participation:* Percentage of civic activities listed in the text in which an average respondent participates
Sweden	66.10	10.94
Norway	65.05	11.74
Finland	62.72	10.66
China	60.30	3.97
Denmark	57.66	11.35
Netherlands	53.47	20.80
Canada	53.07	11.42
United States	51.06	11.72
Ireland	47.36	8.04
United Kingdom	43.68	7.01
Iceland	43.60	11.35
Switzerland	42.64	6.64
Japan	41.71	2.79
Germany	37.85	9.39
Russia	37.45	2.94
India	35.43	N.A.
Italy	35.30	4.49
Poland	34.50	N.A.
Spain	34.24	2.70
South Korea	34.17	10.06
Belgium	33.50	10.05
Mexico	33.45	5.37

Table 11.3 (*continued*)

Country	Trust: The percentage of people that answered "yes" when asked "Generally speaking, would you say that most people can be trusted or that you can't be too careful in dealing with people?"	Participation: Percentage of civic activities listed in the text in which an average respondent participates
Austria	31.82	5.97
Lithuania	30.80	3.70
Bulgaria	30.39	3.13
South Africa	29.00	N.A.
Czech Republic	27.83	N.A.
Estonia	27.57	5.45
Belorussia	25.47	N.A.
Hungary	24.58	2.41
Argentina	23.30	2.58
Nigeria	23.20	N.A.
France	22.79	6.08
Chile	22.70	5.77
Portugal	21.67	4.07
Latvia	19.04	4.42
Slovak Republic	17.38	3.38
Romania	16.06	1.37
Turkey	9.98	N.A.
Brazil	6.45	5.86
Mean	35.30	6.90
Median	33.00	5.86

skeptical that these powerful countervailing institutions fully account for the differences between Russia and Poland in the transition of their governments.[11]

11.4.3 CULTURAL ANTAGONISM TO CAPITALISM

Next, consider the perennial favorite: the theory that the Russians do not believe in capitalism (e.g., Goldman 1994). This theory might not explain government failure in Russia, even if it were true. However, since the theory is so often repeated, one must keep repeating that there is no evidence supporting it.[12] Like gossip, it spreads without substantiation.

Shiller, Boycko, and Korobov (1991, 1992) published the results of surveys they conducted in Russia, United States, Ukraine, Germany, and Japan that tested public attitudes toward capitalism. The fact that the surveys were conducted before radical reforms had begun in Russia is especially valuable; they can thus genuinely assess respondents' attitudes toward markets and capitalism rather than their reaction to the events taking place in their country. The authors of the surveys discovered astonishing similarity across countries in responses to their questions: people everywhere were positively inclined toward markets and incentives, although they also had rather strong sentiments in favor of fairness and equality. There was no evidence of excessive Russian suspicion of capitalism.

The attitude toward markets and capitalism should be distinguished from the attitude toward the short-run economic consequences of transition, such as recession, unemployment, and significant dislocation of labor. Perhaps the clearest way to see this is to recall the unpopularity of integration in East Germany, where the people expressed deep unhappiness in all surveys despite the massive resource transfers they received and despite vast objective increases in their consumption. Aslund, Boone, and Johnson (1996) present the results of annual surveys conducted by the European Commission which asked people in transition economies whether they liked the direction in which their country was going. The authors show that in Poland, for example, 41 percent more people answered no than yes to this question in 1991, right after the radical reform. The sharp excess of pessimists remained until 1995, the year the economy grew by 7 percent. Because Russia's recession lasted longer,

Russia reports a large excess of pessimists through 1995—the last year for which the data are reported—but the numbers are not that different from these for Poland in 1991. Earle and Rose (1996) also report negative attitudes in Russia toward the government's economic policy, combined with complaints that reforms have not been fast enough.

This evidence suggests that the Russians are unhappy with the situation in their country, and not that they are culturally hostile to capitalism. One commonly mentioned reason for this unhappiness is the perception that the government is dysfunctional, corrupt, and incapable of delivering growth and stability. But this shows that government failure is the reason for the concern about the economy, not that skepticism about capitalism is the cause of government failure. The theory of Russian hostility to markets, then, is not supported by the data.

11.4.4 THE HUMAN CAPITAL OF POLITICIANS

Politicians, like the rest of us, require certain skills to practice their craft. Some of these skills are very different in a market economy than in a Communist economy. While all local politicians need to make sure that the garbage is collected and public transport works, politicians in a market economy also need to worry that local entrepreneurs are able to get licenses to operate their businesses, borrow funds from nonfraudulent banks, rent space, go to court, and so on. The public goods of market and Communist economies are not the same.

It is doubtful that a Communist politician can quickly pick up the requisite skills. His difficulties may be even greater if he is of mature age and his learning capacity is diminished (Posner 1995). Many of today's Russian politicians are Communist leftovers experiencing significant hardships in understanding what is expected of them, and fearful that in the new society they will be outsmarted by competitors. Few of these leftover politicians have transformed themselves into capitalist politicians. You cannot teach an old dog new tricks.

The problem of renewing human capital during transition is not unique to politicians: obsolete human capital might be the most significant deterrent to the restructuring of privatized state firms as well. Barberis, Boycko, Shleifer, and Tsukanova (1996) examine the restructuring of Russian shops following privatization, and find that the mere presence of new owners and managers—as opposed to the presence of new incentives—is the best predictor of restructuring. In both the economy and politics, the replacement of obsolete human capital may well be the central problem of transition.

In politics, Poland appears to have gone a good deal further in solving this problem than Russia. Studies of elections and of the turnover of elites corroborate this view. For example, 75 percent of local leaders elected in Poland in 1990 had no record of government service, and 45 percent of newly elected mayors were under the age of forty. Although comparable percentages for Russia are not available, they are certain to be a good deal lower even now. Poland had such substantial replacement of political leadership because of the popularity of Solidarity. In 1990, 47 percent of newly elected politicians came from civic opposition movements (mainly Solidarity) and another 39 percent were independents, with only 8 percent being Communists. In the Russian election to the local soviets in 1990, a much lower 33 percent of the winners came from civil opposition movements and a vastly higher 49 percent were Communists. Indeed, if one looks at local governments in the mid-1990s, in Poland the office-holders have largely changed and been replaced by younger people, with some experience in both democratic politics and the market economy, whereas in Russia, the local leaders are largely the very same people who were there before the reforms began.[13] In this respect, Solidarity changed Poland. Russia would be a very different place politically if it had a similar revolution from below.

A recent Polish study of political elites in the two countries paints a similar picture.[14] The authors interviewed several hundred members of the 1993 political, economic, and cultural elites, and asked them about their current and past activities. For Russia, they discovered that, of the current political elite, 83 percent were former Communist Party members, and, of the current economic elite, 53 percent were former Party members. For Poland, the respective numbers were 30 percent and 57 percent. This together with their other findings shows that the former Polish elite has been largely removed from politics and has dedicated its energies to business. In Russia, in contrast, the former political elite remains in power.

Although this discussion has focused on local governments as the place where the turnover of political elites is essential to make government hospitable to private business, Russia's problems with obsolete human capital affect national economic policies as well. While it is often difficult to disentangle the economic confusion of politicians from self-serving rhetoric, some Russian politicians elaborate their views in little-read scholarly publications, presumably to preserve their insights for history. Take, for instance, the apparently genuine conviction of the former Central Bank governor Geraschenko that inflation in Russia was caused by monopoly pricing rather than by the hyperactivity of his printing presses. Or consider a 1994 article by Yavlinsky (a Gorbachev economist and sometime presidential candidate) and Braguinsky advocating a full-blown Peronist growth strategy for Russia, with large government spending, protection of industry, and massive state investment in "strategic firms." One may conclude that the lack of turnover of human capital in Russian politics may well be a serious reason for the poor performance of its government.

11.4.5 INCENTIVES OF LOCAL POLITICIANS

An equally important problem for government performance is the incentives facing local politicians. For local politicians to support the growth of new business, they need to have either political or financial incentives to do so. These incentives come from several sources. First, if politicians need to collect campaign contributions to run their elections, they might favor new business as a source of potential campaign donations. President Yeltsin's 1996 reelection campaign, for example, was largely financed by private firms. Second, if politicians need to provide public goods to attract votes, and must collect taxes to pay for these public goods, they may support the growth of new business to broaden the tax base. This mechanism may operate even without elections: in China, evidently, local Communist leaders count on taxes from small business to finance public goods required for their localities to function (Oi 1992). Finally, local politicians may support private business if they effectively become shareholders in it and profit personally when it does well. This mechanism is also essential for the political support of Chinese township and village enterprises (Oi 1992; Liu 1992). These three incentive mechanisms—campaign support, local tax base, and personal shareholdings—can all in principle encourage local political support of private business.

Close ties between local government and business are not always conducive to new business formation and entry. The existing firms may use their political connections and campaign contributions to deter entry, to limit trade, or to restrict the opportunities of competitors to grow.[15] At the national level, these ties between government and existing firms have encouraged antigrowth policies in many countries. Still, it is naive to believe that the local politicians in any country would accommodate private business growth unless they have some incentive to do so, and the channels outlined above describe some of the clear-cut incentives.

Along a variety of dimensions, the incentives of local politicians in Russia—unlike those in Poland—do not encourage them to support private business. First, the electoral motive has been rather weak in Russia.[16] Although Russia held local elections for a variety of positions in 1990, President Yeltsin has subsequently assumed control over local governments. In 1991 he signed a decree giving himself power to appoint governors and mayors without elections in most regions, and in 1993 he sharply curtailed the power of the local legislatures. The ostensible reason for these steps was to prevent separatist pressures. As a consequence, the officials Yeltsin appointed were selected for their loyalty and lack of political ambition rather than their market sympathies. Indeed, the appointed governors often undermined private business because they feared the political challenge it might bring about.

This situation of centralized control is slowly changing. In 1996 many regions in Russia elected governors, and many cities elected mayors. Gubernatorial elections are not without costs. The elected governors may use their mandates to threaten political independence and thus extract resources from Moscow. They might also restrict trade to protect local business, much as their Chinese counterparts do (Young 1996). Governors are also too far from small local businesses to rely on them for campaign finance or other forms of political support.[17] Local elections are more obviously beneficial since the officials who would actually benefit from local business support and at the same time do not have separatist or protectionist ambitions are precisely the local politicians.

Poland has held elections more consistently than Russia (Barbone and Hicks 1995; Swianiewicz 1992). Most important, the officials at very local levels—where small business would actually have a political say—are all elected. Because of elections, Polish politicians appear to have much stronger sympathies for private business than their Russian counterparts.

In addition to the problem of insufficient electoral oversight, the incentives arising from local government finance are also very different in Russia and in Poland.[18] In Poland, the principal source of funds for local governments is local taxes and fees, especially property taxes. Grants from the central government and even shared taxes are less important, and arguably are structured so as to encourage local business formation. This system gives local politicians in Poland an incentive to broaden the tax base to increase revenue, and the principal mechanism for broadening the tax base is new business formation and employment.

In Russia, the situation is different. Over two-thirds of local government revenues comes from their share of taxes collected by the central government. Moreover, while this share is in theory fixed, in practice it is negotiated. Regional governments negotiate with Moscow, and local governments negotiate with regions. The effects of such fiscal federalism (which should be contrasted with Chinese fiscal federalism, where sharing rules are evidently firmer) are perverse. Governors have little incentive to broaden their tax bases, and instead devote their efforts to negotiations with Moscow.[19] Moreover, as Treisman (1996, 1998) has persuasively shown, the regions that receive the most revenue are the ones that create trouble for Moscow: they have strikes, labor unrest, and separatist movements, and they vote *against* the incumbent Moscow government. Peace and prosperity in a region do not, evidently, increase the resources of the local government. This situation is likely to get worse when governors are elected, since the president will lose his power of appointment and will retain few mechanisms to keep the country together other than throwing money at the separatist regions.[20] Under these circumstances, it is not surprising that local governments in Russia do not feel pressured to promote small business.[21]

The final potential incentive of the local officials is financial, namely to become effective shareholders in the local businesses and to prosper when they do. This model appears to be widespread in China (Oi 1992), and many people have pointed out its relevance for the city of Moscow. Nonetheless, it seems to be much less widely adopted in Russia than one would have guessed several years ago. Rather than encourage local business and then profit when it does, local officials in Russia often destroy local business through excessive up-front corruption and regulation. They confiscate the wealth before there is any. Why is this so?

The likely reason is that many local officials in Russia see a rather short and insecure future for themselves in politics. If the private economy grows, they are likely to lose power because they will not be acceptable to the new business elites. If elections are held, they are also likely to lose power to the younger generation that can more credibly promise growth to voters. In the absence of political security that would guarantee them access to the future profits of firms, and lacking corporate governance mechanisms that would enable them to take equity and count on future dividends, many local government officials are grabbing what they can while they can. This approach, of course, is devastating for growth.[22]

11.4.6 INITIAL CONDITIONS

The final explanation of the difference in government performance in Russia and Poland is that the two countries started with different "initial conditions." Indeed, Poland has been pursuing economic reforms at least since the 1980s, much longer than Russia has. As a consequence, the Polish private sector was well established by 1990, when radical reforms began. By 1986, one-third of the Polish labor force was employed in the private sector, including agriculture, and a quarter of national output originated in the private sector—not counting the underground economy (Rostowski 1989). When constitutional protection of private property was instituted in 1989, a large share of the economy was already in that form. The large size of the private sector also meant that the government had some experience dealing with it. Many of the Solidarity members who entered the government in 1990 came from the private sector.

Furthermore, Poland had a much more substantial legal history and tradition on which to rely. Many of its commercial laws were adopted as soon as reforms began because they were based on Poland's own pre–World War II laws. Some of the people who were involved in prewar legal practice, and many of their students, were alive and capable in 1990. National tradition made the implementation of at least some institutional reforms a good deal easier.

Russia has been building capitalism for a much shorter time. Gorbachev's reforms allowed some quasi-private firms in Russia, but very few compared with Poland. Russia's history of market institutions is equally sparse. Russia's prerevolutionary laws were an instrument of autocratic control, not a mechanism of protection against it (Owen 1991). The regulatory agencies have been created from scratch, and their employees often view their jobs as mandates for personal enrichment rather than efficient regulation.[23]

But the importance of initial conditions can be overrated. Many countries in Eastern Europe, such as Slovakia and the Czech Republic, grew rapidly in the 1990s even though they had as little private business before the reforms as Russia did. Some countries of the former Soviet Union, such as Kyrghizstan, were also growing despite having a limited history of legal traditions and public institutions. With proper political incentives, initial conditions are often overcome.

11.4.7 SUMMARY

The conclusion that the Russian government is less effective in serving the market economy—as well as its people—than the Polish government is uncontroversial, but the exact cause of poor government performance is difficult to pin down. Nonetheless, arguments to the effect that Russia is historically and culturally incapable of good government—such as Russia's supposed low level of trust or anti–market culture—lack support. The more convincing argument is that Russia has not had as radical a change in its government, in terms of both structure and personnel, as Poland or the Czech Republic. Starting from this perspective, one does not need to give up hope that Russia is capable of a political transition. What, then, are the necessary steps?

11.5 Strategies for Public Sector Reform in Russia

This chapter began by establishing that the speed of economic reform is not the only essential input in the success of the transition to capitalism. The transition of government into one supporting the market economy is a separate, and perhaps as important, element of the transformation. The analysis of section 11.4 points to several reforms of Russia's political system that could accelerate the transition of the government. Before turning to these reforms, however, let us briefly pause on the suggestion that the way to address Russia's problems is to increase the size and power of its government by following the policies of increased spending, government-mandated increases in wages and pensions, public sector investment, and creation of government-supported cartels to foster industrialization. These strategies are advocated by such distinguished writers as Yavlinsky and Braguinsky (1994) and Abalkin and colleagues (1996).

It is possible to make the case that Russia spends too little on education, public safety, and even welfare.[24] Nonetheless, an increase in the size of the government as it exists in Russia today is unlikely to help the public. This state would waste most of its additional resources to support its inefficient agriculture and military industrial complex, to keep declining industries from shutting down, and to stop the reallocation of labor into services and small business. Many of the resources of this larger state would be stolen and transferred abroad. The tax burden from this large, predatory state would also eliminate, or at best drive underground, the small private businesses that have become the engine of the Russian economy despite all the difficulties they face. Russia needs a state focused on a different set of functions, rather than a bigger state doing more of what it already does so badly. And to become a refocused state Russia above all needs political reform.

The analysis of the previous sections points to three essential public sector reforms. Perhaps the most critical is to accelerate elections at the subregional or local levels. Such elections would increase the accountability of local politicians to the public and therefore, through channels such as the need for public revenue and for political contributions, make local government friendlier to business. If the incumbent politicians prove unable to accommodate these political demands, they will lose power. Local elections would thus stimulate the turnover of human capital as well as provide politicians with better incentives. Local elections also have the benefit that cities, unlike regions, do not want to become independent countries, or to protect their business from trade. Polish-style grass-roots democracy has the clearest economic benefits.[25]

Parallel to electoral reform, fiscal federalism—and more generally the tax system—in Russia needs to be reformed as well. If local governments are to be responsive to the needs of their constituents, they must tax their constituents themselves and make their expenditures to a large extent from these proceeds. Taxation and representation would then go together. Such reforms are likely to reduce Russia's currently prohibitive tax rates, but also to stimulate the government's incentive to actually collect the taxes. It is striking how similar Poland and China are in this regard, and how different both of them are from Russia.

Finally, institutional reforms, hard as they are, need to continue. Legal reforms are the most important among those, but creating functional bureaucracies, one at a time, is also crucial.

Russia's mediocre growth record points to the urgency of these reforms. In fact, some have argued that Russia has been mistaken in beginning with economic reforms and delaying political and institutional reforms. To be sure, the transition in Russia would have been easier if it had an effective (not large!) government. But this evaluation ignores a critical interaction between economic and political reforms, namely that economic reforms create pressure for political reforms. In Russia in 1991 and 1992, the pressure for political reforms to support markets simply did not exist, in part because private business barely existed. Today private business accounts for over half of the GNP and has a strong economic interest in making government more accommodating. Accommodation includes regulatory and institutional reforms, such as containment of corruption, creation of a law-based society, and design of a sane regulatory system. Business pressures are likely to play a critical role in the political transition of Russia, and of course they did not exist before economic reforms.

Russia now faces the opportunity to make its political transition. Its growth has lagged because its government has lagged, despite the rapid speed of economic reforms. But time is on Russia's side primarily because it is now a market economy, with a strong and growing private sector asserting its needs. Russia may have lagged in political reforms, and has surely paid the price, but it is difficult to believe that the laggard will fail to catch up.

Notes

1 Perspectives on Government

We appreciate comments from Robert Bates, Olivier Blanchard, Ed Glaeser, Oliver Hart, David Laibson, and Rafael La Porta.

1. Our discussion draws on the *Economist* (1997).
2. There are many other wonderful examples in the book *Bureaucrats in Business* (World Bank 1995), whose title misleadingly suggests that it might be a history of the World Bank itself.
3. For a more general version of the helping hand view of this matter, and in particular the notion that the trouble with state firms is the failure of corporate governance, see Bardhan and Roemer (1992).
4. Current research supports this prediction. Russian firms are making significant progress in establishing corporate governance mechanisms (Blasi, Kroumova, and Kruse 1996). Institutions supporting corporate governance, such as the banking sector and capital markets, are also developing rapidly in part because of the profit opportunities made available by the privatized firms.
5. Of course, many economists and political scientists have pursued these agendas as well. Some of the most helpful contributions in this area include Brennan and Buchanan (1980), Bates (1981), Riker (1964), Huntington (1968), and Wilson (1989).

2 Princes and Merchants

We thank Alberto Alesina, Marco Becht, Claudia Goldin, Carol Heim, Larry Katz, Paul Krugman, Michael Kremer, Sam Pehzman, Robert Putnam, and Robert Waldmann for helpful discussions. We also wish to thank the National Bureau of Economic Research and the National Science Foundation for their support.

1. Smith ([1776] 1976), pp. 284–285.

2. Montesquieu (1748).
3. Kantorowicz (1931) calls Frederick II "the first absolutist monarch in Europe."
4. Boxer (1965); Burckhardt (1958); Croce (1970); Elliott (1963, 1986); Kantorowicz (1931); Palmer and Colton (1984); Parry (1966); Plumb (1967); Runciman (1958); Wedgewood (1944). For the southern Italian autocracy, see Burckhardt; Croce; Kantorowicz; and Runciman. For Spain, see Elliott; Palmer and Colton; and Parry. For the Low Countries (now Belgium and Holland), see Boxer; Palmer and Colton; and Wedgewood. Similarly, for Britain, see Palmer and Colton; and Plumb.
5. Haskins (1915); Kantorowicz (1931); Runciman (1958). We stretch the category of "absolutist" to include such examples as the Norman *regno* of southern Italy. Certainly the state and the administrative apparatus of the d'Hautevilles and the Hohenstaufens were feeble and inefficient compared with the bureaucracies and administrations of the seventeenth- and eighteenth-century states that are usually termed "absolutisms." Nevertheless, there is a qualitative difference between other feudal monarchies and those set up in Norman conquest kingdoms like Sicily. Those who would support our inclusive definition of "absolutism" include not only Kantorowicz but also Haskins and Runciman.
6. Poggi (1978).
7. De Vries (1984).
8. Montesquieu (1748); Smith ([1776] 1976).
9. Montesquieu (1748); Smith ([1776] 1976); Brennan and Buchanan (1980); North (1981); North and Thomas (1973); Olson (1991).
10. Hohenberg and Lees (1985).
11. Bairoch (1985).
12. See ibid.; Braudel (1984); Weber (1968).
13. De Vries (1984).
14. Russell (1972).
15. Bairoch, Batou, and Chèvre (1988); Chandler and Fox (1974); Sundbard (1908).
16. Bairoch, Batou, and Chèvre (1988) reproduce the Bairoch database, and make it available in machine-readable form from the Centre d'Histoire Économique Internationale of the University of Geneva.
17. Poggi (1978), 64.
18. Olson (1991); Brennan and Buchanan (1980).
19. De Commynes (1972). Lords nominally subject to the kings of France, like the dukes of Burgundy or of Aquitaine, could draw on their compact and extensive territorial domains for support and defy the king of France almost at will within their domain—in one famous episode, the Valois king Louis XI "the Spider" was lucky to escape with his life after a visit to the domain of the

duke of Burgundy, Charles "the Rash." By contrast, William I of England and his successors prevented the emergence of such compact territorial lordships, and so were able from a very early date to impose a unified system of royal justice on England and extend their administrative reach throughout the country.

20. Poggi (1978).
21. McNeill (1963).
22. Bloch (1961).
23. Smith ([1776] 1976).
24. De Vries (1984).
25. Southern (1970).
26. McNeill (1963); Palmer and Colton (1984); Strayer (1973). We carried out two separate classification exercises, one by us directly and a second by a research assistant relatively unfamiliar with European history, Hoang Quan Vu. His classification was based on McNeill; Palmer and Colton; and the Encyclopaedia Britannica.

Only two disputes have arisen regarding our classification. The first concerns France: we date the establishment of French absolutist monarchy to the era of Louis XIII and the centralization carried out by Cardinal Richelieu in the first half of the seventeenth century; our research assistant dates it from the twelfth-century defeat of the Anglo-French Angevins by Philip II "Augustus" and the c. 1300 centralization and extension of royal power under Philip IV "the Fair." For an account supporting this point of view, see Strayer. However, Philip IV's work did not last, but was undone by his Valois dynasty successors and by the collapse of royal authority during the Hundred Years' War. Which classification of France is adopted has no significant effect on our statistical estimates.

The second dispute concerns Germany, which we had originally removed from the "absolutist" category on the grounds that the German king—the Holy Roman Emperor—usually had little authority, and when German kings did have power, they tried to project it across the Alps to control northern Italy and papal Rome rather than centralizing and strengthening the royal administration in Germany. This judgment has provoked criticism in several seminars: the absence of royal authority did not make property secure but instead gave subordinate territorial princes free rein to attempt to establish little despotic principalities. See Palmer and Colton. Once again, however, which classification of Germany is adopted has no significant effect on our statistical estimates.

27. These results imply that, under the maintained regression assumptions, there are ninety-five chances out of one hundred that the "true" effect lies in the range from 80,000 to 280,000 urban inhabitants lost per century of absolutism.

28. Under the maintained regression assumptions, there are ninety-five chances out of one hundred that the "true" effect lies in the range from 0.4 to 3.9 cities of 30,000 or more inhabitants lost per century of absolutism.

29. Experimentation with a division into three regime types—constitutional and city-state merchant regimes as one type, absolutist princes as a second, and feudal anarchy as a third—uncovered some evidence that anarchy was worse than absolutism for city growth when the dependent variable was growth in urban populations, but not when the dependent variable was growth in the number of cities. Regions suffering from anarchy lose 59,000 people per century from their largest cities.

30. Personal communication from Robert Putnam, spring 1992.

31. Tilly (1990).

32. Bairoch, Batou, and Chèvre (1988).

33. The database underlying Table 2.3 has 150-year periods; the database underlying Table 2.9 has 100-year periods. However, all coefficients are reported in units of number of people or cities per century in order to facilitate comparisons.

34. Braudel (1972); Tilly (1990).

35. Braudel (1984).

36. Olson (1991).

37. William, however, was the nephew of Edward "the Confessor," king before Harold Godwinson.

38. The Habsburg and the medieval Capetians are the only possible exceptions. Yet the medieval Capetians were nearly powerless. The Habsburg lost Holland and Portugal to revolts, nearly lost Belgium, Bohemia, and Catalonia to revolts, and were always on the verge of losing Belgium and northern Italy to the French.

3 The Allocation of Talent

We are grateful to Robert Barro, William Baumol, Olivier Blanchard, Avinash Dixit, Steve Kaplan, Anne Krueger, Paul Romer, Lawrence Summers, and Robert Waldmann for helpful comments. We also appreciate the support of the National Science Foundation and the Sloan and Bradley Foundations.

4 Why Is Rent Seeking So Costly to Growth?

We thank the Bradley Foundation for financial support and Tim Besley for comments.

1. The idea developed here was briefly described in Chapter 3. A similar argument is made by Acemoglu (1995).

2. In this example, the *number* of rent seekers and cash-crop producers is inde-

terminate; only their ratio is known. With diminishing returns to production, this indeterminacy disappears.

5 Corruption

We are grateful to Lawrence Katz and two anonymous referees for comments, and to the Bradley Foundation for financial support.

1. Importantly, if corruption with theft *replaces* taxes, then the corrupt state might have to replace the lost revenue through very distortionary taxation.

6 Pervasive Shortages under Socialism

We are grateful to Abram Bergson, Maxim Boycko, Larry Katz, Jim Poterba, Larry Summers, and two anonymous referees for helpful comments and to the Bradley and Sloan Foundations for financial support.

1. For an excellent overview of standard explanations, as well as an ingenious new theory, see Rotemberg (1990).
2. A Moscow taxi driver illustrated this point. When asked why all the most convenient turns seem to be prohibited on Moscow roads, resulting in huge traffic jams, he replied immediately: "So that policemen can collect the most bribes from the violators."
3. We could alternatively assume that some or all of the industry's costs have to be paid in bribes in order to procure scarce inputs, or that the industry faces some minimum profitability constraint. These assumptions would make the industry care about its official costs and thus change its choice of output, but would not change the basic conclusion that the industry wants to have a shortage of its output.

7 The Politics of Market Socialism

We are grateful to Alberto Alesina, Alan Krueger, Carl Shapiro, and Timothy Taylor for helpful suggestions.

1. Examples include Yunker (1992), Bardhan and Roemer (1992), and the papers collected in Bardhan and Roemer (1993).
2. The classic work is Buchanan and Tullock (1962). Mueller (1989) surveys the theory and evidence on what governments actually do.

8 A Theory of Privatization

This paper was presented by Andrei Shleifer as the Paish Lecture at the Royal Economic Society 1995 meetings. The authors are grateful to the Bradley, Sage, and National Science foundations for the support of this research, to Eric Maskin for very helpful comments, and to Ilya Segal for excellent research assistance.

1. Grossman and Hart (1986) stress the distinction between control and cash flow rights.
2. See Leff (1964), Rose-Ackerman (1978), and Chapters 5 and 9.
3. For a further discussion of this issue, see Shleifer (1995).
4. An alternative model of privatization is to keep control in the hands of politicians but also to give them personal cash-flow rights. Such "nomenklatura privatization" is easy to analyze in our model, and can be shown to increase efficiency relative to political control with no cash flow rights. Although nomenklatura privatization has sometimes been advocated for Eastern Europe, it is politically too unpopular to make it a viable privatization strategy.
5. Kornai (1979) is the classical study of soft budget constraints. More recent models include Dewatripont and Maskin (1995) and Schmidt (1996).

❾ Politicians and Firms

We are grateful to Oliver D. Hart for many helpful conversations and to Alberto Alesina, Roland Benabou, Abhijit Banerjee, James Hines, Bengt Holmstrom, and an anonymous referee for comments on an earlier draft. This research was supported by the Institute for Policy Reform of the United States Agency for International Development and the National Science Foundation.

1. The relevant political variable need not even be employment. For example, politicians might benefit from low food prices charged to their constituents, as in the case of African dictators who keep down city dwellers' food prices to avoid riots (Bates 1981). Even more generally, the political variable can be something socially good, such as low pollution, in which case the model can accommodate social-welfare-maximizing politicians.
2. In asymmetric information models, it is usually assumed that $C(T) > T$ because the politician is benevolent and the deadweight loss of taxation keeps its cost above revenue. Here the motivation is different: the politician is not benevolent and the public is disorganized. As a result, the political cost of spending a dollar of public money to the politician is less than a dollar.
3. Some studies of corruption include Becker and Stigler (1974), Rose-Ackerman (1978), Mauro (1995), Banerjee (1997), and Chapters 5 and 6.
4. This specification breaks down when the manager owns no equity, that is, when $\alpha = 0$, since then the manager has no interest in the cash flow of the firm. However, even if the manager's equity stake is literally zero, he can still divert more resources for personal consumption (cars, carpets, housing) in a more profitable firm, so he still cares about profits. For this reason, we can restrict attention to the cases where $\alpha > 0$ without loss of substantive generality.
5. A more detailed discussion of this issue is contained in Shleifer (1995).
6. An alternative model that yields this result is in Chapter 8.

10 Privatization in the United States

We are grateful to Mark Duggan for excellent research assistance and to Joshua Angrist, Suzanne Cooper, Oliver Hart, Igal Hendel, James Hines, Caroline Hoxby, Guido Imbens, Steve Kaplan, Rafael La Porta, Anne Piehl, James Poterba, an anonymous referee, and especially Larry Katz and Michael Whinston for many comments, and to the National Science Foundation, the Harvard Institute for International Development, and the Bradley Foundation for research support.

1. Kodrzycki (1994) looks at some of the demographic and labor market determinants of the privatization decision. She does not examine the political issues that are the focus here.
2. While disciplining unionized public employees is notoriously difficult, this is not true of the high-level political appointees who typically run park districts or prisons. Such high-level employees are likely to cater to the wishes of the politicians.
3. Lopez-de-Silanes (1997) describes the role of unions in opposing privatization in Mexico.
4. Unless they prefer to collect bribes and political contributions from potential contractors to winning votes from the beneficiaries of public provision. In U.S. local elections, seeking voter support through patronage is probably more important.
5. For Mexico, Lopez-de-Silanes (1997) empirically shows that public union strikes not only deter bidders from acquiring private enterprises, but also lead to substantially lower privatization prices.
6. The other ideology variables based on congressional, senatorial and presidential voting, however, were significant in neither the privatization switchers regression nor the nationalization switchers regression.
7. We have also estimated an ordered probit, in which nonprovision is modeled as a more extreme option than contracting out. Results are consistent with those in Tables 10.5 and 10.7.

11 Government in Transition

Presented as the Schumpeter Lecture to the European Economic Association's annual meeting in Istanbul. Thanks go to Steven Friedman for excellent research assistance, to HIID for financial support, and to Philippe Aghion, Olivier Blanchard, Maxim Boycko, Timothy Frye, Jonathan Hay, Daniel Kaufmann, János Kornai, Rafael La Porta, Florencio Lopez-de-Silanes, Jeffrey Sachs, Daniel Treisman, and Robert Vishny for helpful discussions.

1. There remains the controversial question of China, which has grown tremendously over the last fifteen years despite reforms that have been slow in some

ways. The relevance of the Chinese experience for Eastern Europe is doubtful, for several reasons. First, China at the beginning of reforms was a poor agricultural economy that did not bear nearly the same burdens as a large state industrial sector (Sachs and Woo 1994). Second, China remains a Communist dictatorship and so does not face the complexities (nor reaps the benefits) of democracy.

2. For discussions of this recession, see Blanchard (1997), Blanchard and Kremer (1997), Kornai (1994), Murphy, Shleifer, and Vishny (1992) and the World Bank (1996).

3. The World Bank worked particularly hard on this reclassification. For example, the background paper by DeMelo, Denizer, and Gelb (1996), which explains the World Bank Development Report classification, ranks Russia behind Poland in privatization in 1994. This is so despite the fact that Russia's mass privatization program was finished by July of 1994, whereas Poland's did not even begin until 1995.

4. There are some potentially important differences between Russia and Poland as well. Geographically, Poland is closer to Western Europe, which made it easier to use Polish labor to assemble goods for the European markets. Politically, Poland had more of a democratic as well as institutional tradition. In particular, Poland had two extremely strong nonstate institutions in 1990: the Solidarity union and the Catholic Church, discussed in section 11.4.

5. An excellent discussion of theory and evidence on transition is Blanchard (1997). McMillan (1997) presents a comprehensive survey of the relevant literature.

6. Kornai (1994) summarizes his classic work on the inefficiency of political control. For more formal discussions, see Chapters 5, 6, 8, and 9.

7. Some systematic empirical evidence in support of this proposition in the context of the choice of private versus public provision of municipal services in the United States is contained in Chapter 10.

8. For a general discussion of the importance of legal reform in the transition to capitalism, see North (1990) and Sachs and Warner (1995). For the Russian case, see Hay, Shleifer, and Vishny (1996).

9. This section draws heavily on Frye and Shleifer (1997).

10. The gray economy is itself evidence of the predatory tax and regulatory policies of the state. According to Kaufmann and Kaliberda (1997), the gray economy accounts for 40 percent of the Russian GDP.

11. Pop-Eleches (1997) has redone the Frye-Shleifer (1997) survey in Romania, a country with no countervailing institutions similar to Poland's, and found that Romania's legal and regulatory environment is much closer to Poland's than to Russia's.

12. For a debunking of this theory in the context of the participation of the Russian public in privatization, see Boycko, Shleifer and Vishny (1995).

13. The city of Moscow—despite the shortcomings of its government relative to

that in Warsaw—is an exception for Russia: in 1990 over half the members of its local soviet had changed. Interestingly, Moscow has been growing much faster than other Russian cities.

14. Szelenyi, Treisman, Wnuk-Lipinski (1995). The numbers here come from a review by Jakub Karpinski (1996).

15. See Young (1996) for a striking account of such anticompetitive policies pursued by provincial governments in China.

16. Details on the electoral process in Russia are contained in McFaul (1993) and Teague (1996).

17. This may be too strong, since the election of governors might also bring in more economic reformers. For example, Moscow's mayor was reelected in 1996 with over 90 percent of the vote. Moscow has grown rapidly over the last few years, and the closeness of the ties between its government and business is legendary. In contrast, the mayor of St. Petersburg was not reelected in 1996, largely because of his mismanagement of the city's economy. He was defeated by an opponent who promised to make St. Petersburg more like Moscow.

18. For details on local government finance in Russia, see Le Houerou (1994) and Wallich (1994). For information on Poland, see Barbone and Hicks (1995).

19. Teague (1996) quotes the former finance minister Fedorov describing Russia as the only country where you can get what you want by standing outside the Ministry of Finance and yelling.

20. For a perceptive and relevant analysis of federalism, see Riker's (1964) classic book.

21. This discussion of fiscal federalism in Russia and of ways to improve it has been strongly influenced by Piketty's (1995) memorandum on this subject.

22. For theoretical and historical analyses of how politicians' horizons affect their tendencies to expropriate wealth, see Olson (1991) and Chapter 2.

23. A typical, though sad, example along these lines is the creation of the Russian antimonopoly agency. As soon as it was created, the agency began compiling lists of companies that it felt fell under its jurisdiction. It started with major national monopolies, and then quickly moved on to local "monopolies" such as bakeries and bathhouses. Business owners quickly understood the situation, and began to bribe antimonopoly officials just to get off the list.

24. For example, in 1992 Russia spent 11.6 percent of consolidated government expenditure on education. This figure fell to 10.6 percent in 1995, the year of extreme fiscal austerity. The somewhat more inclusive figure for Poland in 1991 was 15.6 percent.

25. Another potential benefit of local elections is that they would foster the development of political parties, which some scholars regard as essential both for effective democratic politics and for keeping together federalist states such as Russia (Riker 1964).

References

Abalkin, Leonid, et al. 1996. "A New Economic Policy for Russia." *Nezavisimaya Gazeta*, July 1.

Acemoglu, Daron. 1995. "Reward Structures and the Allocation of Talent." *European Economic Review*, 39, no. 1: 17–33.

AFSCME. *See* American Federation of State, County and Municipal Employees.

American Federation of State, County and Municipal Employees. 1984. *Passing the Bucks: The Contracting Out of Public Services.* Washington, D.C.: AFSCME.

Anastassopoulos, Jean-Pierre C. 1981. "The French Experience: Conflicts with Government." In Raymond Vernon and Yair Aharoni, eds., *State-Owned Enterprise in the Western Economies.* London: Croom Helm.

Arrow, Kenneth J. 1962. "The Economic Implications of Learning by Doing." *Review of Economic Studies,* 29: 155–183.

Aslund, Anders, Peter Boone, and Simon Johnson. 1996. "How to Stabilize: Lessons from Post-Communist Countries." *Brookings Papers on Economic Activity,* 1: 217–314.

Atkinson, Anthony B., and Joseph E. Stiglitz. 1980. *Lectures on Public Economics.* London: McGraw-Hill.

Bairoch, Paul. 1985. *De Jericho à Mexico: Villes at economie dans l'histoire.* Paris: Gallimard.

Bairoch, Paul, Jean Batou, and Pierre Chèvre. 1988. *La population des villes Européenes de 800–1850.* Geneva: Librairie Droz.

Banerjee, Abhijit. 1997. "A Theory of Misgovernance." *Quarterly Journal of Economics* 112, no. 4: 1289–1332.

Banfield, Edward. 1975. "Corruption as a Feature of Government Organization." *Journal of Law and Economics,* 17: 587–605.

Barberis, Nicholas, Maxim Boycko, Andrei Shleifer, and Natalia Tsukanova. 1996. "How Does Privatization Work: Evidence from the Russian Shops?" *Journal of Political Economy,* 104: 764–790.

Barbone, Luca, and J. F. Hicks. 1995. "Local and Intergovernmental Agencies in Poland: An Evolving Process." In Richard M. Bird, Robert M. Edel, and Christine I. Wallach, eds., *Decentralization of the Socialist State: Intergovernmental Finance in Transition Economies.* Washington, D.C.: World Bank.

Bardhan, Pranab K., and John E. Roemer. 1992. "Market Socialism: A Case for Rejuvenation." *Journal of Economic Perspectives,* 6, 3: 101–116.

Bardhan, Pranab K., and John E. Roemer, eds. 1993. *Market Socialism: The Current Debate.* New York: Oxford University Press.

Barone, Enrico. (1908) 1935. "The Ministry of Production in the Collectivist State." Reprinted in Friedrich A. Hayek, ed., *Collectivist Economic Planning: Critical Studies on the Possibilities of Socialism,* 245–290. London: G. Routledge.

Barro, Robert J. 1991. "Economic Growth in a Cross-Section of Countries." *Quarterly Journal of Economics,* 106: 407–444.

Bates, Robert H. 1981. *Markets and States in Tropical Africa: The Political Basis of Agricultural Policies.* Berkeley: University of California Press.

——— 1987. *Essays on the Political Economy of Rural Africa.* Berkeley: University of California Press.

Bauer, Peter T. 1976. *Dissent on Development.* Cambridge, Mass.: Harvard University Press.

Baumol, William J. 1990. "Entrepreneurship: Productive, Unproductive, and Destructive." *Journal of Political Economy,* 97: 893–921.

Becker, Gary S. 1983. "A Theory of Competition among Pressure Groups for Political Influence," *Quarterly Journal of Economics,* 98, 3: 371–400.

Becker, Gary S., and George J. Stigler. 1974. "Law Enforcement, Malfeasance, and the Compensation of Enforcers." *Journal of Legal Studies,* 3: 1–19.

Bhagwati, Jagdish N. 1982. "Directly Unproductive, Profit-Seeking (DUP) Activities." *Journal of Political Economy,* 90: 988–1002.

Blanchard, Olivier. 1997. *Clarendon Lectures: The Economics of Post-Communist Transition.* Oxford: Oxford University Press.

Blanchard, Olivier, and Michael Kremer. 1997. "Disorganization." *Quarterly Journal of Economics,* 112: 1091–1126.

Blasi, Joseph R., Maya Kroumova, and Douglas Kruse. 1996. *Kremlin Capitalism.* Ithaca, N.Y.: Cornell University Press.

Bloch, Marc L. 1961. *Feudal Society,* trans. L. A. Manyon. Chicago: University of Chicago Press.

Boxer, Charles R. 1965. *The Dutch Seaborne Empire, 1600–1800.* New York: Knopf.

Boycko, Maxim, Andrei Shleifer, and Robert W. Vishny. 1993. "Privatizing Russia." *Brookings Papers on Economic Activity,* 2: 139–192.

—— 1995. *Privatizing Russia.* Cambridge, Mass.: MIT Press.

Braudel, Fernand. 1972. *The Mediterranean and the Mediterranean World in the Age of Philip II,* trans. S. Reynolds. New York: Harper & Row.

—— 1984. *The Perspective of the World,* trans. S. Reynolds. New York: Harper & Row.

Brennan, Geoffrey, and Buchanan, James M. 1980. *The Power to Tax: Analytical Foundations of a Fiscal Constitution.* Cambridge: Cambridge University Press.

Buchanan, James M., and Gordon Tullock. 1962. *The Calculus of Consent.* Ann Arbor: University of Michigan Press.

Burckhardt, Jacob. 1958. *The Civilization of the Renaissance in Italy,* trans. S. G. C. Middlemore. New York: Harper & Row.

Business International. 1984. *Introduction to the Country Assessment Service.* New York: Business International Corporation.

Carino, Ledivina V., ed. 1986. *Bureaucratic Corruption in Asia: Causes, Consequences, and Controls.* Philippines: JMC Press.

Chandler, Tertius, and Gerald Fox. 1974. *3000 years of Urban Growth.* New York: Academic Press.

Coase, Ronald H. 1960. "The Problem of Social Cost." *Journal of Law and Economics,* 3: 1–44.

Coleman, James. 1990. *Foundations of Social Theory.* Cambridge, Mass.: Harvard University Press.

Croce, Benedetto. 1970. *History of the Kingdom of Naples,* trans. F. Frenaye. Chicago: University of Chicago Press.

de Commynes, Phillippe. (1498) 1972. *Memoirs: The Reign of Louis XI, 1461–1483.* reprint, New York: Penguin.

De Melo, Martha, C. Denizer, and A. Gelb. 1996. "From Plan to Market: Patterns of Transition." World Bank Policy Research Paper no. 1564.

De Soto, Hernando. 1989. *The Other Path: The Invisible Revolution in the Third World.* New York: Harper & Row.

de Vries, Jan. 1984. *European Urbanization, 1500–1800.* Cambridge: Cambridge University Press.

Demsetz, Harold. 1968. "Why Regulate Utilities?" *Journal of Law and Economics,* 11: 55–66.

Dewatripont, Mathias, and Eric S. Maskin. 1995. "Credit and Efficiency in Centralized and Decentralized Economies." *Review of Economic Studies,* 62, no. 4: 541–556.

Donahue, John D. 1989. *The Privatization Decision: Public Ends, Private Means.* New York: Basic Books.

Downs, Anthony. 1967. *Inside Bureaucracy.* Boston: Little, Brown.

Earle, John, and S. Estrin. 1995. "Privatization vs. Competition: Changing Enterprise Behavior in Russia." Central European University. Mimeo.

Earle, John, and R. Rose. 1996. "Ownership Transformation, Economic Behavior and Political Attitudes in Russia." Stanford University. Mimeo.

Economist. 1994a. "Two Half Revolutions." January 22: 55–58.

—— 1994b. "European Airlines: Flights of Fancy." February 5: 69–70.

—— 1994c. "The Bank That Couldn't Say No." April 9: 21–24.

—— 1997. "Banking's Biggest Disaster." July 5: 69–71.

Ekelund, Robert B., and Robert D. Tollison. 1981. *Mercantilism as a Rent-Seeking Society.* College Station: Texas A&M University Press.

Ekpo, Monday. 1979. *Bureaucratic Corruption in Sub-Saharan Africa: Toward a Search of Causes and Consequences.* Washington, D.C.: University Press of America.

Elliot, J. H. 1963. *Imperial Spain, 1469–1716.* London: Edward Arnold.

—— 1986. *The Count-Duke of Olivares: The Statesman in an Age of Decline.* New Haven: Yale University Press.

European Bank for Reconstruction and Development. 1996. *Transition Report 1995.* London.

Frydman, Roman, and Andrzej Rapaczynski. 1991. "Markets and Institutions in Large-Scale Privatization." In V. Corbo, F. Coricelli, and J. Bossak, eds., *Reforming Central and Eastern European Economies.* Washington, D.C.: World Bank.

Frye, Timothy, and Andrei Shleifer. 1997. "The Invisible Hand and the Grabbing Hand." *American Economic Review Papers and Proceedings,* 87: 354–358.

Fukuyama, Francis. 1995. *Trust.* New York: Free Press.

Gambetta, Diego, ed. 1988. *Trust: Making and Breaking Cooperative Relations.* New York: Basil Blackwell.

Gellner, Ernest. 1994. *Conditions of Liberty: Civil Society and Its Rivals.* New York: Allen Lane/Penguin Press.

Goldman, Marshall. 1994. *Lost Opportunity: Why Economic Reforms in Russia Have Not Worked.* New York: Norton.

Gould, David J., and José A. Amaro-Reyes. 1983. *The Effects of Corruption on Administrative Performance.* World Bank Staff Working Paper no. 580. Washington, D.C.: World Bank.

Grossman, Gene, and Alan B. Krueger. 1995. "Economic Growth and the Environment." *Quarterly Journal of Economics,* 110, no. 2: 353–378.

Grossman, Sanford J., and Oliver D. Hart. 1986. "The Costs and Benefits of Ownership: A Theory of Vertical and Lateral Integration." *Journal of Political Economy,* 94: 691–719.

Hamilton, Alexander, John Jay, and John Madison. (1788) 1961. *Federalist Papers.* Reprinted in C. Rossiter, ed., *Federalist Papers.* New York: New American Library.

Hansmann, Henry. 1990. "When Does Workers' Ownership Work? ESOPs, Law Firms, Codetermination and Economic Democracy." *Yale Law Journal*, 99: 1749–1816.

Hart, Oliver D., Andrei Shleifer, and Robert W. Vishny. 1997. "The Proper Scope of Government: Theory and an Application to Prisons." *Quarterly Journal of Economics*, 112: 1127–1161.

Haskins, Charles H. 1915. *The Normans in European History.* New York: Ungar.

Hay, Jonathan, Andrei Shleifer, and Robert W. Vishny. 1996. "Toward a Theory of Legal Reform." *European Economic Review*, 40: 559–567.

Hayek, Friedrich A., ed. 1935. *Collectivist Economic Planning.* London: Routledge and Kegan Paul.

———— 1944. *The Road to Serfdom.* Chicago: University of Chicago Press.

Heilbroner, Robert. 1962. *The Making of Economic Society.* Englewood Cliffs, N.J.: Prentice-Hall.

Hohenberg, Paul M., and Lees, Lynn. 1985. *The Making of Urban Europe, 1000–1950.* Cambridge, Mass.: Harvard University Press.

Huntington, Samuel P. 1968. *Political Order in Changing Societies.* New Haven: Yale University Press.

International Bank for Reconstruction and Development. 1996. *World Bank Development Report 1996: From Plan to Market.* Washington, D.C.: IBRD.

International City Management Association. 1989. *Service Delivery in the 1990s: Alternative Approaches for Local Governments.* Washington, D.C.: ICMA.

International Monetary Fund. 1991. *A Study of the Soviet Economy,* vol. 3. Washington, D.C.

Kantorowicz, Ernst. (1928) 1931. *Frederick the Second, 1194–1250.* Reprint, New York: Ungar.

Karpinski, Jakub. 1996. "Sociologists Compare Nomenklatura Members in Contemporary Elites." *Transition* (May): 36.

Kaufmann, Daniel, and Aleksander Kaliberda. 1997. "Integrating the Unofficial Economy into the Dynamics of Post-Socialist Economies." In B. Kaminski, ed., *Economic Transition in Russia and the New States of Eurasia.* Armonk: M. E. Sharpe.

Kemp, Roger L., ed. 1991. *Privatization: The Provision of Public Services by the Private Sector.* Jefferson, N.C.: McFarland & Co.

Kikeri, Sunita, John Nellis, and Mary Shirley. 1992. *Privatization: The Lessons of Experience.* Washington, D.C.: World Bank.

Klitgaard, Robert. 1988. *Controlling Corruption.* Berkeley: University of California Press.

———— 1990. *Tropical Gangsters.* New York: Basic Books.

———— 1991. "Gifts and Bribes." In Richard Zeckhauser, ed., *Strategy and Choice.* Cambridge, Mass.: MIT Press.

Kodrzycki, Yolanda K. 1994. "Privatization of Local Public Services: Lessons for New England." *New England Economic Review* (May-June): 31–46.

Kornai, János. 1979. "Resource-Constrained vs. Demand-Constrained Systems." *Econometrica*, 47: 801–819.

——— 1993. "Market Socialism Revisited." In Pranab K. Bardhan and John E. Roemer, eds., *Market Socialism: The Current Debate*, 42–68. New York: Oxford University Press.

——— 1994. "Transformational Recession: The Main Causes." *Journal of Comparative Economics*, 19: 39–63.

Kreps, David, et al. 1982. "Rational Cooperation in the Finitely Repeated Prisoners' Dilemma." *Journal of Economic Theory*, 27: 245–252.

Krueger, Anne P. 1974. "The Political Economy of a Rent-Seeking Society." *American Economic Review*, 64: 291–303.

Kuhn, Peter. 1988. "Unions in a General Equilibrium Model of Firm Formation." *Journal of Labor Economics*, 6: 62–82.

La Porta, Rafael, and F. Lopez-de-Silanes. 1997. "The Benefits of Privatization: Evidence from Mexico." NBER Working Paper no. 6215.

La Porta, Rafael, Florencio Lopez-de-Silanes, Andrei Shleifer, and Robert Vishny. 1997. "Trust in Large Organizations." *American Economic Review Papers and Proceedings*, 87: 333–338.

Laffont, Jean-Jacques. 1994. "Regulation, Privatisation, and Incentives in Developing Countries." Mimeo.

Laffont, Jean-Jacques, and Jean Tirole. 1993. *A Theory of Incentives in Regulation and Procurement*. Cambridge, Mass.: MIT Press.

Landes, David. 1969. *The Unbound Prometheus*. New York: Cambridge University Press.

Lange, Oskar. (1936-37) 1964. "On the Economic Theory of Socialism: Part One/Part Two." *Review of Economic Studies*, 4, 1–2: 53–71, 123–42. Reprinted in Oskar Lange and Fred M. Taylor, *On the Economic Theory of Socialism* (1938). New York: McGraw-Hill, 1964.

Le Houerou, Philippe. 1994. "Decentralization and Fiscal Disparities between Regions in the Russian Federation." World Bank Internal Discussion Paper no. IDP-138.

Leff, Nathaniel. 1964. "Economic Development through Bureaucratic Corruption." *American Behavioral Scientist*, 8: 8–14.

Lindbeck, Assar. 1997. "The Swedish Experiment." *Journal of Economic Literature*, 35: 1273–1319.

Lindbeck, Assar, et al. 1993. "Options for Economic and Political Reform in Sweden." *Economic Policy*, 17: 219–264.

Lipton, David, and Jeffrey D. Sachs. 1990. "Privatization in Eastern Europe: The Case of Poland." *Brookings Papers on Economic Activity*, 2: 293–341.

Little, Ian M. D., Dipak Mazumdar, and John M. Page, Jr. 1987. *Small Manufacturing Enterprises: A Comparative Analysis of India and Other Economies*. New York: Oxford University Press for the World Bank.

Liu, Yia-Ling. 1992. "Reform from Below: The Private Economy and Local Politics in the Rural Industrialization of Wenzhou." *China Quarterly*, 130: 293–316.

Lopez-de-Silanes, Florencio. 1997. "Determinants of Privatization Prices." *Quarterly Journal of Economics*, 112, no. 4: 965–1025.

Lucas, Robert E., Jr. 1978. "On the Size Distribution of Business Firms." *Rand Journal of Economics*, 9: 508–523.

Magee, Stephen P., William A. Brock, and Leslie Young. 1989. *Black Hole Tariffs and the Endogenous Policy Theory*. Cambridge: Cambridge University Press.

Martinelli, Alberto. 1981. "The Italian Experience: A Historical Perspective." In Raymond Vernon and Yair Aharoni, eds., *State-Owned Enterprise in the Western Economies*. London: Croom Helm.

Mauro, Paolo. 1995. "Corruption and Growth." *Quarterly Journal of Economics*, 110: 681–712.

McFaul, Michael. 1993. *Post-Communist Societies: Democratic Process in Russia and Eastern Europe*. Washington, D.C.: Center for Strategic and International Studies.

McMillan, John. 1997. "Markets in Transition." In David M. Kreps and Kenneth F. Wallis, eds., *Advances in Economics and Econometrics: Theory & Applications*, Seventh World Congress, vol. 2. Cambridge: Cambridge University Press.

McNeill, William H. 1963. *The Rise of the West: A History of the Human Community*. Chicago: University of Chicago Press.

Megginson, William L., Robert C. Nash, and Mathias van Randenborgh. 1994. "The Financial and Operating Performance of Newly Privatized Firms: An International Empirical Analysis." *Journal of Finance*, 49: 403–452.

Mises, Ludwig von (1920) 1935. "Economic Calculation in the Socialist Commonwealth." In Friederich A. Hayek, ed., *Collectivist Economic Planning: Critical Studies on the Possibilities of Socialism*, 87–130. London: G. Routledge.

Montesquieu, Charles-Louis de Sécondat, Baron de. 1748. *The Spirit of Laws*.

Mueller, Dennis C. 1989. *Public Choice II*. Cambridge: Cambridge University Press.

Murphy, Kevin M., and Finis Welch. 1992. "The Structure of Wages." *Quarterly Journal of Economics*, 107: 285–326.

Murphy, Kevin M., Andrei Shleifer, and Robert W. Vishny. 1992. "The Transition to a Market Economy: Pitfalls of Partial Reform." *Quarterly Journal of Economics*, 107: 889–906.

Murrell, Peter. 1991. "Can Neoclassical Economics Underpin the Reforms of the Centrally Planned Economies?" *Journal of Economic Perspectives,* 5: 59–76.

Musgrave, Richard A. 1959. *The Theory of Public Finance.* New York: McGraw-Hill.

National Commission for Employment Policy. 1988. *Privatization and Public Employees: The Impact of City and County Contracting on Government Workers.* District of Columbia: NCEP.

Nellis, John. 1988. "Contract Plans and Public Enterprise Performance." World Bank Staff Working Paper no. 118.

North, Douglass C. 1981. *Structure and Change in Economic History.* New York: Norton.

——— 1990. *Institutions, Institutional Change, and Economic Performance.* New York: Cambridge University Press.

North, Douglass C., and Robert Paul Thomas. 1973. *The Rise of the Western World: A New Economic History.* Cambridge: Cambridge University Press.

Oi, Jean. 1992. "Fiscal Reform and the Economic Foundations of Local State Corporatism in China." *World Politics,* 45: 99–126.

Olson, Mancur. 1965. *The Logic of Collective Action,* Cambridge, Mass.: Harvard University Press.

——— 1982. *The Rise and Decline of Nations.* New Haven: Yale University Press.

——— 1991. "Autocracy, Democracy, and Prosperity." In Richard Zeckhauser, ed., *Strategy of Choice.* Cambridge, Mass.: MIT Press.

Owen, Thomas. 1991. *The Corporation under Russian Law, 1800–1917.* New York: Cambridge University Press.

Palmer, Robert R., and Colton, Joel. 1984. *A History of the Modern World.* New York: Knopf.

Parry, John H. 1966. *The Spanish Seaborne Empire.* London: Hutchinson.

Phelps, Edmund S., et al. 1993. "Needed Mechanisms for Corporate Governance and Finance in Eastern Europe." *Economics of Transition,* 1, 2: 171–208.

Piketty, Thomas. 1995. "On Tax Reform and Fiscal Federalism in Russia." Mimeo.

Pinto, Brian, M. Belka, and S. Krajewski. 1993. "Transforming State Enterprises in Poland: Evidence on Adjustment by Manufacturing Firms." *Brookings Papers on Economic Activity,* 213–270.

Plumb, John H. 1967. *The Growth of Political Stability in England: 1675–1725.* London: Macmillan.

Poggi, Gianfranco. 1978. *The Development of the Modern State: A Sociological Introduction.* Stanford, Calif.: Stanford University Press.

Pop-Eleches, Cristian. 1977. "Local Government and Private Business in Sibiv, Romania." Mimeo.

Porter, Michael E. 1990. *The Competitive Advantage of Nations.* New York: Free Press.

Posner, Richard A. 1975. "The Social Costs of Monopoly and Regulation." *Journal of Political Economy,* 83: 807–827.

———— 1995. *Aging and Old Age.* Chicago: University of Chicago Press.

Poterba, James M. 1994. "States' Responses to Fiscal Crises: The Effects of Budgetary Institutions and Politics." *Journal of Political Economy,* 102: 799–821.

Putnam, Robert. 1993. *Making Democracy Work: Civic Traditions in Modern Italy.* Princeton: Princeton University Press.

Raiffa, Howard. 1981. "Decision Making in State-Owned Enterprise." In Raymond Vernon and Yair Aharoni, eds., *State-Owned Enterprise in the Western Economies.* London: Croom Helm.

Riker, William. 1964. *Federalism.* Boston: Little, Brown.

Rose-Ackerman, Susan. 1975. "The Economics of Corruption." *Journal of Public Economics,* 4: 187–203.

———— 1978. *Corruption: A Study of Political Economy.* New York: Academic Press.

Rosen, Sherwin. 1981. "The Economics of Superstars." *American Economic Review,* 71: 845–858.

Rostowski, Jacek. 1989. "The Decay of Socialism and the Growth of Private Enterprise in Poland." *Soviet Studies,* 41: 194–214.

Rotemberg, Julio J. 1990. "Rationing in Centrally Planned Economies." Massachusetts Institute of Technology. Mimeo.

Royko, Mike. 1971. *Boss.* New York: Signet Books.

Runciman, Steven. 1958. *The Sicilian Vespers: A History of the Mediterranean World in the 13th Century.* Cambridge: Cambridge University Press.

Russell, Josiah Cox. 1972. *Medieval Regions and Their Cities.* Bloomington: Indiana University Press.

Sachs, Jeffrey D. 1992. "Privatization in Russia: Some Lessons from Eastern Europe." *AER Papers and Proceedings,* 82: 43–48.

———— 1993. *Poland's Jump to a Market Economy.* Cambridge, Mass.: MIT Press.

———— 1995. "Russia's Struggle with Stabilization." *Proceedings of the World Bank Annual Conference on Development Economics.* World Bank.

Sachs, Jeffrey D., and A. Warner. 1995. "Economic Reforms and the Process of Global Integration." *Brookings Papers on Economic Activity,* 1–95.

Sachs, Jeffrey D., and W. T. Woo. 1994. "Structural Factors and Economic Reforms in China, Eastern Europe, and the Former Soviet Union." *Economic Policy,* 9: 101–145.

Sappington, D. E. M., and Stiglitz, J. E. 1987. "Privatization, Information, and Incentives." *Journal of Policy Analysis and Management,* 6: 567–582.

Savas, E. S. 1982. *Privatizing the Public Sector: How to Shrink Government.* Chatham, N.J.: Chatham House Publishers.

———— 1987. *Privatization: The Key to Better Government.* Chatham, N.J.: Chatham House Publishers.

Schmidt, Klaus. 1996. "The Costs and Benefits of Privatization." *Journal of Law and Economics,* 12: 1–24.

Schumpeter, Joseph A. 1942. *Capitalism, Socialism, and Democracy.* New York: Harper & Row.

Shapiro, C., and Willig, R. 1990. "Economic Rationales for the Scope of Privatization." In E. N. Suleiman and J. Waterbury, eds., *The Political Economy of Public Sector Reform and Privatization.* Boulder, Colo.: Westview Press.

Shiller, R. J., M. Boycko, and V. Korobov. 1991. "Popular Attitudes toward Free Markets: The Soviet Union and the United States Compared." *American Economic Review,* 81: 385–400.

———— 1992. "Hunting for Homo Sovieticus: Situational versus Attitudinal Factors in Economic Behavior." *Brookings Papers on Economic Activity,* 127–181.

Shleifer, Andrei. 1995. "Establishing Property Rights." *Proceedings of the World Bank Annual Conference on Development Economics,* 93–117. World Bank.

Shleifer, Andrei, and Robert W. Vishny. 1986. "Large Shareholders and Corporate Control." *Journal of Political Economy* 94: 461–488.

———— 1994. "Privatization in Russia: First Steps." In Olivier J. Blanchard, Kenneth R. Froot, and Jeffrey D. Sachs, eds., *The Transition in Eastern Europe,* vol. 2. Chicago: University of Chicago Press.

Smith, Adam. (1776) 1976. *The Wealth of Nations.* London: W. Strahan and T. Cadell. Reprinted, Oxford: Clarendon Press.

Southern, R. W. 1970. *Western Society and the Church in the Middle Ages.* Harmondsworth: Penguin Books.

Sowell, Thomas. 1990. *Preferential Policies: An International Perspective.* New York: Morrow.

Stahl, D. O., and Alexeev, M. 1985. "The Influence of Black Markets on a Queue-Rationed Centrally Planned Economy." *Journal of Economic Theory,* 35: 234–250.

Stevens, B. J. 1984. *Delivering Municipal Services Efficiently: A Comparison of Municipal and Private Service Delivery.* Washington, D.C.: Office of Policy Development and Research, Department of Housing and Urban Development.

Stigler, George J. 1964. "A Theory of Oligopoly." *Journal of Political Economy,* 72: 44–61.

———— 1965. "The Economist and the State." *American Economic Review,* 55: 1–18.

——— 1971. "The Theory of Economic Regulation." *Bell Journal of Economics,* 2: 3–21.

Stiglitz, Joseph E. 1989. "On the Economic Role of the State." In A. Heertje, ed., *The Economic Role of the State.* Oxford: Blackwell.

——— 1996. *Whither Socialism?* Wicksell Lectures. Cambridge, Mass.: MIT Press.

Strayer, Joseph R. 1973. *On the Medieval Origins of the Modern State.* Princeton, N.J.: Princeton University Press.

Summers, Robert, and Alan Heston. 1988. "A New Set of International Comparisons for Real Product and Price Levels: Estimates for 130 Countries." *Review of Income and Wealth,* 34: 1–25.

Sundbard, G. 1908. *Aperçus statistiques internationaux.* Stockholm.

Swianiewicz, P. 1992. "The Polish Experience of Local Democracy: Is Progress Being Made?" *Policy and Politics,* 20: 87–98.

Szelenyi, Ivan, D. Treisman, and Edmund Wnuk-Lipinski, eds. 1995. *Elites in Poland, Russia, and Hungary: Change or Reproduction?* Warsaw: Polish Academy of Sciences.

Teague, E. 1996. "Russia and the Regions: The Uses of Ambiguity." In J. Gibson and P. Hanson, eds., *Transformation from Below: Local Power and the Political Economy of Post-Communist Transitions.* Brookfield: Edward Elgar.

Tilly, Charles. 1990. *Coercion, Capital, and European States,* A.D. *990–1990.* Berkeley: University of California Press.

Tirole, Jean. 1991. "Privatization in Eastern Europe: Incentives and the Economics of Transition." *NBER Macroeconomics Annual,* 5: 221–267.

Treisman, D. 1996. "The Politics of Inter-governmental Transfers in Post-Soviet Russia." *British Journal of Political Science,* 26: 299–336.

——— 1998. "Fiscal Redistribution in a Fragile Federation: Moscow and the Regions in 1994." *British Journal of Political Science,* 28: 185–222.

Tullock, Gordon. 1959. "Some Problems of Majority Voting." *Journal of Political Economy,* 67: 571–579.

——— 1967. "The Welfare Cost of Tariffs, Monopoly, and Theft." *Western Economic Journal,* 5: 224–232.

United Nations. 1989. *Corruption in Government.* New York: United Nations.

United States Advisory Commission on Intergovernmental Relations. 1993. *State Laws Governing Local Government Structure and Administration.* Washington, D.C.: USACIR.

Vernon, Raymond, and Yair Aharoni, eds. 1981. *State-Owned Enterprise in the Western Economies.* London: Croom Helm.

Vining, Aiden, and Anthony Boardman. 1992. "Ownership vs. Competition: Efficiency in Public Enterprise." *Public Choice,* 73: 205–239.

Wallich, Christine, ed. 1994. *Russia and the Challenge of Fiscal Federalism.* Washington, D.C.: World Bank.

Weber, Max. 1968. *Economy and Society.* Berkeley: University of California Press.

Wedgewood, Cicely V. 1944. *William the Silent: William of Nassau, Prince of Orange, 1533–84.* New Haven: Yale University Press.

Weitzman, Martin L. 1977. "Is the Price System or Rationing More Effective in Getting a Commodity to Those Who Need It Most?" *Bell Journal of Economics,* 8: 517–524.

———— 1984. *The Share Economy: Conquering Stagflation.* Cambridge: Harvard University Press.

Wilson, James Q. 1989. *Bureaucracy: What Government Agencies Do and Why They Do It.* New York: Basic Books.

Wittman, Donald. 1989. "Why Democracies Produce Efficient Results." *Journal of Political Economy,* 97, 6: 1395–1424.

World Bank. 1995. *Bureaucrats in Business.* Washington, D.C.: World Bank.

———— 1996. "From Plan to Market." World Development Report.

Yavlinsky, G., and S. Braguinsky. 1994. "The Inefficiency of Laissez-Faire in Russia: Hysterisis Effects and the Need for Policy-Based Transformation." *Journal of Comparative Economics,* 19: 88–116.

Young, A. 1996. "The Razor's Edge: Distortions, Incremental Reform, and the Theory of the Second Best in the People's Republic of China." Boston University. Mimeo.

Yunker, James A. 1992. *Socialism Revised and Modernized: The Case for Pragmatic Market Socialism.* New York: Praeger.

Index

Absolutist rule, 21–22, 27–28, 31, 35–42, 51–52
Air France, 130, 141

Barro, Robert, 68, 73
Becker, Gary, 4, 8, 91–92, 95, 130, 133
Bribery. *See* Corruption
British Coal, 129–130, 138
Buchanan, James, 4, 8, 14, 21, 28
Bureaucracy, 17, 55–56, 143, 186, 240; corruption and, 11–12, 97, 107; bureaucratized state, 123, 126; and power, 129

Capital, 56, 71; rent seeking and, 88
Capitalism, 119–120, 244–245; transition to, 72, 227–253; versus socialism, 109, 123, 130; versus market socialism, 126; transition to, 227–253. *See also* Democratic capitalism
Cash-flow rights, 153–154, 157–159, 162, 180; and market socialism, 133–134; privatization and, 138, 143, 147, 148
Central banks, 107, 156, 247
Chicago, 101, 152
China, 55, 247, 248, 253
Clean government laws, 185, 187–188, 197–198, 207, 215, 216–219, 225
Coase theorem, 142, 162, 163–164
Commercialization, 162–163. *See also* Corporatization
Communism, 135, 229–231; collapse of, 87, 91, 97, 102, 132; in Russia, 128
Contracts, 142–143, 186; in public

enterprises, 6; and talent, 54–55, 59–60, 63, 68, 71; procurement, 91, 133; corruption, 138, 142. *See also* Private contracting
Control rights, 133, 153–155, 157–162, 167–171, 180; privatization and, 138, 139–147, 148
Corporate governance, 5–6, 9, 11, 129, 250
Corporatization, 143, 154, 157, 167–168, 171–172, 180. *See also* Commercialization
Corruption, 2, 11–12, 91–108; allocation of talent and, 67; innovation and, 87–89; socialism and, 110–111, 113–117; privatization and, 138, 141–143, 146; and public enterprises, 154–155, 156–157, 162–164, 167–172; and transition economies, 230–231, 245, 250, 253
Crédit Lyonnais, 1, 5–7, 9–10, 152
Czech Republic, 143, 228, 239, 241, 251. *See also* Klaus, Vaclav

Democracy, 4, 102, 124, 126, 128–132, 134. *See also* Democratic capitalism
Democratic capitalism, 132–134, 134–135. *See also* Democracy
Depoliticization, 5, 11, 16, 149, 232
Deregulation, 12, 65. *See also* Regulation
Dictatorship, 4, 48, 107, 125–126, 127–128

Economic growth, 4, 5, 169; in preindustrial cities, 48–52;

275

CPSIA information can be obtained at www.ICGtesting.com
Printed in the USA
BVOW040245270812

298756BV00002B/6/A